The cross-linguistic study of bilingual development

Royal Netherlands Academy of Arts and Sciences
P.O. Box 19121, 1000 GC Amsterdam, the Netherlands

ISBN 0-444-85778-8

Koninklijke Nederlandse Akademie van Wetenschappen
Verhandelingen, Afd. Letterkunde, Nieuwe Reeks, deel 158

The cross-linguistic study of bilingual development

Edited by Guus Extra and Ludo Verhoeven

North-Holland, Amsterdam / Oxford / New York / Tokyo, 1994

Acknowledgements

The present volume contains the proceedings of an International Workshop on Bilingual Development in Amsterdam, which was funded by the Royal Netherlands Academy of Arts and Sciences. The editors owe special gratitude to Jetske Folmer and Miranda Habraken of the Tilburg Research Group on Language and Minorities and the staff of the Editorial Department of the Royal Netherlands Academy of Arts and Sciences for their support in the process of preparing this volume.

Contents

Introduction

Cross-linguistic perspectives on bilingual development

Migration processes in recent history have led to a growing interest in the study of bilingual development. Traditionally, there has been a clear bias in the orientation of scientific research concerning language development in ethnic communities towards the second language. In comparison with the large number of studies in the latter area, the number of studies on the acquisition of ethnic community languages has been extremely small. The biased orientation in research on language development in ethnic communities can be derived from studies in Northern America (Grosjean, 1986), Australia (Clyne, 1982) and Europe (Extra & Verhoeven, 1993). During the past decades there has been a shift from almost exclusive attention to the dominant language to a broader focus on first and second language development. In the present volume recent studies on bilingual development will be presented.

Theoretical perspectives on language acquisition

A fundamental problem of linguistics is to explain how a person can and does acquire knowledge of language. In the tradition of generative grammar an attempt has been made to solve the problem of language acquisition by studying the abstract principles in the complex syntax of adult grammar. In explaining language acquisition it is supposed that the language ability of human beings is constrained by a universal grammar. Such grammar is defined as a set of language-specific principles, based on some sort of language acquisition device: a neural mechanism tailored to the specific task of language acquisition. It is also assumed that language acquisition is a genetically transmitted process, and that the basic structures which make language acquisition possible are uniquely linguistic. As such, the neural substrats of linguistic ability are seen as independent from those structuring human cognitive ability.

There are several problems with the generative approach of language acquisition. First of all, the factor time is totally ignored. While explaining its apparent ease, rapidity and uniformity, language acquisition is seen as an instantaneous phenomenon, idealizing it to a situation in which the child has at his disposal all of the principles and parameters of universal grammar and all linguistic data necessary to fix those parameters (cf. Hyams, 1986). As such, it is by no means clear how and in what order linguistic parameters are set, nor is it clear how apparent delays which characterize the developmental process can be explained. In order to understand the process of child language acquisition an interaction of maturational linguistic factors must be taken into account. With regard to maturation, it seems a reasonable claim that not all of the principles of universal grammar are available at the initial state. As has been proposed by Felix (1987), the emergence of grammatical principles most likely follows a maturational schedule. With respect to the lexicon, it can be assumed that there are certain grammatical developments which are dependent on the learning of lexical properties. Given the fact that lexical entries displaying such features as argument structure and subcategorization restrictions must be learned one-by-one, language acquisition can only be seen as a gradual and time-consuming process.

It can be assumed that the process of language acquisition must represent an interaction between principles of universal grammar and other cognitive functions. If there are no instantaneous linguistic principles underlying language acquisition, it can be questioned how in the course of time children acquire rules which relate syntactic forms and semantic functions. On the basis of an extensive series of cross-linguistic studies Slobin (1985) has proposed a set of universal operational principles for the construction of language. In their initial form these principles are believed to exist prior to the child's experience with language. In the course of applying such principles to perceived speech and associated perception of objects and events, a basic child grammar will evolve, corresponding to the internal organization and storage of linguistic structures.

Recent studies of first language acquisition have made clear that, by the age of 4, children are in command of many of the grammatical principles and rules governing their language use (cf. Goodluck, 1986). However, several studies have provided evidence that, both at the level of competence and performance rules, language development goes on into later school years (Bowerman, 1979, 1982; Karmiloff-Smith, 1979, 1986). Later language development in children can be characterized by a growing command of discourse principles. Around age 5, developmental shifts take place from intra- to intersentential devices, from basic structures to additional functions and from contextualized to decontextualized abilities.

The study of bilingual development

The language patterns of children living in a multicultural and multilingual society can be quite diverse. Some children, brought up by parents bilingually, develop proficiency in two languages more or less simultaneously during their infant years. Most children, however, learn the two languages in a successive manner. They learn the ethnic community language in the home and the wider ethnic community, and gradually the second language enters into their lives through television, peer contact and occasionally through day-care. When they enter school, the language input becomes almost exclusively L2. Children may take part in special second language instruction, but to a greater part they acquire the second language naturally, mainly through interaction with peers and teachers.

Given current theoretical perspectives, the process of bilingual development can at best be studied from an interdisciplinary point of view, combining insights from linguistic theory and developmental theory. From a formal linguistic point of view bilingual development can be defined as an 'instantaneous' process in an ideal situation in which the child has at his disposal all of the principles and parameters of universal grammar and two sets of input data necessary to fix those parameters. Given the obvious fact that languages are not acquired instantaneously, developmental theory must explain the various 'delays' which characterize both first and second language development and the apparent difficulties children encounter in sorting out the principles of two different languages.

The analysis of children's bilingual development at school age will primarily focus on the children's organizing processes over spans of connected utterances. Narratives, in their broader sense, can be taken as relevant exponents of extended discourse. It can be examined how children in this age range learn to master cohesive devices for anchoring discourse structure in narrative comprehension and production, and under what conditions and with what grammatical constraints processes of transfer do occur. The study of bilingual development at school age need not be confined to oral language data. Given the fact that, starting at age 7, the school curriculum is highly devoted to reading and writing, data on emerging literacy can be explored as well.

In the study of bilingual development the following research questions can be addressed:

1. How are first and second language systems built up in the course of time?
2. Under what conditions and with what lexical and syntactic rules do processes of transfer and code-switching occur?
3. In what way does the language input shape the child's grammar?

The first question is concerned with the developmental process itself. It may be investigated how the two language systems get differentiated and developed over time. The second question goes into both functional and structural properties of processes of language transfer and code-switching. The final question concerns the role of language input. In order to investigate the role of language input, an inventory can be made of the interactional patterns the children take part in. It can be determined what language is used under which circumstances by and towards the children. The assumption underlying the final question is that the child may learn directly from positive evidence in the input, as has been proposed by Pinker (1984). The input may influence the process of bilingual development in two ways. First, the structural properties of each language may influence the perception and the cognitive processing of language elements. Second, the specific input which is selected will determine the range of linguistic parameters to be acquired.

With regard to the patterns of language development in bilingual children, it is still unclear what sort of operating principles children use. We have no clear insight into the conditions under which processes of language transfer occur. Previous studies on later bilingual development were limited in sofar that the languages under consideration were highly related (cf. Grosjean, 1982; McLaughlin, 1985; Romaine, 1989). In order to be able to further explore the role of structural properties of languages, we need more research, especially on children's data in typologically distant language pairs.

Linguistic domains

In the study of bilingual development a number of linguistic domains can be taken into account. Cross-linguistic attention may be given to typological differences between the languages under consideration in each of these domains. Without the pretention of being exhaustive, a number of domains that can be considered relevant for the study of bilingual development will be reviewed. These domains have proved to be highly significant in a large body of cross-linguistic studies on language acquisition in both children (cf. Slobin, 1985) and adults (cf. Perdue, 1993).

Clause structure

Within current linguistic theories universal grammar is defined as a parameterized system. A set of universal principles is presupposed, at least some of which are associated with parameters, expressing the limited range of variation that languages exhibit as regards these principles. Bilingual acquisition gives an interesting test of the idea that children come to language learning equipped with a universal grammar which is then modified on exposure to the environment. The ultimate question is how universal principles will lead to mastery of two separate grammars and what the role of environmental factors is in this process. In the analysis of clause structure a distinction can be made between core and peripheral or marked properties of the languages under consideration. As has been shown in work on first language acquisition, children start out with basic sentential phrase structures along with core complements through a principle of canonical mapping (Slobin, 1985; Hyams, 1988). Later on they sort out those aspects of complementation which are peripheral. It is also assumed that the distinction between core and peripheral properties will give better insight into the acquisition of inflectional morphology. On the basis of earlier research (Slobin & Bever, 1982), it can be hypothesized that inflections will be easier learned in languages where inflection is a core property than in languages where inflection is a peripheral property.

Gradually, children learn to use complex syntactic devices, such as relativization and clause linking. Following Comrie (1976) and Keenan & Comrie (1977) a relative clause can be defined as 'any syntactic device specifying a set of objects in two steps: a larger step is specified, called the domain of relativization, and then restricted to some subset of which a certain sentence, the restrictive sentence, is true. The domain of relativization is expressed in surface by the head NP, and the restrictive sentence by the restricting clause'. From a typological point of view, a distinction can be made between external and internal relatives, with the head NP outside and inside the restricting clause respectively. External relatives can further be divided in postnominal and prenominal relatives. Keenan (1985) has shown that there is a general tendency across languages to favour postnominal as opposed to prenominal relative clauses. Postnominal relative clauses are almost uniquely attested in verb-initial languages, and they are most productive in verb-medial languages. In verb-final languages prenominal relative clauses are usually most productive. However, in the latter type of languages postnominal and internal relative clauses often are dominant.

In clause linking, complex sentences are being formed in which two or more predications are combined. From a comparative point of view, two types of complex sentence structures can be distinguished: 'co-ranking structures' and 'chaining structures' (Longacre, 1985). Co-ranking structures, such as those found in typical Indo-European languages, may consist of several verbs of the same rank. A chaining structure, on the other hand, typically ends in a dominating verb of a fuller structure than any of the preceding verbs. The dominating verb is usually known as the final verb, the preceding verbs as medial verbs.

From a syntactic point of view, the acquisition of complex sentences involves insight in the layered structure of clauses and in the concepts of embeddedness and dependence. Given the fact that children start out linking clauses before all operators are understood, it can be expected that the linkage of sub-clausal units will precede the linkage of full clauses. Furthermore, it can be hypothesized that the linkage of autonomous clauses is conceptually simpler than the linkage of clauses with one clause being embedded. Studies conducted by Bowerman (1979) and Goodluck & Tavakolian (1982) give positive evidence for such claims.

The attempts so far to relate typological differences to sentence processing difficulties underscore the need for cross-linguistic studies on the acquisition of clause structure and clause linking. It can be investigated in what order the various types of grammatical relations in simple and complex clauses are acquired. Moreover, it can be explored to what extent there is evidence for language transfer in children's syntactic devices.

Lexicon and word formation

Linguistic competence generally includes a lexicon of well-established words and a repertoire of word formation devices for extending the basic lexicon. New meanings can be expressed with forms which fit the word formation options of that particular language. Basically, two types of word formation devices can be distinguished. On the one hand, stem modification or derivation in which a single base is related to a form which is altered in some way. On the other hand, compounding in which a set of two or more independent bases are combined in some way. Anderson (1985) has stressed the fact that there is a good deal of idiosyncrasy in word formation devices in different languages, and that in any single language word formation rules are quite diverse in terms of input classes and semantic and syntactic relations involved.

In the process of language acquisition, children must learn the diversity of options for coining words in the languages under consideration. In a number of studies the acquisition of word formation devices has been investigated. For such diverse languages as English (Clark, 1981; Clark, Hecht & Mulford, 1986) and Hebrew (Berman & Sagi, 1982; Walden, 1982), it was found that children at an early age start coining words in order to fill lexical gaps. Gradually, children give up some of their early innovative coinages in favour of words established in the lexicon of adult language users. Clark has claimed that at least three general principles govern the course of acquisition of word formation rules. The first principle is semantic transparency stating that known elements with one-to-one matches of meaning and form are most transparent for constructing and interpreting new words. The second principle is regularization saying that children will use the same device everywhere to mark the same meaning. The third principle is productivity predicting that those word formation devices used most often by adults are preferred in children's language for constructing new word forms. Clark (1982, 1983) stressed the importance of cross-linguistic evidence on the structure and use of word formation devices in different types of languages.

The study of lexical development can be elaborated by taking two languages into account, especially in case the two languages are typologically unrelated. First of all, the development of lexical variety and word formation devices in both languages can be explored. With respect to word formation processes a distinction can be made between conventionalized forms and lexical innovations. A major question is to find out what general mechanisms underlie the choice and construction of word forms in L1 and L2. At the same time it can be explored to what extent the processes of lexical development in the two languages interact. Incorporation of lexemes of one language in the other language are then to be analysed.

Reference to entities

In the domain of reference to entities a range of topics can be studied. Two phenomena deserve special interest: pronominal reference and the distinction between definite and indefinite reference.

Languages greatly vary in their conceptual notions and linguistic devices for pronominal reference to entities. There is an optional set of subject, object and possessive pronouns marking role (first/second/third) and number (singular/plural). There is the possibility of gender, status and dual distinction. In various languages demonstratives can be used to refer to entities. In discourse, either pro drop or pronominalization can be seen as the unmarked coding for topic continuity. Moreover, there can be very different markers for indefinite and definite expressions.

In pronominal reference the deictic and anaphoric use of pronouns is under concern. First and second person pronouns usually only function deictically, whereas third person pronouns allow both deictic and anaphoric use. From studies on first language acquisition (cf. Wales, 1986), it has become clear that children start using pronouns deictically at an early age. First and second person pronouns, referring to the domain of joint speaker-hearer attention, are acquired first. Third person pronouns which require gestural support are acquired later. Deictic devices often enter crucially into children's conversational discourse. Karmiloff-Smith (1979) has shown that there is a progression across age in the discourse functions that the same linguistic form may have. Only gradually children learn the crucial constraints in their use of anaphoric expressions.

In the domain of anaphoric reference the developmental patterns of bound and free anaphora in children's first and second language use, as distinguished in Chomsky's (1981) binding theory, can be compared. In a variety of studies the acquisition of lexical anaphors and pronouns have been studied in languages such as English and Dutch. With respect to bound anaphors, a fast pattern of acquisition could be evidenced. It seems that syntactic knowledge of bound anaphora, as part of universal grammar, is guiding the development (Koster, 1988). Furthermore, it has become clear that the development of free anaphor resolution shows a much more irregular and slow development.

In a number of studies the acquisition of anaphoric reference was investigated in languages that are typologically very different from English. From a cross-linguistic point of view those languages which have binding principles that are distinct from English are of special interest, because these languages seem to challenge Chomsky's claims (e.g., Hyams, 1988). More recently, the acquisition of anaphoric reference was explored in a bilingual context. On the basis of empirical data on L2 acquisition of anaphora among Japanese and Spanish learners of English, Flynn (1986) concluded a primacy of the head-initial/head-final parameter's role.

In order to comprehend and use the contrast between definite and indefinite reference children must learn the rules for the establishment and maintenance of connected discourse. In the case a speaker does expect entities to be identifiable, noun phrases will be given the status of definite. However, as is shown by Karmi-loff-Smith (1986), the basic referential markers in many languages are plurifunctio-nal. In order to acquire the right distinctions for reference tracking children must learn to map the right forms and functions. Broeder (1991) studied the acquisition of pronominal reference to person by Turkish and Moroccan adult learners of Dutch. Derived from principles of input frequency, informational complexity, perceptual salience and first language use, he tested a series of predictions on order of acquisition. In cases of competition, the principle of perceptual salience was found to overrule the principle of input frequency and only in few cases first langu-age influence could be evidenced in second language use.

In the study of bilingual development it can be examined how children learn to use the coding devices for pronominal reference and for the expression of definite vs. indefinite reference in their first and second language systems over time. It can also be determined to what extent there is evidence of transfer from the use of referential expressions in one language to the other language. Finally, in the study of children's construction of narratives it can be examined how children learn to use the coding devices for topic continuity in their first and second language systems over time. A distinction can be made between coding devices for the introduction, maintenance and shift of referents on the one hand, and devices for the expression of definite vs. indefinite reference on the other.

Reference to space

The study of reference to space focuses on the use of spatial concepts which are relevant to the expression of location or motion. According to Fillmore (1982: 37), the subject of spatial reference has three natural subtopics. First, systems of demonstratives can be studied so far as these are structured with reference to the location of the communicative act. Second, pre-or postpositional and adverbial devices for constructing locative expressions with an implicit reference to the location of the communicative act can be identified. Third, systems of motion verbs for whose interpretation reference to the communication act is necessary can be investigated. Motion verbs may differ in many respects: direction of the movement, type of movement, object of movement and origin or target of movement.

With respect to the acquisition of devices for spatial reference it can be hypothesized that both cognitive maturation and language-specific factors play a significant role. When referring to the location or motion of entities in space, languages may differ both in their use of spatial concepts and in the ways in which spatial concepts are encoded. Depending on how the sub-systems of spatial reference in a particular language are organized, the developmental sequences can be different. Johnston & Slobin (1979), following the development of seven basic locative relations in English, Italian, Serbo-Croatian and Turkish children, indeed found that both cognitive complexity and language-specific differences play a role in the rate and sequence of acquisition. The relevant language-specific differences they proposed were placement of adposition, lexical diversity, clarity of etymology, morphological complexity and homonymity.

The sub-systems of spatial reference in various languages may differ considerably, both in underlying spatial concepts and in the form of the devices they include. In most Indo-European languages, there is a dyadic system of primary spatial deixis. Furthermore, locative relations are mainly encoded by means of prepositions and adverbs. These linguistic devices express such semantic relations as interior/exterior, region/contact, front/back, left/right, top/bottom and 'between-ness' or interposition. Besides, there are motion verbs expressing a change in the position of the agent or an object. Other languages, such as Turkish, have a three-step system of spatial deixis. Generally, distance contrasts are expressed as proximal, medial and distal. Turkish also has a basic system of case suffixes referring to goal (DAT), location (LOC), and source/path (ABL). There is also a complementary system for the indication of spatial relations which uses a group of nouns denoting places. These nouns enter into a postpositional construction which corresponds in function to a prepositional phrase in Indo-European languages.

In the study of bilingual development it can be explored how children learn to use the distance features of spatial deixis in their first and second language systems over time. Moroever, it can be investigated how the coding devices for the expression of spatial relations in the languages under consideration are developed. An important question is finally to what extent there is transfer from the use of spatial expressions in one language to the other language.

Reference to time

In exploring reference to time three fundamental categories of temporality in language can be distinguished: temporal relations, aspect and internal temporal features. Temporal relations refer to the location of events in relation to a given reference time. Aspect refers to the various perspectives that can be taken towards an event, e.g., perfective vs. imperfective. Internal temporal features refer to quasi-objective time characteristics of an event, such as durativity or transformativity.

With regard to first language acquisition, Weist (1986) has shown that the marking of temporal relations involves a sequence of four stages. The initial temporal system, situated in the here-and-now, does not make a distinction between event time and reference time at the time of speech. The second system is characterized by the child's capacity to represent the event time prior to and subsequent to, or simultaneous with, the speech time. In the third stage of development the concept of reference time emerges. In the initial reference time system, however, event time is restricted to the reference time context. In the final stage, children are able to use a free reference system in which speech time, event time and reference time can represent three different points in time and can be related freely. The acquisition rate of aspect and internal temporal features is highly dependent on the manner in which these devices are coded in the surface structure of the target language (Slobin, 1985).

Tense and aspect oppositions in narratives not only function to locate events relative to the moment of speech, but also as an organizer of narrative structure. Schriffrin (1981) and Fleischman (1985) showed that the use of present tense to refer to past events (historical present) and past tense in narratives is alternated in a regular way. They concluded that the organization of narratives delimits the area in which the historical present can occur, and that various structural and functional constraints determine switches between the two tenses. Wallace (1982) has shown that present tense (vs. non-present) and perfective aspect (vs imperfective) supply the main points or the foreground in the narrative. Klein & Von Stutterheim (1985) proposed that the foreground in narratives is characterized by the conditions of topic and focus which constrain the temporal features of referential movement.

Given the substantial differences of temporal reference in different languages, the acquisition of linguistic devices for temporal reference in a bilingual context can be thought of as highly relevant. A basic question is to find out what operating principles underlie the synthetic and analytic devices for temporal marking at the levels of utterance and discourse in either language and to what extent there is transfer from temporal devices in one language to the other language.

Empirical studies

There is a highly specific tradition of studies on early bilingualism. From reviews by Taeschner (1983: 5-18) and McLaughlin (1985: 72-98) it is clear that most of these studies show the following characteristics:

– single or multiple case studies,
– based on diaries kept by (one of) the parents on
– the simultaneous acquisition of
– two typologically related languages,
– one language being spoken by one parent, the other being the dominant language in the wider community,
– by children from a high socio-economic background.

A landmark in research on early bilingualism is the study of Leopold (1970). Leopold's report was on the language development of his daughter Hildegard who was brought up according to the one person-one language strategy, speaking German to her father and English to her mother. It was found that during her first two years Hildegard did not succeed in keeping the two language systems apart. Her speech sounds were not differentiated by language while German and English words were mixed freely. By the end of the second year the phonological and grammatical systems of the two languages were slowly separated. From the age of two to five, there was an increasing influence of one language (English) over the other (German), because the contacts in the English-speaking environment greatly exceeded her contacts with German.

Volterra & Taeschner (1978) and Taeschner (1983) proposed a three-stage model of language development in bilingual children on the basis of data on two Italian-German speaking children. In stage 1, the child has a uniform lexical system lacking cross-language synonyms, with early mixed-language word combinations as a necessary concomitant. In stage 2, the child has two differentiated lexical systems from which more-word utterances are constructed. However, in this stage there is only one basic grammar in that the same syntactic rules are applied to utterances in either language. In stage 3, there is a differentiation of two grammatical systems. In this stage interference phenomena still occur, especially when the child needs to switch rapidly from one language to the other, or when the information given is usually expressed in the other language.

From a number of studies there is additional evidence that the separation of languages manifests itself by a decrease in mixed utterances (de Houwer, 1990; Redlinger & Park, 1980). Furthermore, Vihman (1982, 1985) showed that the differentiation of syntactic rules in an Estonian-English speaking child starts out with universal rules that apply to both languages. Rules specific to either of the two languages were developed later on. However, Meisel (1986), studying the development of word order regularities and case markings in two French-German speaking children, found that the children were able to differentiate between grammatical properties of the two languages as soon as they began to use multiword utterances. From the beginning the children were able to make use of morphological means to encode syntactic functions.

In several recent studies the process of first and/or second language development of immigrant minority groups in Europe has been investigated. The informants form part of a first, second or third generation of immigrants who originally moved from rural sites in Mediterranean societies to industrialized areas in North-Western Europe. Unlike most of the previous work, the acquisition of typologically unrelated languages in these studies was examined by outside researchers in child or adult learners of a low socio-economic background, L1 being the ethnic community language, and L2 being the dominant language of the environment. In the vast majority of studies the primary focus was on second language development. Perdue (1993) gives a survey of the goals and outcomes of a cross-linguistic and longitudinal study, sponsored by the European Science Foundation, on second language acquisition by adult immigrants in France, Great Britain, Germany, the Netherlands and Sweden. The project focused on the acquisition of French, English, German, Dutch and Swedish by adult speakers of six different source languages. Major topics of analysis were word order principles at the levels of utterance structure and word-formation, the acquisition of spatial and temporal reference, and processes of achieving understanding and giving feedback in interaction. In only a limited number of studies the primary focus was on the acquisition of a specific ethnic community language, such as Arabic (De Ruiter, 1989), Finnish (Lainio, 1987), Italian (Fantini, 1985), Serbo-Croatian (Pavlinic, et al., 1988), Turkish (Boeschoten, 1990; Pfaff, 1991, 1993; Schaufeli, 1991; Verhoeven, 1991).

Previous studies on bilingual development give no reason to believe that the process of language acquisition in bilinguals and monolinguals is different in its basic features. The essential difference is that bilingual children are confronted with two sets of input and that they have the additional task of distinguishing the two language systems. However, the complex process of learning to separate two different languages is still poorly understood. It remains unclear what sort of operating principles children use while acquiring two languages at the same time. It is also unclear under what conditions processes of language transfer and code switching occur. Moreover, most of the studies that have been conducted so far were limited in their scope, given the fact that the languages under consideration were highly related. The analysis of learner data in two unrelated languages will offer new perspectives on the role of structural properties of these languages in the process of acquisition.

The present volume

In this volume empirical studies on bilingual development will be presented. In order to allow for cross-linguistic comparisons, a variety of language contact situations is taken into account and the typological distance between the language pairs under consideration varies widely. English is studied in contact with Dutch, Hungarian, Spanish and Turkish; apart form the American context of English-Spanish contact, English is not the dominant language of the environment. Turkish and/or Arabic are studied in contact with German, Dutch and French; apart from the Moroccan context of Arabic-French contact, Turkish and Arabic are used as minority languages in a European immigration context. The latter context also holds for the study on Finnish-Swedish and Italian-German contact.

The book is divided into two parts. Part 1 gives an overview of studies on early bilingual development. The focus of Part 2 is on bilingual development at school age and beyond.

Part 1: Early bilingual development

The first part of the book opens with a retrospective on the study of early bilingualism by Barry McLaughlin. In chapter 2, he summarizes research related to the following theoretical issues: the (supposed) effects of bilingual development, the notion of 'semilingualism', language mixing, rate of language development and the notion of a 'critical period' for second language learning.

In chapter 3, Annick de Houwer discusses the separate development hypothesis. On the basis of a case-study of a young Dutch-English bilingual child, she first of all focuses on morphosyntactic development, language choice, mixed utterances and metalinguistic awareness. On the basis of the available evidence for the separate development hypothesis, she suggests further ways to explore its validity.

In two subsequent chapters, the acquisition of Turkish in an immigrant setting is dealt with. In chapter 4, Hanneke van der Heijden and Ludo Verhoeven present first outcomes of a study on the early bilingual development of Turkish children in the Netherlands. Their analysis of both Turkish and Dutch language data focuses on the domains of clause structure, lexicon and reference to entities, space and time. In all domains of research the proficiency level in Turkish was higher than in Dutch. Evidence for language transfer turned out to be limited.

In chapter 5, Carol Pfaff considers the interplay of structural and pragmatic factors in Turkish and German discourse of preschool and early school age bilingual children attending a day-care centre in Berlin. The presented data reveal the effects of language dominance on both the choice of expressive devices and on the conversational strategies employed by the children in each of their languages.

In the next chapter, Özden Ekmekçi goes into the strategies conveyed in bilingual development of two native English-speaking preschool children in Turkey. She found the subject's language choice to be a function of the language of the interlocutor. Modification of talk, questioning and clarification turned out to be the most observed caretaker strategies. Typical learner strategies observed were shift to the native language, nonverbal feedback and the use of stereotype words.

The next study is on code-switching at an early age. In chapter 7, Ali Bentahila and Eirlys Davies report on the French-Arabic language varieties used by 4-5-year-old bilingual children in Morocco. They found code-switching to be a commonplace strategy of communication, apart from the use of Arabic or French. The Moroccan children showed a strong preference for phrasal and clausal switches as opposed to single-word switches.

The final study presented in Part 1 deals with the acquisition of early literacy in a bilingual child, living in Hungary. In chapter 8 Kathleen Wodala describes the reading acquisition in English and Hungarian between the age of 5 and 7. Particular attention is paid to the kinds of positive and negative transfer in the acquisition of reading skills.

Part 2: Bilingual development at school age and beyond

Part 2 of the volume opens with a contribution on sociolinguistic variables that determine the rate of first and second language development. In chapter 9, Kenji Hakuta and Lucinda Pease-Alvarez focus on patterns of language proficiency and language choice, and on language attitudes of bilingual Hispanic students in two Californian communities. Data were based on both observed and reported language behaviour. Evidence was found for increases in English proficiency and decreases in Spanish proficiency across groups, for a consistent shift towards English in the language choice of both the children and their parents, and for birth order effects on language choice.

In chapter 10, Jeroen Aarssen, Petra Bos and Ludo Verhoeven describe a study in which the acquisition of complex syntax in Turkish and Moroccan children in the Netherlands is dealt with. They focus on the preliminary results of two experimental tasks. The first experiment investigates the development of bound and free anaphors in Turkish and Moroccan-Arabic as a first language and Dutch as a second language. The second one gives insight into relative clause comprehension, with respect to the grammatical roles of the constituents in the sentences and the linear arrangement of words in the same languages.

In the next chapter, Åke Viberg goes into bilingual development at school age of Finnish children in Sweden. Oral and written language data of students in the fourth and sixth grade of primary school were analysed. The focus of the analyses was on clause linking. Evidence could be found for age-related differences in the usage of sequential markers in the children's first and second language discourse.

In chapter 12, Anneli Schaufeli focuses on first language text cohesion in a Turkish-Dutch bilingual setting. She compared the structural properties of oral and written narratives of bilingual Turkish children living in the Netherlands with those of monolingual Turkish children living in Turkey.

In chapter 13, Aldo di Luzio deals with the temporal structure in L1 narratives of Italian migrant children in the age range of 8-12, living in Germany. He found that the temporal structures used by the children were regular and systematic, conforming to the mother tongue development of a monolingual native peer group in Italy. The differences between the two groups are related to different patterns of linguistic and cultural socialization.

In the two final studies interlingual processes in morphosyntactic development are explored. In chapter 14, Hendrik Boeschoten makes an attempt to account for L2 influence on L1 development in the case of Turkish children in the age range of 8-12, living in Germany. He concludes that the syntactic level found in the L1 data was not deeply affected by the children's contact with German. Some impact from German was evidenced for surface word order. In addition, simplifications in the children's use of Turkish could be found, both of a syntagmatic and paradigmatic nature.

In the final chapter, Peter Broeder, Guus Extra and Roeland van Hout try to find evidence for L1 influence on L2 development with reference to Turkish and Moroccan adults living in the Netherlands. They focus on word-formation devices used in (semi-) spontaneous speech. They found that the acquisition of composition devices precedes the acquisition of derivation devices. In using the former devices learners rely both on source-language related principles and on target-language related principles. Opposite word order principles in Turkish (head-final) versus Arabic (head-initial) emerge as source-language effects in the learners' approaching of the target language norm.

References

Anderson, S., 1985. Typological distinctions in word formation. In: T. Shopen (ed.), *Language typology and syntactic description.* Cambridge: University Press.

Berman, R. & Y. Sagi, 1982. Word formation processes and lexical innovations of young children. *Hebrew Computational Linguistics Bulletin,* 18, 36-62.

Boeschoten, H., 1990. *Acquisition of Turkish by immigrant children.* Wiesbaden: Herassowitz.

Bowerman, M., 1979. The acquisition of complex sentences. In: P. Fletscher & M. Garman (eds), *Language Acquisition.* Cambridge: University Press.

Bowerman, M., 1982. Starting to talk worse: Clues to language acquisition from children's late speech errors. In: S. Strauss (ed.), *U-shaped behavioral growth.* New York: Academic Press.

Broeder, P., 1991. *Talking about people.* Lisse: Swets & Zeitlinger.

Chomsky, N., 1981. *Some aspects and consequences of the theory of government and binding.* Cambridge, MA: MIT Press.

Clark, E., 1981. Lexical innovations: How children learn to create new words. In: W. Deutsch (ed.), *The child's construction of language.* London: Academic Press.

Clark, E., 1982. The young word maker: A case study of innovation in the child's lexicon. In: E. Wanner & L. Gleitman (eds.), *Language acquisition: The state of the art.* Cambridge: University Press.

Clark, E., 1983. Convention and contrast in acquiring the lexicon. In: T. Seiler & W. Wannenmacher (eds.), *Concept development and the development of word meaning.* Berlin: Springer Verlag.

Clark, E., B. Hecht & R. Mulford, 1986. Coining complex compounds in English: Affixes and word order in acquisition. *Linguistics,* 24, 7-29.

Clyne, M., 1982. *Multilingual Australia.* Melbourne: River Seine Publ.

Comrie, B., 1976. *Aspect.* Cambridge: University Press.

De Ruiter, J., 1989. *Young Moroccans in the Netherlands (Ph.D. Thesis).* University of Utrecht.

De Houwer, A., 1990. *The acquisition of two languages from birth: a case study.* Cambridge: University Press.

Extra, G. & L. Verhoeven (eds), 1993. *Immigrant languages in Europe.* Clevedon: Multilingual Matters.

Fantini, A., 1985. *Language acquisition of a bilingual child.* Clevedon: Multilingual Matters.

Felix, S., 1987. *Cognition and language growth.* Dordrecht: Foris.

Fillmore, C., 1982. Towards a descriptive framework for spatial deixis. In: R. Jarvella & W. Klein (eds.), *Speech, place and action.* London: Wiley and Sons.

Fleischmann, S., 1985. Discourse functions of tense-aspect oppositions in narrative: Toward a theory of grounding. *Linguistics,* 23, 851-882.

Flynn, 1986. *A parameter-setting model of second language acquisition.* Dordrecht: Reidel.

Goodluck, H., 1986. Language acquisition and linguistic theory. In: F. Fletscher & P. Garman (eds), *Language Acquisition.* Cambridge: University Press.

Goodluck, H. & S. Tavakolian, 1982. Competence and processing in children's grammar of relative clauses. *Cognition,* 11, 1-27.

Grosjean, F., 1986. *Life with two languages.* Cambridge, MA: Harvard University Press.

Hyams, N., 1986. *Language acquisition and the theory of parameters.* Dordrecht: Reidel.

Hyams, N., 1988. A principles and parameter approach to the study of child language. *Paper presented at the 27th Child Language Research Forum in Stanford.*

Johnston, J. & D. Slobin, 1979. The development of locative expressions in English, Italian, Serbo-Croatian and Turkish. *Journal of Child Language,* 6, 529-545.

Karmiloff-Smith, A., 1979. *A functional approach to child language.* Cambridge: University Press.

Karmiloff-Smith, A., 1986. From meta-processes to conscious access: Evidence from children's metalinguistic and repair data. *Cognition,* 23, 95-147.

Keenan, E., 1985. Relative clauses. In: T. Shopen (ed.), *Language Typology and Syntactic Description.* Cambridge: University Press.

Keenan, E. & B. Comrie, 1977. NP accessibility and universal grammar. *Linguistic*

Inquiry, 8, 63-100.

Klein, W. & C. Von Stutterheim, 1985. *Text structure and referential movement*. Nijmegen: MPI.

Koster, C. (1988). An across experiments analysis of children's anaphor errors. In: G. de Haan & W. Zonnenveld (eds.), Formal Parameters of Generative Grammar, 1988. Dordrecht: ICG.

Lainio, J., 1987. Language use of Finns in Sweden. Implicational patterns in four domains. *Scandinavian Working Papers on Bilingualism*, 7, 11-28.

Leopold, W., 1970. *Speech development of a bilingual child*. Vols. 1-4. New York: AMS Press.

Longacre, R., 1985. Sentences as combinations of clauses. In: T. Shopen (ed.), *Language typology and syntactic description*, Vol. II, 235-286.

McLaughlin, B., 1985. *Second Language Acquisition in Childhood*. Hillsdale, N.J.: LEA.

Meisel, J., 1986. Word order and case marking in early child language. Evidence from simultaneous acquisition of two first languages: French and German. *Linguistics*, 24, 123-183.

Pavlinic, A., K. Brcic & N. Jeftic, 1988. Supplementary mother tongue education and the linguistic development of Yugoslav children in Denmark. *Journal of Multilingual and Multicultural Development*, 9 (1-2), 151-167.

Perdue, C. (ed.), 1993. *Adult language acquisition: cross-linguistic perspectives*. Vol. 1: Field methods, Vol. 2: The results. Cambridge: University Press.

Pfaff, C., 1991. Turkish in contact with German: Language maintenance and loss among immigrant children in West Berlin. *International Journal of the Sociology of Language*, 90, 97-129.

Pfaff, C., 1993. Turkish language development in Germany. In: G. Extra & L. Verhoeven (eds), *Immigrant languages in Europe*. Clevedon: Multilingual matters.

Pinker, S., 1984. *Language learnability and language development*. Cambridge: Harvard University Press.

Redlinger, W. & T. Park, 1980. Language mixing in young bilinguals. *Journal of Child Language*, 7, 337-352.

Romaine, S., 1989. *Bilingualism*. Oxford: Basil Blackwell.

Schaufeli, A., 1991. *Turkish in an immigrant setting. A comparative study of the first language of monolingual and bilingual Turkish children (Ph.D. Thesis)*. University of Amsterdam.

Schiffrin, D., 1981. Tense variation in narratives. *Language*, 57, 1, 45-63.

Slobin, D., 1985. *The cross-linguistic study of language acquisition*. Hillsdale: LEA.

Slobin, D. & T. Bever, 1982. Children use canonical sentence schemas: A cross-linguistic study of word order and inflections. *Cognition*, 12, 229-265.

Taeschner, T., 1983. *The sun is feminine. A study on language acquisition in bilingual children*. Berlin: Springer.

Verhoeven, L., 1991. The acquisition of Turkish in a mono- and bilingual setting. In: H. Boeschoten & L. Verhoeven (eds), *Turkish linguistics today*. Leiden: Brill.

Vihman, M., 1982. The acquisition of morphology by a bilingual child. *Applied Psycholinguistics,* 3, 141-160.

Vihman, M., 1985. Language differentiation by the bilingual child. *Journal of Child Language,* 12, 297-324.

Volterra, V. & R. Taeschner, 1978. The acquisition and development of language by bilingual children. *Journal of Child Language,* 5, 311-326.

Walden, Z., 1982. *The root of roots: Children's construction of word formation processes in Hebrew.* Harvard: Ph.D. Thesis.

Wales, R., 1986. Deixis. In: P. Fletscher & M. Garman (eds), *Language acquisition.* Cambridge: University Press.

Wallace, S., 1982. Figure and ground: The interrelationships of linguistic categories. In P. Hopper (ed.), *Tense-Aspect. Between Semantics and Pragmatics.* Amsterdam: Benjamins.

Weist, R., 1986. Tense and aspect. In: P. Fletscher & M. Garman (eds), *Language acquisition.* Cambridge: University Press.

Part 1

Early bilingual development

Barry McLaughlin

Retrospective on the study of early bilingualism

The study of childhood bilingualism has come a long way since the early case studies of Ronjat (1913), Pavlovitch (1920), and Leopold (1939-49). More recent research, highly influenced by the expanding field of first-language acquisition, has led to a proliferation of studies dealing with specific linguistic dimensions of bilingual acquisition (Hamers & Hablanc, 1989). The result has been that the field of second-language acquisition has also witnessed a marked expansion. The revised version of an earlier review of the field (McLaughlin, 1978) required two volumes five years later (McLaughlin, 1984; McLaughlin, 1985). Today several volumes would be required.

This paper discusses five perennial issues in the study of childhood bilingualism. The thesis is that, although we have learned a great deal and have slain many dragons, there is still a great deal to learn about each of these issues.

The effects of a second language on first language proficiency

Parents in an increasing number of families face an interesting choice: that of raising their children in a bilingual or monolingual environment. In some cases parents who have learned a second language for educational purposes may wonder about the advantages or disadvantages of raising their children bilingually. In many cases husband and wife have different first languages and may wish to give their children access to both languages by using both in the home. In other cases the parents may have immigrated to a new country and may want to maintain the language of the old country while at the same time providing the conditions in the home for the children to learn the language of the new country.

How advisable is it to raise children bilingually? What consequences are there to bilingual upbringing? In his classic study, Jules Ronjat (1913) reported that his son Louis showed only positive consequences from having been raised in a bilingual, French-German home environment. Louis Ronjat learned to speak both languages as a native-speaking child would. He showed very few signs of interference between languages. Nor did his bilingualism have a deleterious effect on his cognitive development. His development was quite normal and it has been reported that by the age of 15 Louis Ronjat had equal fluency in both languages (Vildomec, 1963), preferring French for technology and German for literature. Many other researchers after Ronjat have come to the same conclusion that early bilingualism has positive consequences for linguistic and cognitive development.

In contrast, a large number of studies in the 1920s and 1930s concluded that bilingualism had negative consequences on children's development. As Hakuta (1986) has pointed out, these studies were flawed by serious methodological problems; currently most scholars are convinced that a bilingual experience has positive consequences on the child's linguistic development. The effects on cognitive development are more controversial (McLaughlin, 1984; Reynolds, 1991).

Several books have appeared in the past decade for parents who want to raise their children bilingually (Saunders, 1982; Harding & Riley, 1986; Arnberg, 1987). One of the questions that many parents want to know is what effect bilingualism will have on their children's first-language development. This is not a new concern. The ancient Romans had the same anxieties, and Quintilian and Cicero both expressed the view that the emphasis placed on Greek in the education of young Romans would interfere with their development in the Latin language.

However, the research evidence should allay parents' concerns. There is simply no evidence for what has been dubbed the 'single space' theory, according to which an individual has room in the brain for a single language. Aside from the experience of Europeans and most of the rest of the world outside of the United States, the achievement of primitive tribes who master a number of different languages of great complexity (Hakuta, 1986) would seem to bear eloquent witness to the human's capacity in this respect. Quintilian, Cicero, and many parents vastly underestimate human capabilities. Nonetheless, there are reports in the literature of less positive outcomes. This brings us to a second 'perennial' issue.

The issue of semilingualism

The children of many who have written diary accounts of bilingual children were raised in academic families in middle class socio-economic circumstances. What of children from working-class families? What of the children of guest-workers, for instance? The Scandinavian linguist, Skutnabb-Kangas (1978), wrote of a Finnish child whose language abilities at the age of five were very different from those typically reported in the literature. She observed the child in a Swedish day care centre and described his language abilities as follows:

'He couldn't count to more than three in any language, after that he said: many. He didn't know the names of any colours in any language. He didn't know the names of most of the things around him, either at the day care centre or outside (I often took him out and downtown for walks) in any language. In Finnish he used only present tense, in Swedish present and past. Instead of the person inflection in Finnish he often used the infinitive form. Finnish has fifteen cases, and usually children master the 11 most common of them, around the age of three. He used only 6 of them, which meant that he for instance was unable to say that something was on something, or that somebody was going to a place or coming from a place' (Skutnabb-Kangas, 1978: 224).

Skutnabb-Kangas maintained that this child was 'semilingual' and that she had seen many children like him - immigrant children in Swedish-speaking school, pre-schools, and daycare centres. She went on to argue that many of the approximately 5 million immigrant children in industrialized Western European countries 'do not know any language properly, at the same level as monolingual children. The language tests and estimates show that they often lag up to four years behind their monolingual peers in language tests in both languages' (Skutnabb-Kangas, 1978: 229).

The children Skutnabb-Kangas is speaking of are not from middle-class families; their bilingual experience is not 'additive' (to use Lambert's (1977) terminology), but 'subtractive'. For many lower-class immigrant children, experience with a second language does more harm that good, according to this view; the child becomes semilingual.

Skutnabb-Kangas defined semilingualism as 'a linguistic handicap which prevents the individual from acquiring the linguistic skill appropriate to his original linguistic capacity in any language' (Toukomaa & Skutnabb-Kangas, 1977: 20). More specifically, certain aspects of linguistic competence are affected by semilingualism - the ability to understand the meaning of abstract concepts and synonyms, and the ability to deal with highly decontextualized language (Toukomaa & Skutnabb-Kangas, 1977). Thus, semilingualism is thought of as a low level of linguistic competence that impedes continued development in the first language, interferes with development in the second, and promotes cognitive deficiency and low levels of school achievement.

This use of the semilingualism concept has been attacked by a number of authors on various grounds. Several critics have argued that the notion de-emphasizes social factors and expresses a middle-class bias that does not reflect the sociolinguistic realities of lower-class minority-language children (Brent-Palmer, 1979). It implies conformity to norms implicit in standard language use, i.e., the language of the school and academic and social advancement (Stroud, 1978). Other critics have questioned the empirical validity of the research used by Skutnabb-Kangas to ground the semilingualism term, and have argued that the concept has become a term of opprobrium that has led to discriminatory thinking and behaviour towards immigrant children (Ekstrand, 1983).

Most linguists are sceptical of the semilingualism concept. There may be instances of extreme linguistic and communicative deprivation that lead to the kinds of language pathology that Skutnabb-Kangas observed. Indeed, the child that she described in her case study had little language input outside of daycare. He lived with his mother who travelled two hours each way to her work place and came home exhausted late in the evening. His situation may be less atypical than we would like to believe. Because of the economic situation their parents find themselves in, some children from poor working-class families suffer from being raised in impoverished linguistic environments.

However, many working-class children are surrounded by a rich linguistic environment. There may be a period when first language proficiency declines because of lack of opportunity to use this language and, at the same time, knowledge of the second language has not yet reached an age-appropriate level. Semilingualism is a useful way to refer to this developmental phase. Instead, the use of the term 'semilingualism' should be restricted to those cases where, through extreme social deprivation, bilingual children do not learn to function well in either language.

What is more common is *language imbalance*. That is, at certain points in the development of their languages bilingual children do not perform as well as native speakers in either language. Edith Magiste (1979), studying German-speaking children learning Swedish, reported on the basis of reaction time measures that as these measures improved in the second language they declined in the first. Indeed, using these kinds of subtle measures of proficiency it appears that language balance - in the sense of equivalent native-like proficiency in two languages - is impossible to obtain in practice, and there may be points when neither language is at native-like levels.

But this is not semilingualism. We are talking here of very subtle measures. Many bilingual children, obviously, would be judged as native-like in their ability in both of their languages. There may be shifts back and forth in which language is more proficient, depending on language use and exposure, but most children are able eventually to come up to age-level proficiency given more exposure and opportunities for use of the weaker language.

Even in those cases where it appears that children are 'semilingual', on closer examination, one of their languages is usually well-developed. Many teachers of Spanish-speaking children in the United States, for example, say that their children do not know either language at age-appropriate levels. However, in a study of six-year-old first-grade Spanish-speaking children living in poverty on San Antonio's west side, Pena (1967) found that the children's Spanish was more developed than it appeared at first glance.

'In most instances when the children were asked to respond spontaneously to an object or given situation pertinent to their experiential background, they responded in complete and correct grammatical constructions. It was also evident that even though the children possessed complete grammatical constructions in their language, the noun and verb slots were often filled with words borrowed from English or English words they had Hispanicized' (Pena, 1967: 158).

This brings us to the next issue.

The issue of language mixing

What of those instances where the child seems to confuse the two languages, where the child's language seems to be a hodgepodge of constructions and vocabulary

Retrospective on the study of early bilingualism

items, some drawn from one language and some from the other? Here are some examples from the speech of the famous Hildegard, the daughter of Werner Leopold, whose four volume work on his child's bilingualism (1939, 1947, 1949a, 1949b) remains one of the most important sources in the field. Hildegard spoke English with her mother and German with her father.

Die Milch pouren (Pour the milk).
Musik practicen (Practice music).
Ich habe geyawnt (I yawned).
For two monthe (For two months).

A number of authors have argued that such language mixing is an inevitable consequence of bilingual development, although estimates of the amount of mixing found in bilingual children's language vary. Marilyn Vihman reported that 34 per cent of her son's utterances were mixed at 20 months (Vihman, 1982); Redlinger and Park (1980) found up to 20 per cent mixed utterances in one of four case studies. However, Swain (1974) observed the linguistic interaction of a French-English bilingual child over a nine-month period beginning at 3;1 and found lexical mixing to occur in only four per cent of the child's utterances. Lindholm and Padilla (1977) found that only 2 per cent of the utterances produced by five Spanish-English bilingual children ranging in age from two to six years contained mixes.

Reported rates of mixing are difficult to interpret because of several factors (Genesee, 1987):

1. differential exposure to the languages in question;
2. the possibility of inequitable sampling of the child's language;
3. the lack of an acceptable metric of language development with which to identify children at comparable stages, and
4. different operational definitions of mixing.

In addition, the typological distance between the languages in question should be considered. Furthermore, there may be more mixing in the language of some children than others because adult bilinguals in their environment also mix languages in the same sentence.

In an interesting study of the language development of Mexican-American children, McClure (1977) observed that young bilinguals tended to code-mix more - that is to insert single items from one language in another:

I put the tenedores on the table.
I want a motorcycle verde.

These mixes tended to be nouns and, to a lesser degree, adjectives, and - contrary to the above examples - tended to be English words in a Spanish utterance. Children over the age of nine tended to code-change - that is, the switched languages for at least a phrase or a sentence - as much as they code mixed. McClure noted that younger children switched languages to resolve ambiguities and clarify statements, but that older children switched to convey social meanings. For older speakers code-switching is a rhetorical strategy used in such communicative tasks as persuading, explaining, requesting, and controlling. It is preferred to other rhetorical devices because it has greater semantic power deriving from metaphorical allusion to shared values and to the bilinguals' common problems vis-a-vis the society at large (Penalosa, 1980).

Susan Ervin-Tripp (1967) observed that where bilinguals have been interacting mainly with other bilinguals for a long time, the model for each of their languages is not monolingual usage of these languages but rather the languages as spoken by the bilinguals themselves. In this view, the mixed speech can be seen as a code of its own - a 'contact language' (Haugen, 1953) that is used in a bilingual setting when appropriate - that is, whenever speakers wish to stress in-group behavior or emphasize informality or rapport.

Such mixing of Spanish expressions in English and English expressions in Spanish is a speech style common in many Mexican-American communities, especially in the Southwest. This is nothing new: the same thing occurs in other ethnic groups. American Jews use certain Yiddish expressions and Italians certain Italian expressions to mark in-group identity.

There is general acceptance today that such code-switching is not a sign of linguistic confusion, but of linguistic vitality (Romaine, 1989). Studies of code switching in adults show it to be a sophisticated, rule-governed communicative device used by linguistically competent bilinguals to achieve a variety of communicative goals, such as conveying emphasis, role playing, or establishing socio-cultural identity (Genesee, 1987; Grosjean, 1982).

The issue of language mixing and code-switching continues to intrigue researchers studying early bilingualism. Genesee's critique is especially valuable in making us aware of the complexity involved in comparing children in different conditions of language presentation, but also of our responsibility for operationalizing what is meant by mixing and code-switching.

To this point, the discussion has focused on topics that relate to the general question of the effect on the child of being raised bilingually, with particular attention to linguistic issues. Another issue concerns the cognitive consequences of bilingualism. However, as Reynolds (1991) has recently pointed out, this body of research is plagued by procedural shortcomings, by pre-experimental and quasiexperimental designs that produce selection artifacts, and by problems in defining bilinguality. In this area, as one critic said of Hegel's philosophy, we are in a night where all cows are black.

How long does it take to learn a second language?

The next 'perennial' issue is the question of how long it takes to learn a second language. Research with preschool children indicates that in about a year most children acquire a second language in a naturalistic context. With older children there is more to learn - a nine-year-old child has a considerably larger vocabulary than a five-year-old - and so fluency is harder to achieve. Most authors say it takes about two years for school-age children to be able to communicate fluently in a second language with their peers (McLaughlin, 1985).

But we are talking here of fluency in the sense of person-to-person communication, or what Cummins (1981) refers to as context-embedded communicative skills. Literacy-related skills, the skills needed for reading and writing - what Cummins refers to as context-reduced linguistic proficiency - is another story. In a school context, it is not enough to be fluent in person-to-person discourse.

The child needs to be proficient in the context-reduced aspects of language as well. Cummins argued that bilingual programs in which children are exited early on the basis of language assessment instruments that tap only context-embedded skills do children a serious misservice. He noted that many educators have a confused idea of what it means to be proficient in English. Simply because a minority-language child shows proficiency in certain aspects of English-person-to-person communication does not mean that the child is ready for the all-English classroom, which demands linguistic proficiency in more abstract and disembedded communication. Cummins cited research evidence from a study of 1,210 immigrant children in Canada indicating that it takes minority-language children approximately five to seven years to master the context-reduced cognitive skills required for the regular English curriculum, whereas it takes only about two years to master the context-embedded aspects of English proficiency.

Three other studies bear on the question of how long it takes school-age children to learn a second language. The first study compared Navajo children exposed to monolingual instruction in English with an ESL component with Navajo children in a bilingual program in which they were instructed in reading in their native language and then transferred to English (Rosier, 1977). Initially children in the bilingual program performed worse on tests of English language ability, but subsequently they surpassed children in the ESL condition. It took, on the average, about three or four years of bilingual instruction for the effects of the program to show up.

Wong Fillmore, who has conducted research with a large number of children in bilingual classrooms (1982; Wong Fillmore et al., 1984) reported that minority-language children can generally acquire oral communicative skills in the second language fairly quickly. Within two or three years most children could at least give the impression that they speak the language well. However, it required much longer to attain the level of proficiency required for understanding the language in its instructional use. She reported that typical learners took as many as four to six years to acquire the language skills needed for school.

A final study was conducted by Collier (1987), who analysed the length of time required for LEP students to become proficient in cognitive-academic English. Her sample included data from 1977 to 1984 on 1,548 minority-language children who had received part-time ESL instruction. On the basis of her analysis of these data, Collier concluded that it takes no less than 4 years, and may take as many as 8 or more years, for the most advantaged LEP students to acquire full learning proficiency in a second language at the level of native speakers, as measured by standardized tests. Furthermore, Collier argued that all LEP children would profit from a minimum of two years of continuing cognitive-academic development in their native languages.

What this research suggests is that learning a second language takes a lot more time that people generally acknowledge. There is a widespread belief, even among highly educated individuals, that children are miraculous second language-learners. Research contradicts this view. At least in the contexts of Canadian and American schools, it takes immigrant children several years to develop the language skills they need to be on a par with native English speakers. Many children never develop the reading comprehension skills they need to do well in high school and beyond.

Is there a critical period for second language acquisition?

This brings us to the final 'perennial' issue. For a long time, it was commonly believed that young children are superior to older children and adults in second-language learning. The notion was that there was a 'critical period' for second-language learning and that older children and adults, having passed the critical period, could not learn second languages as easily and quickly as young children. However, when direct comparisons were made between older learners and child second-language learners, results usually indicated that adult (and adolescent) learners performed better on measures of morphology and syntax than did child learners. Children typically - but not always - showed superiority in the learning of phonology (McLaughlin, 1984).

Krashen, Long, and Scarcella (1979) - in an oft-cited article - have argued that adults acquire the morphology and syntax of a second language faster than young children, but that child learners will ultimately attain higher proficiency levels. They endorsed a 'younger-is-better' position, according to which child second-language learners are expected to be superior to adolescents and adults in terms of ultimate achievement. The research they cited, however, indicates that ultimate proficiency in morphology and syntax is highest among informal learners who have begun acquisition during early adolescence - from 12 to 15.

Furthermore, research with school children learning second languages contradicts the younger-is-better hypothesis. In the largest single study of children learning a second language in a school context, 17,000 British children learning French were compared on the basis of when they started the language (Stern, Burstall & Harley, 1975). After five years of exposure, children who began at eleven years were found to be more successful language learners than children who began at eight years. This study leads one to conclude that, given the same amount of exposure, older children are better second-language learners than younger ones. A number of other studies in the European context have produced the same findings, which is why second-language instruction in many European countries begins when children are nine or ten, rather than earlier.

One possible reason for these findings is that the instructional techniques used for young children were inappropriate. In much European second-language instruction, heavy emphasis is placed on formal grammatical analysis, and it may be that older children are more skilled in dealing with such an instructional approach. This argument is contradicted, however, by the findings from Canadian immersion programs, which indicate that children in late immersion programs (in which the second language is introduced when children are eleven or twelve) have been found to perform just as well on tests of second-language proficiency as children who began their immersion experience at kindergarten or grade one and who have had more than twice as much exposure.

This Canadian research is especially important because, in the immersion classroom, little emphasis is placed on the formal aspects of grammar, and, therefore, older children should have no advantage over younger ones. Although not all research indicates that late immersion students do as well as early immersion students (McLaughlin, 1985), differences in performance are by no means as great as relative amount of classroom exposure would lead one to expect. It appears that older children, because of more developed cognitive strategies, may do better than younger children at the task of learning a second language in the school context (Wong Fillmore, 1982).

The question of when to begin second-language instruction is still a topic of considerable debate in the literature. It is important to note that research on this issue involves the comparison of age groups in which other variables - such as amount of exposure and opportunities for use -are controlled. But in practice, there is a general consensus that the more exposure and the greater the opportunities for second-language use, the better. This would imply that the sooner a child starts a second language, the better. Younger children have more time at their disposal and no variable is as important as time on task.

Conclusions

Most scholars agree that bilingualism is of positive benefit to children and that the beliefs about negative effects of bilingualism held in a previous era are incorrect. Many scholars would also support the notion that, in the case of children schooled in a second language, it is important to use the child's first language for a longer period of time than is usually done -indeed, to maintain that language whenever possible. As Kenji Hakuta (1991) has pointed out, bilingualism is a valuable gift, and all children should be given the opportunity to develop bilingual competence.

To one looking back on the past several decades of research on childhood bilingualism - as I have attempted to do in this paper - a number of perennial concerns recur. Most of these concerns are represented in research discussed in this volume. In addition, there are other areas that have attracted interest in recent years - bilingual communication strategies, language loss and language choice, narration in a second language - topics that also are treated in this volume.

What will be the future of research on childhood bilingualism? My prognosis is that the field will be greatly influenced in the next decade by work in cognitive psychology and developmental psychology. Increasing attention will be given to cognitive processes in childhood bilingualism, for example lexical development in bilingual children, metacognition, reading and writing in a second language. It is also likely that more attention will be given to socio-emotional development in bilingual children, the home-school mismatch, adolescent bicultural identity. These are challenging issues and one can look forward to exciting work in childhood bilingualism.

References

Arnberg, L., 1987. *Raising children bilingually: The Preschool Years.* Clevedon, Avon:Multilingual Matters.

Brent-Palmer, C., 1979. A sociolinguistic assessment of the notion of 'immigrant semilingualism'; from a social conflict perspective. *Working Papers in Bilingualism,* 17, 135-180.

Collier, V., 1987. Age and rate of acquisition of a second language for academic purposes. *TESOL Quarterly,* 27, 617-641.

Cummins, J., 1981. *Bilingualism and minority-language children.* Toronto: The Ontario Institute for Studies in Education.

Ekstrand, L., 1983. Maintenance or transition - or both? A review of Swedish ideologies and empirical research. In: T. Husen (ed.), *Multicultural and multilingual education in immigrant countries.* London: Pergamon Press.

Ervin-Tripp, S., 1967. An Issei learns English. *Journal of Social Issues,* 23, 78-90.

Genesee, F., 1987. *Learning through two languages: Studies of Immersion and Bilingual Education.* New York: Newbury House.

Grosjean, F., 1982. *Life with two languages: An introduction to bilingualism.* Cambridge MA: Harvard University Press.

Hakuta, K., 1986. *The mirror of language: The debate on bilingualism.* New York: Basic Books.

Hakuta, K., 1991. *Bilingualism as a gift.* Paper presented at the Esther Katz Rosen Symposium on the Psychological Development of Gifted Children. Lawrence, KA: University of Kansas.

Hamers, J. & M. Blanc, 1989. *Bilinguality and bilingualism.* Cambridge: Cambridge University Press.

Harding, E. & P. Riley, 1986. *The bilingual family: A handbook for parents.* Cambridge: Cambridge University Press.

Haugen, E., 1953. *The Norwegian language in America.* Philadelphia: University of Pennsylvania Press.

Krashen, S., M. Long & R. Scarcella, 1979. Age, rate, and eventual attainment in second language acquisition. *TESOL Quarterly,* 13, 573-582.

Lambert, W., 1977. The effects of bilingualism on the individual: Cognitive and sociocultural consequences. In: P. Hornby (ed.), *Bilingualism: Psychological, social and educational implications*. New York: Academic Press.

Leopold, W., 1939, 1947, 1949a, 1949b. *Speech development of a bilingual child: A linguist's record*. Vol. 1: *Vocabulary growth in the first two years*. Vol. 2: *Sound learning in the first two years*. Vol. 3: *Grammar and general problems in the first two years*. Vol. 4: *Diary from age two*. Evanston, IL: Northwestern University Press.

Lindholm, K. & A. Padilla, 1977. Language mixing in bilingual children. *Journal of Child Language,* 5, 327-335.

McClure, E., 1977. *Aspects of code switching in the discourse of bilingual Mexican American children*. Technical Report No. 44. Cambridge, MA: Berancek and Newman.

McLaughlin, B., 1978. *Second-language acquisition in childhood*. First edition. Hillsdale, N.J.: Lawrence Erlbaum Associates.

McLaughlin, B., 1984. *Second-language acquisition in childhood. Volume 1: Pre-school children*. Hillsdale, N. J.: Lawrence Erlbaum Associates.

McLaughlin, B., 1985. *Second-language acquisition in childhood. Volume 2: School-age children*. Hillsdale, N. J.: Lawrence Erlbaum Associates.

Magiste, E., 1979. The competing language systems of the multilingual: A developmental study of decoding and encoding processes. *Journal of Verbal Learning and Verbal Behavior,* 18, 79-89. Pavlovitch, M., 1920. *Le langage enfantin: Acquisition du serbe et du francais par un enfant serbe*. Paris: Champion.

Pena, A., 1967. *A comparative study of selected syntactic structures of the oral language status in Spanish and English of disadvantaged first grade Spanish-speaking children*. Ph.D. Thesis, University of Texas at Austin.

Penalosa, F., 1980. *Chicano sociolinguistics: A brief introduction*. Rowley, MA: Newbury House. Redlinger, W. & T. Park, 1980. Language mixing in young bilinguals. *Journal of Child Language,* 7, 337-352.

Reynolds, A., 1991. The cognitive consequences of bilingualism. In: A. Renolds (ed.), *Bilingualism, multiculturalism, and second language learning: The McGill Conference in honor of Wallace E. Lambert*. Hillsdale, N. J.: Lawrence Erlbaum Associates.

Romaine, S., 1989. *Bilingualism*. Oxford: Basil Blackwood.

Ronjat, J., 1913. *Le developpement du langage observe chez un enfant bilingue*. Paris: Champion.

Rosier, P., 1977. *A comparative study of two approaches of introducing initial reading to Navajo children: The direct method and the native-language method*. Doctoral Dissertation, Northern Arizona University.

Saunders, G., 1982 *Bilingual children: Guidance for the family*. Clevedon, Avon: Multilingual matters.

Skutnabb-Kangas, T., 1978. Semilingualism and the education of migrant children as a means of reproducing the caste of assembly line workers. In: N. Ditmarr, H. Haberland, T. Skutnabb-Kangas, & U. Teleman (eds), *Papers from the first*

Scandinavian-German symposium on the language of immigrant workers and their children. Roskilde: Universitetscenter.

Stern, H., C. Burstall & B. Harley, 1975. *French from age eight or eleven?* Toronto: Ontario Institute for Studies in Education.

Stroud, C., 1978. The concept of semilingualism. *Working Papers,* 16, 153-172. Lund, Sweden: Lund University, Department of General Linguistics.

Swain, M., 1974. Child bilingual language learning and linguistic interdependence. In: S. Carey (ed.), *Bilingualism, Biculturalism, and Education.* Edmonton: University of Alberta Press.

Toukomaa, P. & T. Skutnabb-Kangas, 1977. *The intensive teaching of the mother tongue to migrant children at pre-school age.* University of Tampere. UNESCO. Tutkimusia Research Reports, Sweden.

Vihman, M., 1982. The acquisition of morphology by a bilingual child: The whole-word approach. *Applied Psycholinguistics,* 3, 141-160.

Vildomec, V., 1963. *Multilingualism: General linguistics and psychology of speech.* Leyden: Sijthoff.

Wong Fillmore, L., 1982. *The development of second language literacy skills.* Statement to the National Commission on Excellence in Education. Houston, Texas.

Wong Fillmore, L., M. Ammon, P. Ammon, B. McLaughlin, 1984. *Learning English through bilingual instruction: Final Report. (Contract, 400-80-0030).* Washington, DC: National Institute of Education.

Retrospective on the study of early bilingualism

The Separate Development Hypothesis:
method and implications

This paper starts with a general overview of the main findings of a recent longitudinal case study of a young Dutch-English bilingual child (De Houwer, 1990). This case study provides strong support for the Separate Development Hypothesis (SDH), but the Kate study alone does not offer entirely sufficient nor necessarily generalizable evidence for it. It is the primary purpose of this paper to explore how the SDH can be further investigated. In this exploration due attention is given to methodological considerations. Finally, suggestions are made concerning the relevance of the SDH for child language studies in general.

Case study of a Dutch-English bilingual child: an overview

Subject and method

The mini-bilingual referred to in the title of this paper is a little girl, Kate, who was tape-recorded in her home during 19 spontaneous interaction sessions in the 8 month period between the ages of *2;7* and 3;4. The recordings mostly took place while Kate was interacting with her mother and the investigator, although there are also a few (parts of) recordings made while Kate was alone with one adult. Occasionally Kate's father was present during recording.

From birth onwards Kate was addressed in Standard American English by her American mother, and Kate's Flemish father always spoke to her in standard Dutch. Kate's case, then, is one of Bilingual First Language Acquisition or BFLA (Meisel, 1989; De Houwer, 1990: 3).

The investigator addressed Kate in a fairly standard colloquial variety of Dutch. Kate lived in Antwerp, Belgium, at the time of the recordings. Whereas the 'street environment' was Dutch speaking, Kate had a lot of contact with English outside the home through a thriving English speaking community which included a church, a playgroup and a small school, all of which Kate visited regularly. All in all, the amount of Dutch and English that Kate heard from the various people around her was fairly balanced for both languages.

Kate's two languages were clearly separated in the input, i.e., the people around Kate usually addressed her in one of two languages only. Thus, Kate grew up in a one person/one language environment.

All the recorded material was transcribed in full in normal spelling. The child utterances were then entered on computer disks, coded along various dimensions and analysed using specially designed programs. Detailed methodological information can be found in De Houwer (1990: 71-85).

Analyses and findings

Main points

Kate's linguistic portrait around the age of three, as it emerges from the various analyses performed, can be sketched as follows: Kate was a child who could equally well function in English as in Dutch, and she could at least partially be described as being two monolinguals in one. In effect, Kate's language production for each language closely resembled that of her monolingual peers. In addition, however, Kate was a competent code-switcher, and the relatively few utterances with lexical material from both languages were mostly well-formed according to the grammatical rules of either Dutch or English. Kate also showed quite a few signs of metalinguistic awareness.

The conclusions mentioned above were arrived at on the basis of highly detailed analyses of the following aspects: most of the morphosyntactic characteristics present in the material, those aspects in the material that were directly related to the language contact situation, and signs of metalinguistic awareness.

Morphosyntax

Apart from one area, namely syntagmatic relations within noun phrases, all the morphosyntactic subsystems analysed are quite distinct and different from each other in adult English and Dutch. Hence it becomes possible to investigate whether the child is acquiring these subsystems within each language, or whether, conversely, there is any influence from one language on the other. After all, one can only approach the issue whether development proceeds intra- or interlinguistically on the basis of areas that are quite different from one another in the respective input systems (see also Meisel, 1989).

The particular subsystems investigated in the Kate study concern both paradigmatic and syntagmatic relationships within noun phrases and verb phrases, the use of sentential word order, and the nature and complexity of sentences. More specifically, the following areas were studied:

– the marking of gender by means of pronouns, determiners and the $<\partial>$ morpheme as used on Dutch modifying adjectives
– plural formation
– the use of diminutives
– noun phrases with an adjective as head
– paradigmatic and syntagmatic characteristics of verb forms

- the conjugation of finite verbs (lexical verbs; HEBBEN/HAVE; ZIJN/BE; modals; auxiliary DO)
- syntagmatic relationships within verb phrases
- the expression of past time reference by means of verbs
- the expression of future time reference by means of verbs
- the order of subject, finite/non-finite verb, and object in declarative main clauses
- word order in clauses with a multi-component VP
- word order in subordinate clauses
- word order in questions
- question words in WH-questions
- sentence types
- clause types
- the use of clause connectors
- the type and frequency of clause constituents.

The analysis of the morphosyntactic characteristics of Kate's language production showed that each of Kate's two languages developed separately from the other: Kate's two languages at the time of investigation constituted two distinct, structurally closed sets. There was no evidence of structures, patterns or rules of the one language being applied to the other. This major finding led to the formulation of what I have called the Separate Development Hypothesis, which will be discussed in more detail later in this paper. Detailed comparisons of the data with published reports on language usage by monolingual pre-schoolers around the age of three showed that, at least as far as morphosyntax was concerned, Kate's English data were highly similar to those reported for English speaking children, while her Dutch data were highly similar to those reported for Dutch speaking children. My impression is that Kate's phonology was 'native'-like (see Davies, 1991 for a discussion of this notion) for both of her languages, but no comparisons were made with data from her monolingual American English and Flemish Dutch speaking peers to further substantiate this claim.

Language choice and mixed utterances

A second main focus of analysis were those aspects in the material that were directly related to the language contact situation, namely language choice and the linguistic characteristics of mixed utterances. Mixed utterances are here defined as utterances containing lexical material from both languages.

It was found that Kate's language choice was mainly determined by the interlocutor: Kate addressed each person in her environment mostly in the language that that person tended to address her in. On those relatively few occasions when she did not, Kate apparently took into account language behaviour of the interacting person that was not directly addressed to her. More precisely, she allowed herself to be quite 'relaxed', in a sense, about her language choice with persons that she knew to be fluent bilinguals, such as the investigator and her father. These individuals spoke English and Dutch frequently and with great ease and fluency in Kate's hearing range: they would often use English with Kate's mother and with English speaking visitors. With Kate, however, they would use mostly Dutch. Kate largely accommodated these bilinguals by mostly addressing them in Dutch, too, but in about 10 per cent of the cases she addressed them in English, which, as she probably assumed, would not hamper communication. Kate was rather less inclined to use the 'wrong' language with persons that she knew to be basically monolingual (her mother and her paternal grandparents). In both her willingness to lean on two linguistic systems alternatingly in interactions with known bilinguals and her reluctance to do so in conversations with monolinguals, Kate strongly resembles older bilinguals (see, e.g., Romaine, 1989). Mixed utterances occur throughout the Kate study and constitute an average of 7 per cent of all child utterances in the material.

A formal analysis was made of mixed utterances that could clearly be described as consisting of a 'guest' and a 'host' language. The 'host' language is considered the main language of the utterance, i.e., if more than 50 per cent of all the morphemes in an utterance are in language X, then X is the host language. Any morphemes from language Y are defined as insertions from the guest language. It was found that the 'guest' language insertions in the Kate data typically consisted of single nouns.

Both the finding that language choice is mainly determined by interlocutor and the finding that in mixed utterances it is most frequently a noun that is inserted from the guest language are confirmed by many other studies of very young bilingual children (see, e.g., Kielhöfer & Jonekeit, 1983; Saunders, 1982; Swain & Wesche, 1975; Taeschner, 1983).

Metalinguistic awareness

As a third major strand in the analysis of the corpus the data were scanned for possible signs of metalinguistic awareness. These signs were found in spontaneous and elicited repairs, explicit metalinguistic statements, hesitations and self-repetitions. The main reason for the investigation of these possible signs of metalinguistic awareness, apart from the fact that they are inherently interesting in the study of child language (see, e.g., Cazden e.a., 1984), was the finding that in both languages Kate made a dramatic jump in morphosyntactic development after her third birthday. Until then, she had been relatively stagnant, but after her third birthday many new forms appeared, while old forms were used more appropriately and more frequently. This development was clearly noticeable in many areas of morphosyntax at the same time, regardless of what language Kate was using. Following Clark (1982), it was hypothesized that such a striking development that was going on in both languages at once might be due to a general increase in metalinguistic awareness.

Signs of metalinguistic awareness were indeed quite noticeably on the increase after Kate's third birthday, both in terms of frequency and in terms of type, and this again regardless of what language Kate was using. However, the existence of a causal relation between metalinguistic awareness on the one hand and morphosyntactic development on the other could unfortunately not be proven. On the positive side, though, empirical evidence was provided for the hypothesis that there is a language-independent mechanism, namely the monitor (in the sense of, e.g., Clark & Andersen, 1979 and Marshall & Morton, 1978 rather than Krashen, 1978), which provides a basis for the development of language awareness. The language-independent nature of this mechanism had hitherto not been empirically proved, since it had only been investigated in monolingual speakers.

The Separate Development Hypothesis

Definition

The Separate Development Hypothesis claims that 'the morphosyntactic development of a pre-school child regularly exposed to two languages from birth which are presented in a separate manner proceeds in a separate fashion for both languages' (De Houwer, 1990: 339; the SDH is not to be confused with the Independent Development Hypothesis as defined by Bergman, 1976).

Although the SDH does not specifically refer to any age range, it was intended to apply to normally developing bilingual children between the ages of, more or less, two to four. It cannot be predicted what happens once a bilingual child's two languages are firmly established as far as basic morphosyntax goes. In the field of BFLA so far, the issue of separate development on the morphosyntactic level has only been approached for subjects under the age of four. Because of the greater level of competence in both languages at around the age of four and the concomitant great expansion of linguistic knowledge and capabilities on all levels, it may become harder for the bilingual child to keep both rule systems apart. Contact with bilingual speakers who do not keep their languages systematically apart might also trigger interference phenomena in the hitherto 'double monolingual bilingual child'. These intriguing possibilities are well worth pursuing.

Evidence for the SDH until now

The results of the Kate study certainly fit the Separate Development Hypothesis (SDH). There is ample evidence in the Kate corpus that clearly shows the existence of two separate, morphosyntactically closed linguistic systems. Furthermore, the very fact that detailed comparisons with comparable data for English and Dutch speaking children showed Kate to be highly similar to monolingual children in each of her languages gives further strong support for the SDH. The one element in the definition of the SDH that is less straightforward is the element referring to the role played by the input.

Kate happened to be a child who heard her two languages from separate input sources. In formulating the SDH this fact had to be taken into account. It would not have been profitable to state the SDH as: 'the morphosyntactic development of a pre-school child regularly exposed to two languages from birth proceeds in a separate fashion for both languages'. Such a hypothesis would implicitly and, I believe, wrongly deny the possible role of the type of input that the bilingual child is receiving. In the final formulation of the SDH, therefore, the role of the input was strongly emphasized.

However, although the SDH as it stands now does in fact explain the data for Kate, it goes far beyond those data, since it is stated in a very general fashion. This begs the question of how generally applicable the SDH actually is. To the best of my knowledge, there have so far been no methodologically sound reports in the Western literature on children growing up with two separate languages from birth who do not develop these two languages separately as far as morphosyntax goes. In fact, the little evidence that is available fully supports the SDH, but the data base for this evidence is quite small, since it concerns only a handful of bilingual children (outside the Kate study, see mainly Meisel, 1985, 1986, 1989, 1990; Parodi, 1990; Schlyter, 1990).

In the following we shall explore ways of finding more positive evidence that could further substantiate the SDH.

Ways to further explore the SDH

Additional evidence for the Separate Development Hypothesis could be gained primarily from more case studies of bilingual children acquiring two languages from birth that are separated in the input (i.e., of children growing up in a one person/one language situation).

Selection of subjects

Morphosyntactic development can be studied in children from quite a young age. From monolingual acquisition data it appears that there is quite a wide variation in the onset of productive morphosyntactic markers, depending both on the individual child and the particular language being acquired (see, e.g., Mills, 1986; Peters, 1983; the papers in Slobin, 1985, Volume 1; Wells, 1985). Thus, it is not inappropriate to suggest that bilingual children be studied from the age of approximately two and a half years onwards, at which time they should be at the end of the two-word stage and/or in the beginning (or even the middle) of the multi-word stage (see, e.g., Ingram, 1989, Schaerlaekens & Gillis, 1987).

In choosing a young bilingual subject one must, of course, be fairly sure that one is dealing with a child who has no hearing impediment or other noticeable dysfunction. If, for instance, by the age of two and a half years one's possible bilingual subject is still only producing mainly single word utterances, there can be serious doubt as to whether the child's hearing is normal. In this case the child should not be studied to approach the SDH, since the SDH, if not explicitly so, was formulated to capture a reality for children who are developing normally.

Another point is that in the search for further evidence for the SDH the language pairs that young bilingual subjects are learning should be as diverse as possible. Obviously, the more linguistic variety there is in the total body of data from young bilingual children that fit the SDH, the greater the chance is that the SDH captures a general acquisition principle in young bilingual children. After all, if only a small number of languages are investigated, there might still be a chance that any apparent confirmation of the SDH is in fact an effect of the specific languages in one's sample.

Although longitudinal studies are still sorely needed in the field of BFLA in general, in order to specifically address the SDH I think it is important that many different children learning many different languages be studied, rather than that the focus be solely on longterm individual case studies, which are very time-consuming. Though these long-term case studies can, of course, be used to test the SDH, they are not necessarily the only possible way to approach it or the most efficient one.

Data base and analysis

The SDH can be approached as soon as one has available a substantial number of utterances in each language that the child is exposed to. These utterances should be longer than a single word. After all, syntax or internal phrase structure do not show up in single word utterances, and bound morphemes only minimally so.

The question is what counts as a substantial number of utterances in each language. The answer here is not straightforward, but I would think that for one child about 300 fully transcribed, fully clear utterances in each language would give one a sufficiently large basis to work from. These 600 utterances would have to be collected in a relatively short time span, say one to one and a half months, so as to produce internal consistency. The central issue when addressing the SDH is, after all, not developmental processes over time, but the relationship between the child's two languages at any given moment within the age range indicated earlier (approximately from two to four).

In analysing the data one can look only at those cross-linguistically comparable areas that are clearly different for the two languages (cf. also Meisel, 1989). If the SDH is correct, the child data should show a difference for those different areas, and there should be no clear influence from the one language on the other. There will be ambiguous cases, however, in which the child produces forms that could be interpreted as being either the result of transfer or the result of development. One way of getting around this interpretative problem could be to look at data from monolingual acquisition: if the bilingual child uses ambiguous forms similar to a monolingual peer there is a possibility that the forms are developmentally, i.e., intralinguistically, determined. However, such a comparative approach can never entirely settle the issue since a similarity of form does not necessarily indicate a similarity in processing. Hence, intrinsically ambiguous forms in the bilingual data will have to remain just that, and their source(s) will have to remain unresolved.

For the SDH to be found valid, all or most of the morphosyntactic elements used by a particular bilingual child must be shown to be primarily intralinguistically determined. Hence, I think it is important in exploring the SDH further that one looks at all or most of the morphosyntactic features that are present in the data. After all, it is possible that there is separate development in one area of language functioning (e.g., subject-finite verb agreement) but heavy use of transfer in another one (e.g., the use of sentential word order). Should one find this to be the case, it is not obvious what the conclusions would be with regard to the SDH.

Interpretation

Suppose, then, that all or most of tyhe morphosyntactic features present in a particular bilingual child's data have been analysed. If it is established that in the majority of the areas studied there is indeed a separate development, and that there are only a few ambiguous areas whose interpretation is not straightforward (and there normally will be a few areas like these), one has indeed found strong evidence for the SDH.

If, on the other hand, most of the material analysed is uninterpretable, and only some of it is straightforward, i.e., shows separate development, then there is clearly less strong support for the SDH. In this case, further analyses could be carried out based on morphosyntactic elements that are highly similar for the two languages involved, in het hope that these will reveal differences in the child data. These differences would, I expect, more often than not show up in the absence of a particular form in the one language while it is clearly present in the other. If indeed differences could be found there would be more of a basis to tilt one's former interim conclusion in favor of the SDH. In interpreting the analyses for the features that are similar in the input languages one would however have to tread very carefully indeed.

Finally, it is clear that the more children of widely diverse bilingual and socio-psychological backgrounds there are whose data fit the SDH, the more positive evidence there is for it, more so than if one has found many bilingual children of very similar backgrounds learning the same set of languages whose data fit the hypothesis.

Why further explore the SDH?

Any attempt to find supportive evidence for the SDH will be quite time-consuming and involve a great deal of effort. Apart from the obivous benefit from such attempts, in the sense that they would contribute to a greater knowledge of the bilingual acquisition process, the question can be asked whether the SDH is relevant within the larger framework of child language acquisition studies.

In the field of child language acquisition the search for explanations of the language development process continues steadily (see e.g. Gleason et al., 1989; Ingram 1989; Kuczaj 1985/86). Many different and interacting factors are obviously

The Separate Development Hypothesis

involved in this process. Depending on the school of thought that a particular researcher identifies with, or depending on one's training as a researcher (Bennett-Kastor, 1985/86), the most important factors are identified as being either cognitive, social, psychological, language-specific, language-universal, interactive or input-related.

In trying to gauge the weight of specific factors in acquisition, different children must be compared with each other. Lately, there have been many cross-linguistic studies which attempt to isolate differences or similarities in acquisition patterns across monolingual children from different language backgrounds (see, e.g., Simon & Fourcin, 1978; Slobin, 1985). In these studies, however, it is extremely difficult, if not impossible, to control for extralinguistic characteristics such as level of cognitive, emotional, and social development, and to ensure that the only variable is the feature 'language'.

It is notoriously difficult to fully match young children to each other. Identical twins come the closest to being a fully matched pair, but if they are brought up monolingually, it is impossible to investigate the relative importance of linguistic vs. non-linguistic factors in acquisition. It is rather young bilingual children that offer the ideal laboratory for studying this issue. The main variable in their case is the factor language. The use of bilingual subjects to approach theoretical issues in the study of child language acquisition in general can thus be seen as a highly recommendable methodological step (see, e.g., Levy, 1985 for a similar line of argumentation).

What, then, is the significance of the Separate Development Hypothesis for explanations of child language acquisition in general? The repeated confirmation of the SDH would, I think, provide very strong evidence for the importance of the input-related nature of the language learning task as far as morphosyntax is concerned. After all, the young bilingual child who shows evidence of the SDH clearly approaches his or her two languages as distinct, closed sets. This highly language-specific development is only possible on the basis of the existence in the input of two closed linguistic systems, and the child's subsequent perception and processing of these systems as being separate.

If more universal processes were strongly at work in the acquisition of morpho-syntax, one would expect these universal processes to be able to override any input-related, and hence language-specific, strategies in acquisition. Thus, one would expect to see forms in the data that were clearly the result of the transfer of patterns from the other language. A confirmation of the SDH would clearly go against this, and hence also against the importance of universal strategies as a *primary* explanation for morphosyntactic development.

Universal strategies may play an important role in the acquisition of morphosyntax, but these universal strategies must be held captive, so to speak, by the particular language that is being acquired. Within the separate acquisition of each of a bilingual child's two languages, similar processes may be at work; however, there are no comparison procedures going on between the actual forms that are being acquired. These forms are relatable only to the specific input that the child is receiving in each of his or her languages. It appears to me that for a better understanding of morphosyntactic development in both monolingual and bilingual children we would do well to find out more about the specific characteristics of that input.

Conclusions

This paper started off with a review of the main findings from a case study of a young bilingual girl, Kate, who developed her two languages, English and Dutch, in an entirely language-specific manner as far as morphosyntax is concerned. Kate grew up in a one person/one language situation.

On the basis of the findings from the Kate study the Separate Development Hypothesis was formulated. This hypothesis claims that in the pre-school acquisition of two separate languages from birth the morphosyntax of each language develops independently from the other. As such, the SDH draws a direct link between the nature of the input in bilingual acquisition and the nature of morphosyntactic development.

Since the current evidence for the SDH is quite limited, suggestions were made for ways to further explore its validity. It was argued that in order to do this many short-term but highly detailed studies focusing on morphosyntactic development are needed of young bilingual children between the ages of two to four growing up with two separate languages from birth. These languages should be as diverse as possible. The main emphasis in studies addressing the SDH should be on those aspects in the two languages under investigation that are structurally different.

It was further argued that the confirmation of the SDH has theoretical repercussions for explanations in the field of child language acquisition in general. Language is part of socialization. This social aspect of language becomes much more foregrounded when bilingual children are studied than when one is dealing with monolingual children. With monolingual children it is easy to disregard this social dimension, and to concentrate solely on, for instance, cognitive factors. In addition, with monolingual children it is easy to overlook the inputrelated, language-specific nature of the acquisition process. It is my hope that more researchers in the field of child language research will start to turn their attention to the study of bilingual children, who can furnish us with a better basis to look for explanations in acquisition.

Acknowledgement

The author would like to thank W. Wölck, State University of New York, for very helpful comments and discussions about this paper.

References

Bennett-Kastor, T., 1985/86. The two fields of child language research. *First language, 6,* 161-174.

Bergman, C., 1976. Interference vs. independent development in infant bilingualism. In: G. Keller, R. Teschner and S. Viera (eds), *Bilingualism in he bicentennial and beyond,* 86-96. New York: Bilingual Press/Editorial Bilingüe.

Cazden, C., S. Michaels & T. Patton, 1984. Spontaneous repairs in sharing time narratives: the intersection of metalinguistic awareness, speech event and narrative style. In: S. Freedman (ed.), *The acquisition of written language: revision and response.* Norwood, N.J.: Ablex.

Clark, E., 1982. Language change during language acquisition. In: M. Lamb & A. Brown (eds), *Advances in developmental psychology. Volume 2,* 171-195. Hillsdale, New Jersey: Lawrence Erlbaum Associates.

Clark, E. & E. Andersen, 1979. Spontaneous repairs: awareness in the process of acquiring language. *Papers and reports on child language development,* 16, 1-12.

Davies, A., 1991. The notion of the native speaker. *Journal of Intercultural Studies,* 12, 35-45.

De Houwer, A., 1990. *The acquisition of two languages from birth: a case study.* Cambridge: Cambridge University Press.

Gleason, J., D. Hay & L. Cain, 1989. Social and affective determinants of language acquisition. In: M. Rice & R. Schiefelbusch (eds), *The teachability of language,* 171-186. Baltimore: Brookes.

Ingram, D., 1989. *First language acquisition. Method, description, and explanation.* Cambridge: Cambridge University Press.

Kielhöfer, B. & S. Jonekeit, 1983. *Zweisprachige Kindererziehung.* Tübingen: Stauffenberg Verlag.

Krashen, S., 1978. Individual variation in the use of the monitor. In: W. Ritchie, (ed.), *Second language acquisition research,* 175-183. New York: Academic Press.

Kuczaj II, S., 1985/86. General developmental patterns and individual differences in the acquisition of copula and auxiliary *be* forms. *First Language,* 6, 111-117.

Levy, Y., 1985. Theoretical gains from the study of bilingualism: a case report. *Language learning,* 35, 541-554.

Marshall, J. & J. Morton, 1978. On the mechanics of Emma. In: A. Sinclair, R. Jarvella & W. Levelt (eds), *The child's conception of language,* 225-239. Berlin: Springer-Verlag.

Meisel, J., 1985. Les phases initiales du développement de notions temporelles, aspectuelles et de modes d'action. Étude basée sur le langage d'enfants bilingues français-allemand. *Lingua,* 66, 321-374.

Meisel, J., 1986. Word order and case marking in early child language. Evidence from simultaneous acquisition of two first languages: French and German. *Linguistics,* 24, 123-183.

Meisel, J., 1989. Early differentiation of languages in bilingual children. In: K.

Hyltenstam & L. Obler (eds), *Bilingualism across the lifespan. Aspects of acquisition, maturity and loss,* 13-40. Cambridge: Cambridge University Press.

Meisel, J., 1990. INFL-ection: Subjects and subject-verb agreement. In: J. Meisel, (ed.), *Two first languages – early grammatical development in bilingual children,* 237-298. Dordrecht: Foris Publications.

Mills, A., 1986. *The acquisition of gender. A study of English and German.* Berlin: Springer-Verlag.

Parodi, T., 1990. The acquisition of word order regularities and case morphology. In: J. Meisel, (ed.), *Two first languages – early grammatical development in bilingual children,* 157-192. Dordrecht: Foris Publications.

Peters, A., 1983. *The units of language acquisition.* Cambridge: Cambridge University Press.

Romaine, S., 1989. *Bilingualism.* Oxford: Blackwell.

Saunders, G., 1982. *Bilingual children: guidance for the family.* Clevedon: Multilingual Matters.

Schaerlaekens, A. & S. Gillis, 1987. *De taalverwerving van het kind. Een hernieuwde oriëntatie in het Nederlandstalig onderzoek.* Groningen: Wolters-Noordhoff.

Schlyter, S., (1990), The acquisition of tense and aspect. In: J. Meisel, (ed.), *Two first languages – early grammatical development in bilingual children,* 87-122. Dordrecht: Foris Publications.

Simon, C. & A. Fourcin, 1978. Cross-language study of speech-pattern learning. *Journal of the Acoustical Society of America,* 63, 925-935.

Slobin, D. (ed.), 1985. *The cross-linguistic study of language acquisition.* Hillsdale, New Jersey: Lawrence Erlbaum Associates.

Swain, M. & M. Wesche, 1975. Linguistic interaction: case study of a bilingual child. *Language sciences,* 37, 17-22.

Taeschner, T., 1983. *The sun is feminine: A study on language acquisition in bilingual children.* Berlin/Heidelberg: Springer.

Wells, G., 1985. *Language development in the pre-school years.* Cambridge: Cambridge University Press.

Hanneke van der Heijden and Ludo Verhoeven

Early bilingual development of Turkish children in the Netherlands

Most studies on bilingual development that have been conducted so far were limited in their scope, given the fact that the languages under consideration were highly related. The present study[1] differs in several respects from this research tradition. First of all, in order to uncover the role of structural properties of two languages in early bilingual acquisition two typologically distant languages will be studied. Furthermore, unlike most of the work that has been done so far, the process of bilingual acquisition is studied by outside researchers in children of a low socio-economic background, L1 being the ethnic community language spoken by both parents, and L2 being the dominant language of society. The focus in this study will be on the analysis of children's speech data in Turkish and Dutch. The children participating in this study are born in the Netherlands and form part of a third generation of immigrants who originally moved from rural sites in Turkey to in-dustrialized areas in the Netherlands.

The process of bilingual development will be studied from an interdisciplinary point of view, combining insights from linguistic theory and developmental theory. Starting from a longitudinal perspective, it will be investigated how the two langua-ge systems get differentiated and developed over time. Moreover, the apparent difficulties children encounter in separating the two languages will be examined. An attempt will be made to answer the following two research questions:

1. How do the systems under consideration develop over time in both L1 and L2?
2. To what extent and in what direction does transfer between L1 and L2 occur?

The focus will be on a number of linguistic domains that have proved to be highly significant in a large body of cross-linguistic studies on language acquisition in both children (see chapter 1). Before going into the design and preliminary results of the present study, a short description of the structural properties of the domains selected in Turkish and Dutch will be given and earlier research findings on early bilingualism in these domains will be reviewed.

[1] This study is supported by the Foundation for Linguistic Research, which is funded by the Nether-lands organization for research, NWO

Theoretical background

The present study will focus on the following linguistic domains: clause structure, reference to time, lexicon and word formation, reference to entities and reference to space.

With respect to *clause structure,* the central question is how universal principles will lead to two separate grammars. The fact that structural properties of clauses in Turkish and Dutch are partly different will help in answering this question. As is clear from generative work (e.g., Koster, 1975), the underlying pattern of Dutch is SOV, manifesting itself in various surface structures and in a verb movement rule which will usually move the verb to the second position in main clauses. In spoken Dutch, verb-initial occurs as well, due to the non-appearance of a pronominalized NP-object (cf. Jansen, 1981). Dutch also takes prepositions. The basic structure of Turkish is SOV, V taking clause final position (Kornfilt, 1984; Ergüvanlı, 1984). As is usual for SOV languages, Turkish takes postpositions.

In exploring *reference to time* two categories of temporality in language will be distinguished: temporal relations and aspect. Temporal relations refer to the location of events in relation to a given reference time. Aspect refers to the various perspectives that can be taken towards an event, e.g., perfective vs. imperfective. In the process of temporal development children gradually learn to distinguish between speech time, event time and reference time (Weist, 1986). The acquisition rate of temporal features turns out to be highly dependent on the manner in which these devices are coded in the surface structure of the target language (Slobin, 1985). The temporal systems of the three languages under consideration differ considerably. Dutch can be characterized as a language with a very limited aspect system and a restricted tense system. Basically, there is a contrast between present, simple past and perfect. Aspect plays a role in so far as progressive can be contrasted with imperfective aspect by using a locative expression of durative aspect. Turkish grammaticizes more temporal distinctions than Dutch does. With respect to tense there are different markers for past, present and perfect. Within the past there is a modal distinction between the expression of direct and indirect evidence: *-Dİ* vs. *-MİŞ* (cf. Slobin & Aksu, 1982). Past events can also be marked as imperfective or perfective. The perfective form *-Dİ* can also be used for unmarked, aspectually neutral past reference. The imperfective view on past events can be further specified as regards the factuality of an event *(-İyordu* vs. *-İRDİ).* A comprehensive overview on Turkish aspect is given in Johanson (1971). Aksu-Koç (1988) goes into the acquisition of aspect in Turkish.

In the *lexical domain* children must extend their storage of well-established words and a repertoire of word formation devices for extending the basic lexicon. New meanings can be expressed with forms which fit the word formation options of that particular language, such as stem modification and/or compounding. As has been claimed by Anderson (1985), there is a good deal of idiosyncrasy in word formation devices in different languages, while in any single language word formation rules are quite diverse in terms of input classes and semantic and syntactic relations involved. In the process of language acquisition, children must learn the diversity of options for coining words in the language under consideration. Clark (1982, 1983) stressed the importance of cross-linguistic evidence on the structure and use of word formation devices in different types of languages. Taking a cross-linguistic point of view as a starting point, Clark & Berman (1984) compared word formation strategies in English and Hebrew. They found that English and Hebrew speaking children acquiring their first language indeed rely on universal principles: semantic transparency, regularization and productivity. However, such principles must gradually be modified in light of the typological properties of the language being learned. What is general in acquisition appears to be gradually shaped by each particular language, as children learn how different options are developed in the conventional lexicon and how to put these options to work in constructing new words.

In the present study Clark's principles will be elaborated by investigating the lexical development of Turkish children. The basic devices for word formation in Turkish and Dutch are very different (cf. Broeder e.a., 1988). Word formation in Turkish highly depends on affixation. Affixes are postponed, syllabic, regular and distinct. Turkish phonology does not subsequently obscure the borders between formatives. Turkish also favours compounding (Dede, 1978). The basic syntactic structure of a nominal compound is a head noun with a possessive, preceded by a modifying noun. From data on monolingual children we have some information about the process of lexical development in Turkish. Ekmekçi (1987) analysed the lexical innovations made by Turkish children in the age range from 3;0 to 6;0. She found that in creating new words children acquire the most productive suffix first and then apply it in place of other less productive suffixes which serve the same function. Children failed to recognize exceptions to the rules. The application of the most productive suffixes was also pre-empted in loan words.

In the domain of *reference to entities* pronominal reference and the distinction between definite and indefinite reference will be explored. In pronominal reference we will study the deictic and anaphoric use of pronouns. Studies on first language acquisition (cf. Wales, 1986) have shown that children start using pronouns deictically: first and second person pronouns, referring to the here-and-now, are learned first, while third person pronouns are learned later. According to Karmiloff-Smith (1979, 1986), children learn only gradually children the discourse functions that are involved in the use of anaphoric expressions. In order to comprehend and use the contrast between definite and indefinite reference children must learn that noun phrases get the status of finite in case entities are thought of being identifiable.

Dutch and Turkish vary in their conceptual notions and linguistic devices for pronominal reference to entities (cf. Broeder, 1992). Dutch makes use of a set of pronouns marking person (first/second/third) and number (singular/plural). There is a gender distinction for third person (singular) and a politeness form for second person (singular and plural). In object position most of the pronouns get inflected. Under certain conditions demonstratives can be used to refer to entities. Pronominalization in discourse is conventional. Dutch has explicit markers for indefinite and definite expressions. Turkish has a set of pronouns, marking person and number, that get inflected for case depending on their grammatical role in the sentence. There is no distinction for gender. Demonstratives can also be used for reference to an entity. Subject agreement in Turkish is marked on the verbal element by means of a person suffix. The use of pronouns is optional. In case the subject has an emphatic or contrastive function, a pronominal form becomes obligatory. In discourse, pro drop can be seen as the unmarked coding for topic continuity. In Turkish, there is no constant marker of the status of definite vs. indefinite reference. Dede (1986) and Czató (1990) make clear that the distinction is realized through an interplay of morphosyntactic and pragmatic factors.

The study of *reference to space* will focus on the use of spatial concepts which are relevant to the expression of location or motion. As has been shown by Johnston and Slobin (1979) both cognitive maturation and language-specific factors can play a role in the development of spatial terms. The relevant language-specific differences they proposed were placement of adposition, lexical diversity, clarity of etymology, morphological complexity and homonymity. The sub-systems of spatial reference in Dutch and Turkish differ considerably, both in underlying spatial concepts and in the form of the devices they include. In Dutch, there is a dyadic system of primary spatial deixis. Furthermore, locative relations are mainly encoded by means of prepositions and adverbs. These linguistic devices express such semantic relations as path, containment, interior, exterior, neighbouring, inferior/superior, front/back and interposition. Besides, there are motion verbs expressing a change in the position of the agent or an object. Turkish has a three-step system of spatial deixis. Generally, distance contrasts are expressed as proximal, medial and distal. Furthermore, Turkish has a basic system of case suffixes referring to goal (DAT), location (LOC), and source/path (ABL). There is also a complementary system for the indication of spatial relations based on a group of nouns denoting places. These nouns enter into a postpositional construction which corresponds in function to a prepositional phrase in Indo-European languages. Semantic relations, such as containment, interior/exterior, neighbouring, inferior/superior, front/back, interposition, up/down, high/low and left/right can thus be expressed.

Design of the study

Informants

The research is set up as a multiple case study with a longitudinal design. There are three groups of informants:

1. a core group of four Turkish girls born in the Netherlands, growing up with two languages, Turkish and Dutch;
2. a comparison group of two monolingual Dutch girls;

3. and a comparison group of two monolingual Turkish girls living in Turkey. The
   data of this group are collected by dr. Özden Ekmekçi and Hatice Sofu.

In the analyses to be presented in this chapter only the data of one of the children
of the core group of informants, Berrin, are under consideration.

Berrin is the youngest daughter of a Turkish family living in a middle large town
in the eastern part of the Netherlands. Both her parents are of a low educational
level. They originate from Central Anatolia and live in the Netherlands for about 20
years now. Berrin has two elder sisters, who were about 16 and 14 years old at the
time of recording, and one elder brother, who was 13 years of age. Berrin has
attended a so-called international day care centre ever since she was six weeks old.
From the beginning of the period of data collection Berrin visited the centre during
five days a week. In Berrin's group as in the other groups at the centre, both a
Dutch and a Turkish caretaker had been appointed. Thus, the ethnic background of
staff more or less represented the ethnic composition of the group of children, most
of whom were of Dutch or Turkish origin as well. As a consequence Berrin
received both Turkish and Dutch language input at the day care centre. Turkish
input originated from her Turkish caretaker and from her Turkish playmates. The
Turkish caretaker always used standard Turkish to the children. Dutch input was
given by the Dutch caretakers, by the Turkish caretaker when she addressed a
Dutch child or a mixed group of children and by the Dutch children. The language
choice of the caretakers as a function of addressee is given in Table 1. The Dutch
caretakers expressed a clear regional accent in their Dutch.

Table 1. Language choice of caretakers as a function of ethnic background of addressed child(ren).

Addressee	Dutch caretaker	Turkish caretaker
(group of) Dutch child(ren)	Dutch	Dutch
mixed group of children	Dutch	Dutch
(group of) Turkish child(ren)	Dutch	Turkish

Both of Berrin's parents were not very proficient in Dutch. In the summer of 1990,
when Berrin was aged 2;6-2;8, the family spent its holiday in Turkey, which implied a sharp increase of Turkish input from monolingual speakers of Turkish.

Data collection

Twice every month an audio recording was made of the speech of each child of the
group of core informants: one aimed at eliciting Turkish speech and one aimed at
eliciting Dutch speech from the informant. In order not to provoke codeswitching
from the child as an artefact, recordings were made by a native speaker of the target
language. Intervals between two recordings in the same target language varied
between 20 to 40 days. The period of data collection covered the informant's age

range from 2;0 (in years; months) to 3;6. This resulted in a data base of 38 recordings (19 months, 2 languages). Every recording lasted at least one hour.

During the recording session the informant wore a jacket with a small microphone and a wireless transmitter. Her speech was recorded by means of a receiver connected to a tape recorder. By using this technique the speech recorded is not restricted to researcher - informant interactions alone. All of the informant's utterances are recorded as long as the equipment is switched on. Thus, the child's free conversations with peers and caretakers as well as her monologues are included in the recordings also.

An activity which was performed in all recording sessions consisted in the reading of a picture book. The researcher and the informant together looked at the book. At the same time the researcher tried to elicit speech from the informant by asking wh-questions directly relating to the events depicted or to the real life experience of the child.

Recordings were transcribed and stored into the computer according to the conventions of CHAT, Codes for the Human Analysis of Transcripts (MacWhinney, 1991). This transcription and coding format has been designed to establish a uniform database of child language acquisition data, called CHILDES (Child language Exchange System).

Preliminary data will be presented of the first twelve months of recording of Berrin. All recordings of Berrin were made at the day care centre. Because there was both native input of Turkish and Dutch, neither of the target languages of the recordings was artificial. From this age range four transcripts of each language will be analysed in this paper. The recording sessions were divided into blocks of three months each. From every block one transcript was selected, as is shown in Table 2.

Table 2. Analysed transcripts of Dutch and Turkish based recordings of Berrin's speech.

Age range	2;0-2;2	2;3-2;5	2;6-2;8	2;9-2;11
Dutch	2;2	2;5	2;8	2;10
Turkish	2;2	2;5	2;6	2;10

Due to the natural setting of data collection and the degree of language proficiency, transcripts show considerable variation in length. In the analyses this problem is dealt with either by using qualitative analyses and making comparisons within sessions on the one hand, or by standardising frequencies for 100 utterances on the other.

Results on Turkish language acquisition

Clause structure

The distribution of left branching and alternative word order in verbal and nominal clauses is presented in Table 3. Due to the relatively big share of elliptic utterances the total number of neither verbal nor nominal clauses amounts to 100. With the child's progression of age there is a gradual decrease of nominal clauses together with a gradual increase of verbal clauses. At age 2;2 there is a balance of nominal and verbal clauses. At age 2;10 verbal clauses outnumber nominal clauses.

Table 3. Distribution of word order in verbal and nominal clauses per 100 Turkish utterances as a function of age.

Age	2;2	2;5	2;6	2;10
Verbal clauses	26.3	28.1	28.5	40.2
SOV	26.3	28.1	26.3	34.7
Non-final V	–	–	2.2	5.5
Nominal clauses	26.3	14.6	11.0	11.2
S - Predicate	26.3	14.6	10.6	7.8
Other order	–	–	.4	3.4

There is more variation in word order as the child grows older. Until the age of 2;5 there is a uniform pattern of left-branching word order patterns both in verbal and nominal clauses, resulting in SOV and S - predicate order respectively. From the very beginning, the child strictly applies the rule that indefinite or non-referential objects occur right before the verb and can not be removed.

From age 2;6 onwards the proportion of alternative word order patterns gradually increases. In verb non-final word order patterns of verbal clauses a broad range of constituents can be placed after the verb: subjects (ex. [1]), objects (ex. [2]), directives, locatives and adverbial constituents:

1. *neye*   *gidiyo*   *bebek?*   (2;10)
   where-DIR   go-PRES-3SG   doll
   'where goes the doll?'

2. *ben*   *atmadım*   *bunu.*   (2;10)
   I   throw-NEG-PAST-1SG   this-OBJ
   'I didnot throw this.'

Generally, the same constraints that apply to variation in word order of monolingual Turkish children can be found in Berrin's utterances (cf. Ekmekçi, 1986). In the vast majority of cases word order turns out to be semantically or pragmatically motivated. There is a tendency to place new information right before the verb, both in SOV- and in non-verb final clauses. In some cases, however, the alternation of word order seems counterintuitive with respect to the given-new contract (cf. Chafe, 1980), such as in [3], where the new information, i.e., the information that is asked for by the adult, is placed after the verbal predicate. The symbol '#' in this and following examples indicates a pause, the symbol ':' stands for a lengthening of the preceding phoneme.

3. adult: *mert*   *nerde?*   (2;6)
             mert   where-LOC
             'where is mert?'

    child: *gitti.*
             go-PAST-3SG
             'he is gone.'

             gitti   *tuvate #*   *me:t.*
             go-PAST-3SG   toilet-DIR   mert
             '(he) went to the toilet   mert.'

             me:t gitti tuvate me:t.
             'mert went to the toilet mert.'

In [4], when commenting on the motion of a milky liquid in a toy bottle, Berrin seems to vary word order in order to emphasize the various semantic roles in the utterance:

4. *ama*   *süt*   *içinde*   *dökülüyor.*   (2;10)
   but   milk   in-POSS3SG-LOC   spill-PASS-PRES-3SG
   'but the milk inside is spilled.'

   dökülüyor süt içinde.
   '(it) is spilled the milk inside.'

   içinde dökülüyor süt.
   'inside (it) is spilled the milk.'

Most of the alternative word order patterns in nominal clauses are of the type locative-subject [5] or predicate-subject [6], whereas Berrin in the earlier stages only used subject-locative and subject-predicate word order:

5. *nerde*   *elman?*   (2;10)   vs.   *halil*   *nerde?*   (2;5)
   where-LOC   apple-POSS2SG   halil   where-LOC
   'where is your apple?'   'where is halil?'

6. *sirke   mi   o?*   (2;10)
   vinager QUES that
   'is that vinager?'

   o   pasta?   (2;5)
   that paste
   'is that paste?'

   kimin   yumurtası?   (2;10)
   who-GEN   egg-POSS3SG
   'whose egg is that?'

   bu kimin?   (2;5)
   this who-GEN
   'whose is this?'

We should remark here that the word *pasta* in example [6] is a dutch loan, used to refer to a kind of nutpaste that is spread on sandwiches.

With respect to case marking, it can be concluded that the general rules for inflecting nouns are acquired at an early age. Errors seem to go along with the expansion of the child's linguistic repertoire. With respect to the lexicon, it is clear that lexical entries displaying such features as argument structure and subcategorization restrictions must be learned one-by-one. Examples of deviant learner varieties of case marking governed by the verb are *ondan şevedem (= seveceğim)* for standard *onu* ('I will love that'), and *onda istiyom* for standard *ondan* or *onu* ('I want (something from) that'). This struggle with the acquisition of argument structure is also apparent from the fact that intransitive verb forms sometimes occur in combination with an object (as in [7] and [8]), although at the same time instances of these verbs occurring with correct argument structure can be found:

7. *kaydı   bunu.*   (2;10)
   slide-PAST-3SG this-OBJ
   'he slid this.'

   standard: *kaydırdı bunu.*
             slide-CAUS-PAST-3SG
             'he made this slide.'
   or: *kaydı bu.*
             this-SUBJ
             'this slid.'

8. *şayata bit.*   (2;5)
   salad   finish(INTR)-IMP
   'salad, finish.'

   standard: *salatayı   bitir.*
             salad-OBJ   finish-CAUS-IMP
             'finish the salad.'
   or: *salata bitti.*
             finish(INTR)-PAST-3SG
             'the salad is finished.'

Reference to time

The results with respect to temporal marking of verbs are presented in Table 4. With the child's progression of age the range of linguistic means for expressing tense and also aspect gradually expands.

Table 4. Distribution of verbal inflections in Turkish as a function of age.

Age	2;2	2;5	2;6	2;10
-İyor	2	16	36	80
-Dİ	–	10	22	51
-mİş	1	2	5	–
-EcEk	–	5	2	11
-R	–	–	7	15
conjunctive	–	–	16	10
imperative	2	22	30	25

Starting at age 2;5 the child appears to use -İyor for marking events in the present and the suffix -Dİ for events in the past. -mİş is occasionally used in aspectual opposition to -Dİ as is illustrated in [9]. This example was taken from a fragment of picture telling. The child looks at two pictures of a man holding balloons. On the first picture he has three of them, on the second he has only two balloons in his hand. The inflection -mİş is used to mark an inferential (IFR) connotation.

9. adult: *bunun yok balonu.*   (2;6)
             'this one does not have a balloon.'
             bunun var.
             'this one has.'

    child: *biyi   patamış   değil mi?*
            burst-IFR-3SG
            'one of them bursted, did not it?'

The future tense -EcEk is also mastered at an early age. The aorist -R and the conjunctive appear at age 2;6. These suffixes not only denote tense, but also modal concepts (cf. Boeschoten, 1990: 81 ff.).

At age 2;10 we find another example of aspectual marking. With the imperfective marking of -İyordu in [10] the child seems to point to the fact that in the predicate of 'falling' there is no beginning and no end point (cf. Johanson's, 1971 notion of *Intraterminalität*).

10.   *bak   düşüyordu.*   (2;10)
       look   fall-PRES-PAST-3SG
       'look, he was falling.'

As the denotation of imperative meaning is concerned, an expansion of the set of linguistic means can be observed, starting from the sole verb stem to the use of the suffixes *-sEnE* and *-ElE* (which is a contraction of the verbstem and the particle *hele),* both giving extra emphasis to the imperative (Lewis, 1986). Therefore this expansion can be taken to be a modal expansion of the imperative system.

Lexicon

With respect to lexical diversity the number of different nouns and verbs in 100 utterances was counted. The results are given in Table 5. As the child grows older, the numbers of both nominal and verbal word types increase.

Table 5. Nominal and verbal word types in 100 Turkish utterances as a function of age.

Age	2;5	2;6	2;10
Nominal types	16	13	22
Verbal types	16	17	21

In Table 6 the numbers and proportions of transitive and intransitive verb types used by the child are given. There is a relative increase of the use of intransitive verbs with the child's progression of age.

Table 6. Distribution of transitive and intransitive verb types in numbers (left) and percentages (right) as a function of age.

Age	2;2		2;5		2;6		2;10	
Transitive verbs	4	100	14	67	18	60	27	54
Intransitive verbs	0	0	7	33	12	40	23	46

The development of the verb lexicon seems to start with the acquisition of transitive verbs. Gradually, relatively more intransitive verbs are used. At age 2;10 there is almost a balance of the number of transitive and intransitive verbs used.

In a number of cases the child shows evidence for lexical innovations. Examples of derivation are given in [11]:

11.	N > V:	*gemi* ('boat')	>	*gemiş=* as in *gemişiyor*	(2;5)
				('to get the shape of a boat')	
	V > N:	*kay=* ('to slide')	>	*kaya* as in *kayada* ('on the slide')	(2;6)

Other cases concern the construction of verbs by composing a noun with the auxiliary *yap=* ('to make'), such as in *boya yap=* ('to paint'; from *boya* 'paint'). A special case is the innovation *kayıksı yap=,* which Berrin uses to refer to the act of sliding on a slide, along with the standard verb *kay=*. Since this innovation consists of a noun in combination with the verb *yap=* it can be categorized as a compound. At the same time the noun itself is the result of derivation of the noun *kayık* ('(shaped like a) caique') with the suffix *-sī*, which in Standard Turkish is used to indicate (a high degree of) similarity. Probably the phonological resemblance of this noun to the verb *kay=* plays an import role in the creation of this lexical innovation.

Reference to entities

Table 7 presents the results on the use of verbal markers for person in subject agreement as a function of age. There is an expansion of use of personal markers on the verb in the age range from 2;2 to 2;10. The child predominantly uses singular markers with a preference for first and third person.

Table 7. Verbal markers for person in subject agreement as a function of age.

Age	2;2	2;5	2;6	2;10
Singular				
first person	2	4	29	36
second person	–	2	4	23
third person	1	27	54	109
Plural				
first person	–	–	1	–
second person	–	–	–	–
third person	–	–	–	1

In a number of cases the child uses a subject pronoun. In Table 8 a survey is given of the contexts in which the singular first and second person pronouns *ben* and *sen* are used.

Table 8. Contexts in which the Turkish pronouns 'ben' and 'sen' are used as a function of age.

Age	2;2	2;5	2;6	2;10
Emphasis	–	7	14	14
Contrast	–	3	2	5
Response to interlocutor	–	3	2	7
Other	–	1	2	13

The child starts using overt pronouns by the age of 2;5. Most pronouns are used in order to give emphasis, such as in [12]:

12.   adult: *bakiyim.*   (2;6)
                    'let me see.'

       child: *sen*   *de*   *yap.*
                   you   too   do-IMP
                   'you do it as well!'

Other occurrences of overt pronouns can be explained by such contexts as contrast (as in [13]), and response to the interlocutor who starts the introduction of an overt pronoun (as in [14]):

13.   *ben*   *küçük* *sen*   *böyük.*   (2;10)
       I   small   you   big
       'I (have the) small (one), you (the) big (one).'

14.   adult: *sen*   *de*   *elma*   *yedin.*   (2;10)
                   you   too   apple   eat-PAST-2SG
                   'you ate (some) apple as well.'

                   şimdi   *armut yiyeceksin.*
                   now   pear   eat-FUT-2SG
                   'now you are going to eat (some) pear.'

       child: *ben*   *evde*   *yidim*   *ama.*
                   I   house-LOC   eat-PAST-1SG   but
                   'but I ate (it) at home.'

A remarkable use of an overt pronoun emerges in the sequence of utterances in [15]. Though the gist of the discussion is not *who* is to eat but *what* is going to be eaten, exactly the subject is emphasized by the use of an explicit pronoun:

15.   adult: *hadi bi de armut ye.*   (2;10)
                   'come on, eat (some) pear as well.'

       child: *elma.*
                   'apple.'

       adult: *al ondan bundan.*
                   'take from that and from this.'

       child: *ben*   *elma*   *istiyom.*
                   I   apple   want-PRES-1SG
                   'I want (some) apple.'

Reference to entities can be expressed by means of nominal constituents, or by means of the demonstrative pronouns *bu, şu* and *o*. In order to determine the relation between the two types of coding devices a deixicality coefficient was computed. This coefficient is the ratio of the tokens of demonstrative pronouns (used non-attributively) and the sum of this number plus the number of content noun tokens, all occurring in 100 utterances. Demonstrative pronouns were only counted if they were used deictically, i.e., referred to the here-and-now of the speech situation. Pronouns used anaphorically were excluded. The results are given in Table 9. There is a gradual decrease of the deixicality coefficient as the child grows older.

Table 9. Deixicality coefficient in Turkish as a function of age.

Age	2;2	2;5	2;6	2;10
Deixicality coefficient	57.1	54.4	33.9	27.6

Finally, the use of definite and indefinite reference in relation to the expression of possession was examined. In Table 10 a survey is given of the coding devices for possession used by the child as a function of age. In Turkish, whenever a possessive relationship refers to a definite owner, the (pro)noun referring is inflected with genitive case; nouns referring to an indefinite entity are not inflected.

Table 10. Use of devices for possession in Turkish as a function of age.

Age		2;2	2;5	2;6	2;10
(1)	N-poss	-	8	12	26
(2) PRO-gen	N-poss	-	4	6	10
(3) N	N-poss	-	3	-	1
(4) N-gen	N-poss	-	-	-	1
(5) N-poss-gen	N-poss	-	-	1	-

The first two devices are used at an early age. The other three devices appear to cause more difficulties. Constructions of type (3) occurring in Berrin's utterances at age 2;5 are used in contexts where type (4) is obligatory (see [16]). In these cases the definite noun, in all cases a proper name, is handled as if it were indefinite. The same applies to construction (5). Correct realization of this type occurs only once in the data set. Again it seems to be the genitive case which causes the problem. Berrin appears to avoid the construction by leaving out the genitive case and placing either the head noun or the modifying noun as a kind of afterthought after the predicate, as is exemplified in [17] and [18]:

16. *ike*   *annesi.*   standard: *ilkerin*   *annesi*   (2;5)

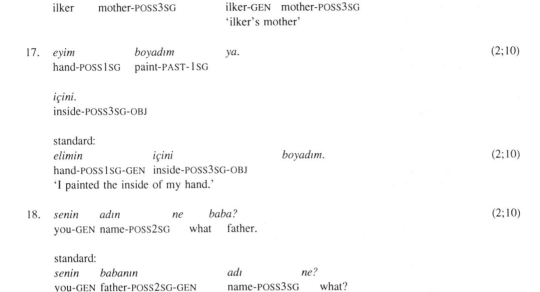

ilker   mother-POSS3SG   ilker-GEN mother-POSS3SG
                                  'ilker's mother'

17. *eyim*   *boyadım*   *ya.*   (2;10)
     hand-POSS1SG   paint-PAST-1SG

     içini.
     inside-POSS3SG-OBJ

     standard:
     elimin   *içini*   *boyadım.*   (2;10)
     hand-POSS1SG-GEN inside-POSS3SG-OBJ
     'I painted the inside of my hand.'

18. *senin*   *adın*   *ne*   *baba?*   (2;10)
     you-GEN name-POSS2SG   what   father.

     standard:
     senin   *babanın*   *adı*   *ne?*
     you-GEN father-POSS2SG-GEN   name-POSS3SG   what?
     'what is your father's name?'

Reference to space

With respect to locative expressions an analysis was made of the non-attributive use of *bu, şu* and *o* as deictic locative expressions. The number of occurrences of these linguistic markers in 100 utterances as a function of age is presented in Table 11.

Table 11. Number of occurrences of bu, şu and o in 100 Turkish utterances as a function of age.

Age	2;2	2;5	2;6	2;10
bu	-	15	13	14
şu	25	7	4	-
o	35	9	2	2

At age 2;2 the child uses a two-step demonstrative system. The use of *şu* and *o* decreases, whereas *bu* gains in importance. In correspondence with the findings of Verhoeven (1987) it is found that when the child grows older, *bu* gradually becomes the unmarked case, whereas *o* is used for reference to persons, especially if persons do not fulfil the role of agents in the utterance (as in [19]), and for the expression of a contrast of views (as in [20]):

19. adult: *en çok kimi seviyorsun?*   (2;10)
             'who do you love most?'

child: *onu.*
'him/her.'

20.   child: **bu**   *tuz*   *mu?*   (2;10)
                this   salt   ques
                'is this salt?'

adult: *tuz değil.*
'not salt.'

child: **o**   *ne?*
            that   what?
            'what is that?'

Furthermore, the number of unmarked and marked nominal references in locative expressions was determined as a function of age.

Table 12. Numbers of locative expressions with unmarked and marked nominal references and adverbial reference as a function of age.

Age	2;2	2;5	2;6	2;10
Unmarked nominal reference (case)				
-E	–	10	12	16
-DE	–	2	7	10
-DEN	–	1	1	1
Marked nominal reference (postpositions)				
içine/içinde ('in(to)')	–	1	3	5
dışarıda ('outside')	–	4	–	–
yanında ('next to')	–	–	1	–
Adverbial reference				
buraya/burada ('here')	–	–	4	2
şurada ('over here')	–	–	1	–
orada ('there')	–	–	1	1

These frequencies show that the child uses nominal reference to space before she uses adverbial expressions. As with deictic reference to entities, *buraya/burada* is used more often than *şurada* and *orada*. Furthermore, at all age levels unmarked nominal reference is the most frequently used device. In general, the number of locative expressions in the child's language seems to be very low, especially as the number of marked nominal expressions referring to space is concerned. The only expression which seems to be used productively is the postpositional construction with *iç,* referring to containment.

Results on Dutch language acquisition

The amount of Dutch data varies considerably between the sessions. The first session at age 2;2 contained very little Dutch data. The same holds for session 2;8, when Berrin had just arrived in the Netherlands after a two-month holiday she had spent in Turkey. In these cases both linguistic and emotional factors are due to the small amount of Dutch utterances of Berrin.

Clause structure and temporal reference

The number of Dutch utterances with a verbal predicate is quite low. The inflectional system of the verb is gradually expanded, though even at age 2;10 it is still limited to present tense (3rd person singular). At age 2;2 the child uses only clauses of the type subject - verb(infinitive) (see [21]):

21. *he   die   pop #   zitten.*   (2;2)
     hey   that   doll   sit-INF

At age 2;5 the child uses utterances with finite verb forms in present tense as well. The obligatory third person singular marker, however, is not realized (see [22]):

22. *deze   saap.*   (2;5)
     'this   sleep.'

At age 2;10 the third person singular marker in present tense is realized, whereas infinitive verb forms are only used in utterances starting with an adjunct. Examples are given in [23] and [24]:

23. *bebe   saapt.*   (2;10)
     baby   sleep-PRES3SG
     'the baby sleeps.'

24. *niet   zitten.*   (2;10)
     not   sit-INF

In nominal clauses the copula *zijn* 'to be' is not used (as is exemplified in [25]). In all instances of this type word order is left branching, resulting in subject-predicate order:

25. *deze mij.* standard: *deze* *is* *van* *mij.* (2;5)
   this be-PRES3SG from I-OBL
   'this is mine.'

   jij ziek. standard: *jij bent* *ziek.* (2;10)
   you be-PRES2SG ill
   'you are ill.'

Auxiliaries are incidently used in formulaic speech (e.g., [26]). Otherwise modal auxiliaries are not realized.

26. *mag* *niet.* (2;8, 2;10)
   is allowed not
   'is not allowed.'

Lexicon

As a measure of lexical diversity the number of nominal and verbal types was counted. The results are given in Table 13. As the child is growing older, only the number of nominal types increases.

Table 13. Numbers of nominal and verbal types in 100 Dutch utterances as a function of age.

Age	2;5	2;10
Nominal types	7	12
Verbal types	5	5

In Table 14 the numbers of transitive and intransitive verbs used by the child are given. As all numbers are very low, proportions were not counted. There is only a small difference in the use of transitive and intransitive verbs used. Nevertheless, the class of intransitive verbs seems to be slightly ahead of that of the transitive ones, unlike the development in the Turkish verb lexicon.

Table 14. Distribution of transitive and intransitive verb types in Dutch as a function of age.

Age	2;2	2;5	2;8	2;10
Transitive verbs	-	2	-	1
Intransitive verbs	1	3	1	4

Reference to entities

Table 15 presents an overview of Berrin's use of subject pronouns in Dutch as a function of age. Just as in the Turkish data was the case, only singular pronouns are used.

Table 15. Distribution of subject pronouns in Dutch as a function of age.

Age	2;2	2;5	2;8	2;10
Singular				
first person	–	+	+	–
second person	–	+	–	+
third person	–	+	–	+
Plural				
first person	–	–	–	–
second person	–	–	–	–
third person	–	–	–	–

Determiners are only used to refer to objects. Table 16 presents the frequencies of the Dutch determiners used. The determiners *deze* and *dit* express proximity, whereas *die* and *dat* express distance. Furthermore, the use of *dit* and *dat* is restricted to neuter nouns in singular; *deze* and *die* can be combined both with masculine and feminine nouns, either in singular or plural, and with neuter nouns in plural.

In the data-set these determiners are all used predicatively either in combination with a noun (as in [25] and [27]) or as an independent utterance, accompanied by gestures.

Table 16. Use of Dutch determiners as a function of age.

Age	2;2	2;5	2;8	2;10
deze	1	28	–	36
dit	–	1	–	–
die	1	12	–	1
dat	–	2	–	2

As can be seen from the table the expressions referring to proximity (*deze* and *dit*) are much more frequent in the data than the expressions for distance (*die* and *dat*). Again a deixicality coefficient was computed as a function of the child's age in order to evaluate the relative use of nominal and pronominal constituents. The results are given in Table 17. It can be seen that the coefficient decreases as the child grows older.

Table 17. Deixicality coefficient in Dutch as a function of age.

Age	2;5	2;10
Deixicality coefficient	0.64	0.47

Finally, the expression of possessive relations was examined. The general possessive construction was Det - N, starting at age 2;5. The determiner is used predicatively to refer to the object possessed, the noun refers to the possessor. An example is given in [27].

27.　*deze papa.* standard:　*deze　is　　　　van　papa.*　　　　　　　　(2;5)
　　　　　　　　　　　　this　be-PRES3SG　from　daddy
　　　　　　　　　　　　'this is daddy's.'

Reference to space

Spatial expressions are very scarce in the data under consideration. The few realized ones nearly all refer to location. The commonly used device for locative reference is the deictic term *daar* 'there', in standard Dutch referring to distant locations. More specific locative reference by means of prepositions occurs only once in the data (at age 2;5), in combination with the deictic term *daar*. Even in reproductions of adult speech prepositions may be left out (as in [28]):

28.　adult:　*zullen we deze hierin　　zetten?*　　　　　　　　　　　　(2;2)
　　　　　　　　　　　　　　here-into
　　　　　　'shall we put this one into this?'

　　　child:　*hier　zetten.*
　　　　　　here　put(INF)
　　　　　　'put here.'

To motion Berrin refers once in the present data-set. Remarkably enough she then uses a Turkish device: the Turkish directive suffix is placed after a Dutch noun (see [29]). A verb of motion is not realized.

29.　*vivian　sapkamaya.*　　　　　　　　　　　　　　　　　　(2;5)
　　　　　　　bedroom-DIR
　　　'vivian (is) to the bedroom.'

Conclusions

From the present study several conclusions can be drawn. First of all it is clear that Berrin's dominant language is Turkish. In all domains analysed her level of proficiency in Turkish is higher than her level of proficiency in Dutch. In Turkish she has a wider range of linguistic means to express meaning than she has in Dutch. A good example of this is the verb inflectional system. In Dutch she only realizes infinitives and present tense forms in third person singular, whereas in Turkish she uses standard devices to refer to present, past and future with certain aspectual properties involved. Secondly, the rate of development in Turkish is higher than in Dutch. The structural development of the Dutch utterances clearly shows less expansion in the age range analysed than the Turkish ones do.

The dominance of Turkish over Dutch might lead to the expectation of a high degree of transfer from L1 to L2. At the lexical level very few instances of mixing of both language systems were found. Berrin used only incidentally single Turkish words when speaking to a native speaker of Dutch. Instances of Dutch lexical items addressed to a native speaker of Turkish were not found at all. That there exists nevertheless some relationship between the two lexicons is nicely illustrated by the songs Berrin invented right after her return from holiday in Turkey, and which consisted of strings of Turkish and Dutch equivalent words like *anne* and *mama* ('mother'). On the morpho-syntactic level traces of transfer are harder to detect. In several domains striking similarities have been found, e.g., the preponderance of deictic terms denoting proximity over those denoting distance. However, in order to distinguish properly between effects of transfer and general language learning phenomena we first need monolingual comparative data. The data on the development of Turkish, e.g., the development of the verb inflectional system and the acquisition of word order, show parallels with what is known about the acquisition of Turkish by monolingual children. On the other hand, the system for spatial reference seems to be relatively undeveloped. Comparative data are also needed to evaluate the rate and structure of development in both languages.

One of the ways in which this study will be elaborated will consist in a comparison of the data obtained from the coregroup of informants with those of monolingual Turkish and Dutch children. Furthermore, the data of Berrin will be compared to those of the other three bilingual core-informants in the Netherlands, who all differ in the respective amount of Turkish and Dutch language input. Finally, data from the full period of data collection will be taken into account.

References

Aksu-Koç, A., 1988. *The acquisition of aspect and modality.* Cambridge: University Press.

Anderson, S., 1985. Typological distinctions in word formation. In: T. Shopen (ed.), *Language typology and syntactic description.* Cambridge: University Press.

Boeschoten, H., 1990. *Acquisition of Turkish by immigrant children.* Tilburg: Ph.D. Thesis.

Broeder, P., 1992. *Talking about people.* A multiple case study on adult language acquisition. Amsterdam/Lisse: Swets & Zeitlinger.

Broeder, P. e.a., 1988. *Processes in the developing lexicon.* Tilburg/Göteborg: ESF-report.

Chafe, W., 1980. *The pear stories: cognitive, cultural and linguistic aspects of narrative production.* Norwood, NJ: Ablex.

Clark, E., 1982. The young word maker: A case study of innovation in the child's lexicon. In: E. Wanner & L. Gleitman (eds.), *Language acquisition: The state of the art,* 390-425. Cambridge: University Press.

Clark, E., 1983. Convention and contrast in acquiring the lexicon. In: T. Seiler & W. Wannenmacher (eds), *Concept development and the development of word meaning,* 67-89. Berlin: Springer Verlag.

Clark, E. & R. Berman, 1984. Structure and use in the acquisition of word formation. *Language,* 60, 3, 542-590.

Czató, E., 1990. Referential properties of some Turkish determiners. In: S. Koç (ed.), *Studies on Turkish Linguistics, Proceedings of the Fourth International Conference on Turkish Linguistics,* August 17-19, 1988, Ankara.

Dede, M., 1978. Why should relativization distinguish between subject and non-subject head nouns. *BLS,* 4, 67-78.

Dede, M., 1986. Definiteness and referentiality in Turkish verbal sentences. In: D. Slobin & K. Zimmer (eds), *Studies in Turkish linguistics,* 147-163. Amsterdam: Benjamins.

Ekmekçi, Ö., 1986. Significance of word order in the acquisition of Turkish. In: D. Slobin & K. Zimmer (eds), *Studies in Turkish Linguistics,* 265-72. Amsterdam: Benjamins.

Ekmekçi, Ö., 1987. Creativity in the language acquisition process. In: H. Boeschoten & L. Verhoeven (eds), *Studies on modern Turkish,* 203-210. Tilburg: University Press.

Ergüvanlı, E., 1984. *The function of word order in Turkish.* Berkeley: University Press.

Jansen, F., 1981. *Syntactische konstrukties in gesproken taal.* Amsterdam: Huis aan de drie grachten.

Johanson, L., 1971. *Aspekt im Türkischen. Vorstudien zu einer Beschreibung des türkeitürkischen Aspektsystems.* Uppsala: Acta Universitatis Upsaliensis, Studia Turcica Upsaliensia 1.

Johnston, J. & D. Slobin, 1979. The development of locative expressions in English, Italian, Serbo-Croatian and Turkish. *Journal of Child Language,* 6, 529-545.

Karmiloff-Smith, A., 1979. *A functional approach to child language.* Cambridge: University Press.

Karmiloff-Smith, A., 1986. From meta-processes to conscious access: Evidence from children's metalinguistic and repair data. *Cognition,* 23, 95-147.

Kornfilt, J., 1984. *Case marking, agreement and empty categories in Turkish.* Harvard: Ph.D Thesis.

Koster, J., 1975. Dutch as a SOV language. *Linguistic analysis,* 1, 2, 11-136.

Lewis, G., 1986. *Turkish grammar.* Oxford: University Press.

MacWhinney, B., 1991. *The CHILDES project: Tools for analyzing talk.* Hillsdale: Erlbaum.

Slobin, D., 1985. *The cross-linguistic study of language acquisition.* Hillsdale: LEA.

Slobin, D. & A. Aksu, 1982. Tense, aspect and modality in the use of the Turkish evidential. In: P. Hopper (ed.), *Tense-aspect: Between semantics and pragmatics,* 185-200. Amsterdam: Benjamins.

Verhoeven, L., 1987. The acquisition of spatial reference in Turkish. In: H. Boeschoten & L. Verhoeven (eds), *Studies on modern Turkish,* 217-230. Tilburg: University Press.

Wales, R., 1986. Deixis. In: P. Fletcher & M. Garman (eds), *Language acquisition,* 401-428. Cambridge: University Press.

Weist, R., 1986. Tense and aspect. In: P. Fletcher & M. Garman (eds), *Language acquisition,* 356-374. Cambridge: University Press.

Carol W. Pfaff

Early bilingual development of Turkish children in Berlin

Since the beginning of 1970's, Berlin has been an important centre of concentration of the migrant population from the Mediterranean countries, especially of migrants from Turkey and, by now the population is composed of adult immigrants and their second and third generations children. Further, as a result of the most recent population movements within the European Community and from Eastern Europe, bilingual issues will remain crucial for some time to come.

Both theoretical and practical aspects of bilingualism are thrown into sharp focus against the background of natural language contact situation in which the children of migrants spend their formative years. Prominent among these are questions of language development and language use.

In the present circumstances, we find simultaneous or early sequential acquisition of a variety of pairs of languages of greater or lesser typological and genetic similarity, allowing the linguist to focus on issues of language-specific, universal and general cognitive strategies in cross-linguistic studies.

A second set of acquisitional issues concerns the linguistic effect of factors such as the extent and quality of discourse with native speakers of both languages on processes of language acquisition and processes of language attrition and language loss.

A third aspect of protracted societal bilingualism concerns the nature and extent of mutual influence of bilinguals' languages on each other. This ranges from the psycholinguistic issue of separation vs. fusion of linguistic systems in very young bilinguals to the linguistic constraints on language mixing in older children, adolescents and adults, and the relationship of these factors to historical change in languages in the speech community by way of the development of ethnic varieties, convergence, etc.

In addition to these theoretical issues, practical problems associated with bilingualism are of particular importance. Among the problems most relevant for the second and third generation children and adolescents are those which centre around education, including the question of whether, when and how mother tongue instruction is to be provided, the implementation of German as a second language instruction, possible modifications in the instructional methods or materials for instruction to accommodate to the linguistic needs of the pupils.

For all of these purposes, basic information about the language development of the children is essential, but to date there has been relatively little empirical evidence on the languages of the bilingual children. The project presented here is an attempt to partially fill this gap for the children of migrants from Turkey as well as to address the theoretical and practical issues in bilingualism in childhood.

This chapter presents an overview and survey of selected results of a longitudinal study of pre-school and early school age Turkish/German bilingual children in Berlin, the 'KITA' study[1]. The chapter is organized as follows. First of all, an overview of the KITA study with its research questions, social setting and methodology is presented. In addition, the major findings regarding the development of both Turkish and German are summarized, focusing on some aspects of development of the lexicon, nominal and verbal morphology, and on the use of these linguistic structures in narrative and conversational discourse. Moreover, the issue of the relationship between morphosyntactic development and communicative competence is taken up and illustrated with comparison of parallel texts in Turkish and German for one child.

The KITA study

The KITA study was a five-year longitudinal investigation (1987-92) of the speech of preschool and early school-age children who attend(ed) a bilingual day-care centre ('Kindertagesstätte', or 'Kita') in Berlin-Kreuzberg. This district has a high proportion of migrant children, especially of families from Turkey. About 90 per cent of the children in the Kita speak Turkish at home. A brief overview of the setting in West Berlin during the period of data collection is given in the next section.

Demographic and sociolinguistic overview

(Immigrant) children's patterns of language acquisition and language use are shaped not only by linguistic and cognitive universals, but also by the environmental and social framework they grow up, which, in turn is to a large extent determined by the demographic characteristics of the community and its educational policies and practices.

The special situation of Berlin as an 'island' within East Germany before reunification accentuated the general tendencies of population decline of the native German population. Among the important demographic factors which play a role in the processes of maintenance or loss of a minority language as well as of patterns of acquisition and use of the majority language are the density and age distribution of

---

[1] The KITA study, *Natürlicher bilingualer Spracherwerb von Kita-Kindern: Vom Krippenalter bis zu den ersten Grundschuljahren,* was funded by the Deutsche Forschungsgemeinschaft (DFG), under its *Language Acquisition* research program, 1987-1992.

the minority population and its spatial distribution in the place of settlement. These characteristics not only determine the opportunities for contact between the speakers of the majority and minority languages, but also influence the degree of pressure on the political policy makers to take special measures to provide for the education of minority as well as majority children.

Table 1 gives a demographic overview of West Berlin, and of Kreuzberg, the district with the highest foreign population, where the children in our KITA study live. As Table 1 shows that the minority population is unevenly distributed geographically.

Table 1. Percentage of non-Germans in Berlin (West) and selected districts

Year	W. Berlin	Kreuzberg	Wedding	Tiergarten	Schöneberg	Neukölln
1978	9.41	23.94	17.38	15.35	14.29	9.30
1980	11.20	27.31	19.88	18.33	17.59	11.61
1986	12.51	28.43	20.85	19.85	18.31	13.30
1990	14.32	30.60	23.72	21.71	19.96	16.03

In 1990, non-Germans of all ages represented 14.32 per cent of the population of West Berlin but the proportion of minority children under 6 was 22.4 per cent. In Kreuzberg, the figures are 30.6 per cent for all non-Germans, but 42.5 per cent for children under 6. The figures are even higher for certain neighbourhoods such as Mariannenplatz, where the KITA is located, nearly 2/3 of the population under 6 is non-German, primarily Turkish-speaking.

These population statistics alone suggest that children growing up in this neighbourhood live in a multilingual community in which Turkish plays a prominent role in the interactions at home, in the neighbourhoods and, also at school, while German may play a subsidiary role. This tendency is exacerbated by the local educational policies, which result in many foreign children attending classes without any German peers. (For a recent discussion of these school policies and their consequences for language development, see Kardam and Pfaff, 1993).

Kita language policy

It can be readily understood that language development is seen as one of the most important educational issues in Berlin. It is widely recognized that contact with German peers plays a major role here and there has been an attempt in recent years to provide such contact in day-care centres. Most Kitas in Berlin (or Germany) follow a language policy which is German-dominant, though some caretakers who can also speak Turkish (or other home language) may also be employed.

In contrast, the VAK Kita, in which our study was conducted[2], had adopted a bilingual policy of 'equal rights for both languages'. During the time of our investigation, while the proportion of children of migrants from Turkey was about 90-95 per cent, the rest German children a few children of mixed marriages, the caretaker staff was composed of equal numbers of native speakers of Turkish and of German who generally followed the policy of speaking their mother tongue to all children, whether Turkish or German.

In the Kita, the children were thus exposed to native adult varieties of both Turkish and German from a very early age, as young as six months in some cases. Although they were also exposed to a number of different native and non-native, child and adult varieties of both these (and other) languages at home and in the neighbourhood, the fact that many of the children spent the majority of each weekday at the Kita made this an ideal setting in which to examine what might be simultaneous acquisition of two first languages in a very different setting from the usual one-parent-one-language situation. This is what we initially expected, but, as will become clear, not what we found.

Sample

Our sample covered the age range from 2-8 and included Turkish children (n=22), German children (n=5), and children of mixed marriages (n=4), coded T, D and TD, respectively, as shown in Table 2.

Table 2. KITA sample

	German		Turkish		Turkish - German	
	N	Age range	N	Age range	N	Age range
Sample	5	1;07-4;10	22	1;01-8;05	4	1;10-6;09
Subsample	3	1;10-4;06	6	1;08-8;05	1	4;02-6;09

Note that our sample overrepresented the proportion of German native speakers to facilitate the cross-linguistic and cross-acquisition type comparisons.

Methodology

Recordings averaging half an hour, longer for the older children, were made separately for each language every month--at the Kita for those preschool children and, for those who had started school, at home, after school.

---

[2] The Kita is organized by the Verein für die Förderung ausländischen und deutschen Kinder (VAK).

The children were recorded, individually or with another child, by teams of two Turkish or two German investigators, who used a variety of toys, books, pictures, etc. and who engaged the child in conversation about these as well as about events and topics which went beyond the 'here and now' of shared experience as much as possible. Interactional contexts were identified as A (Actions, playing with toys) B (looking at books), C (Conversation) and N (Narrative), but actually, these tended to blend into each other, and this was in fact encouraged in order to maximize the naturalness of our 'conversations' with the children.

These recordings were transcribed for quantitative analysis. (See Pfaff et al., 1987 for details.)

Research issues and linguistic features investigated

As noted above, our general research interests were concerned with (1) cross-linguistic comparison of the acquisition of Turkish and German, (2) cross-acquisition type comparison of first and early second language acquisition patterns and (3) the investigation of language contact phenomena.

The focus of the investigation was the development of language mixing, morphosyntax and discourse strategies in both languages. Our initial focus was on development of the lexicon and nominal and verbal morphosyntax; later, as we came to know the children better, we were able to incorporate observations of conversational strategies.

Morphosyntax was of particular interest to us because of the typological divergence between Turkish and German.

Thus, we examine several areas in which Turkish and German differ strikingly in grammatical typology. In both nominal and verbal morphosyntax, Turkish differs from German, in general, in being agglutinative, with regular and transparent morphology, and specifically by having a different set of grammaticized categories in the adult languages.

In nominal morphosyntax, Turkish case and number marking are expressed by nominal suffixes, while German expresses case, number and gender fusionally on articles. In Turkish, gender does not occur at all as a grammatical category; neither natural nor grammatical gender is morphologically marked, while German marks both natural and grammatical gender.

In verbal morphosyntax, Turkish marks tense, mood, aspect, voice, and so on as verbal suffixes while German uses paraphrastic auxiliary plus main verb constructions. In addition, Turkish marks a progressive category which is not marked in German. In addition, Turkish uses non-finite forms, variously termed 'deverbal adverbs', 'gerunds' or 'converbs' to express grammatical relations between clauses expressed by subordinating conjunctions or adverbials in German. In contrast, German non-finite forms, infinitives and past participle are used with finite auxiliary verbs to form modal expressions, perfectives and passives, all of which are expressed by suffixes on the main verb stem in Turkish. The two languages are similar in that subject agreement is marked with inflectional suffixes, however Turkish is a prodrop language while German is not.

Cross-linguistic investigation of first language acquisition, e.g., Slobin ((ed.), 1985) have identified significantly different patterns of development of the morpho-syntactic marking of parallel notions by children acquiring languages of different types. We compare the development of these young Turkish/German bilingual children with the results of investigations of monolingual Turkish children (Aksu-Koç, 1988; Aksu-Koç and Slobin, 1985; Ekmekçi, 1979, 1986; etc.) and German children (Clahsen, 1982, 1988; Mills, 1985; Tracy, 1991; etc.) and, additionally with studies of simultaneous bilingual acquisition involving these languages, (Leopold, 1949; Meisel, 1989, 1990; Saunders, 1983; Taeschner, 1983 etc. for German) and with the growing number of studies of the sequential acquisition of Turkish and/or German or Dutch by migrant children.

Obviously these topics require far more than a short article to explicate. In the following section, I will simply summarize some of our major findings on the development of Turkish and German, illustrating the points with examples from two KITA children who differ in language dominance[3]. In the final section, I briefly comment on a pair of comparable passages in both languages from one child.

Developmental Patterns

Bilingual acquisition

Although their early exposure to both languages initially led us to expect that the children would display the characteristics of 'simultaneous acquisition of two first languages', our analysis of their developing competence to date reveals that their language acquisition patterns differ significantly from those 'Type 1' bilingual children of mixed marriages most frequently reported in the literature on early child bilingualism (see Romaine, 1989).

Instead, we find a pattern of successive first and second language acquisition with clear patterns of language dominance, strikingly different for the Turkish and the German children. After an initial phase of producing only Turkish, all the Turkish children acquired productive competence in German, though, as we will see, this may be quite nonstandard. The German children, with one exception, did not develop productive competence in Turkish despite the fact that they were vastly outnumbered in the KITA by their Turkish peers, most of whom almost always spoke Turkish to each other and to the Turkish caretakers.

[3] The children, coded T05 and T16 are German and Turkish dominant respectively. For more detailed information, see Pfaff et al., 1988, 1991 and Pfaff, 1993.

The obvious conclusion is that co-presence in the KITA of German and Turkish native speakers was clearly not sufficient to effect native-like acquisition in the other languages. Clearly the values and language use patterns of the surrounding community came through even to these very young children.

Language dominance

Language dominance varies and turns out to be significant for the patterning of all the linguistic and interactional variable investigated.

The majority of the Turkish children are clearly Turkish-dominant. Their acquisition of Turkish proceeds essentially like that reported for monolinguals (Aksu-Koç, 1988; Aksu-Koç & Slobin, 1985; Ekmekçi, 1979, 1986) while their acquisition of German differs strikingly from that reported for monolinguals (Mills, 1985; Clahsen, 1988) and is in some respects similar to the patterns characteristic of natural second language acquisition of German by adults and older children (Klein & Dittmar, 1979; Clahsen, Meisel & Pienemann, 1983; von Stutterheim, 1986; Kuhberg, 1987; and others).

For Turkish children who are German-dominant, the acquisitional patterns for Turkish morphosyntax are like those of monolinguals only in some respects, while some structures do not develop to the same extent, if at all, a pattern termed 'stagnation' by Verhoeven and Boeschoten (1986). This stagnation goes along with a tendency to avoid or limit their interaction in Turkish in favour of German, as we will discuss below.

Development of lexicon and language mixing

We analysed instances of mixing of Turkish and German in the individual interviews. As these were conducted primarily in one of the other language, it is not surprising that our findings majority of mixes are lexical items and short phrases from one language in the context of the other, in a form consonant with the Matrix Language Frame model proposed in recent papers by Myers-Scotton (1990, 1992). That is, we find there is always a clear base language which dominates morphosyntax.

Thus we find word morphological integration of German nouns with Turkish case inflections, e.g., *U-Bahn'da* 'in the U-Bahn (subway)' in Turkish interviews or of integration of German verbs, nouns or adjective as verbs in Turkish by means of a postposed 'dummy verb' *yapmak* 'make or do' which carries the tense/aspect and agreement information, e.g., *tanzen yapıyo* 's/he's dancing'. Similarly, we find Turkish nouns occur in German with preposed definite articles, e.g., *der köpek* 'the dog'[4]. Such structures, which are violations of Poplack's the free morpheme constraint (German stems with Turkish inflections) or of the equivalence constraint (Turkish auxiliary postposed to German verb stem) are frequent but these can readily be accounted for in her framework as patterns of 'nonce' borrowing.

The extent of mixing, as indicated by an analysis of type-token ratios, was clearly related to the children's developing language proficiency, but also notably toward the requirements of communication in the wider community outside the KITA. The children rapidly develop toward distinct norms in Turkish and German, approximating the requirements of the 'monolingual mode' in German, with decreasing admixture of Turkish elements in German but approaching a 'bilingual mode community norm' which permits the incorporation of lexical items from German into Turkish (see Pfaff et al., 1988, and Pfaff, 1990b).

It is of interest that mixing patterns differ with language dominance and highly indicative of the situation in Berlin-Kreuzberg that the patterns we find for Turkish-dominant children are very similar to those found for Turkish-speaking adult migrants in the Netherlands, while only the few German-dominant children's patterns are parallel to those they found in Turkish children in the Netherlands (Boeschoten and Verhoeven, 1985).

Nominal and verbal morphology

As far as the development of morphological marking is concerned, our finding clearly reflect the typological differences between Turkish and German. Briefly acquisition of Turkish inflections poses no problem, as is found for Turkish monolingual children (Aksu-Koç and Slobin, 1985), while acquisition of the appropriate case, number, gender marking in German is complicated by the syncretism of the article system, as is true for monolinguals as well (Mills, 1985).

The bilingual children make relatively few errors in Turkish morphology. This is particularly striking for the suffixes which express case, subject-verb agreement and tense-mood-aspect. Those errors which do occur are characteristically different for Turkish-dominant and German-dominant children. Further distinctions are to be found when one examines the frequency and distribution of the suffixes quantitatively or in context.

The acquisition of German morphology, however, is far more difficult for the bilingual children we studied than would be predicted by the typological syncretism of the system. Their patterns of acquisition differ strikingly from those observed for monolinguals, even for the German-dominant T05 and is more like patterns of second language acquisition of German observed for adults and older children.

[4] Many children, however, especially at first do not use articles in German, see the section on 'Development of nominal morphology in Turkish and German'.

The following sections briefly illustrate these points with material from the KITA study.

Development of Nominal Morphology in Turkish and German

Before turning to the acquisition of morphosyntactic marking of nominals, it is appropriate to look briefly at the development of argument structure of utterances in Turkish and German.

Figure 1 summarizes the use of NPs in both Turkish and German by two children over a period of nearly a year, T16 (3;10-4;9) and T05 (4;4-5;2). The overall length of the bars in the graph corresponds to the number of instances of NPs with lexical heads produced by each child in each language and the size of the patterned segments within each bar represents the percentage of the indicated semantic / case functions[5].

Language dominance is reflected in the proportion of overt NPs in Turkish and German. T16 has more NPs in Turkish than in German, while T05 has more NPs in German than in Turkish.

Further, the distribution of overt NPs over the different case functions differs systematically for Turkish-dominant and German-dominant children. The proportion of naming (NP-essives and cop-essives) is notably higher in the non-dominant language. These observations about the distribution of overt NPs actually reflect differences in the discourse strategies employed by the children in their dominant and non-dominant languages. We will return to this topic later.

As far as the development of morphological marking in Turkish is concerned, as noted above Turkish poses no problems; even the German-dominant T05 makes few 'errors'; only a few of those, notably instances of possesives marked only on a preceding possessive pronoun but not by the standard Turkish inflection on the possessed noun, e.g., T05 4;10 *benim para (=param) var* 'I have money' can arguably be taken to represent transfer from German and, even here it equally plausible to claim that this represents a universal tendency toward more analytic marking. The Turkish-dominant children sometimes overgeneralize lexically idiosyncratic possessive forms, e.g., T16 4;6 *sonra bebeğin kolusunu (=kolunu) koparmak istiyo* 'then he wants to take the doll's arm off'. Forms such as *kolusunu* are not 'errors' in case marking, *per se,* but represent overgeneralization of the

---

[5] Semantic/case categories used are defined in Pfaff et al., 1988. For Turkish, in which the case markings more nearly correspond to underlying semantic functions, we have used the traditional case labels for the marked cases. For German, where the correspondences are more complex, we used semantic labels. In both languages, we distinguish naming (essives) from other uses of the nominative such as agent, experiencer, and so on.

NP essives are isolated nouns, possibly with indefinite articles, while Cop(ular) essives are nouns used as predicate nominals. The latter are realized without overt copula forms in Turkish and, frequently, though nonstandardly, in German (see Pfaff et al., 1988 for examples and discussion).

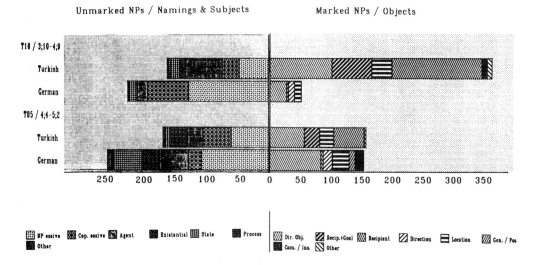

Figure 1. Case function of NPs in Turkish and German for T16 & T05.

regular rules to certain lexical items. Such forms are also reported in monolingual pre-schoolers' speech (Ekmekçi, 1986). (See Pfaff and Savaş, 1988; Pfaff, 1993 for further discussion).

Acquisition of German nominal marking, discussed at length in Pfaff 1992, is problematic for these children and patterns differ strikingly from L1, even for the German-dominant T05.

The proportion of Ø article usage, e.g., Ø *Eisenbahn* is kaputt '(the) train is broken.' by Turkish children is much higher than for the German monolinguals and persists longer.

The use of definite article forms as demonstrative pronouns, rather than personal pronouns, e.g., ich habe *den* gesehen nich (=ich habe ihn nicht gesehen, 'I haven't seen *him*' are much more predominant for Turkish children than for German L1 learners.

While case marking does seem to be acquired, as illustrated by the above example, the choice of article form is nonetheless very frequently nonstandard, as a result of its being confounded with the category gender.

Gender is difficult in German because of the high degree of apparent arbitrariness of the distribution of nouns among the grammatical gender classes[6]. This grammatical subsystem is of special interest because of the psycholinguistic problems it poses for the learner. Mills (1986) has pointed out, that, although gender errors in German first language persist until 8 or 9, the rules are essentially acquired around age 2. In contrast, for second language learners of German, this area of grammar is notoriously difficult and may never be fully mastered. Turkish has no grammatically marked category gender, neither natural nor grammatical. However, the subset of natural gender items could be expected to be mastered early if the semantic primacy hypothesis holds in either L1 or L2.

It is very striking in our study that the category of gender does not seem to be acquired at all. This pertains not only to grammatical gender items, e.g., *dann hab hier stellt, die Hund* (std masc, *den Hund* 'then (he) put (it) here, the dog' T16, but also to natural gender items, e.g., *dann wieder sind kommen, die Mutter und die Vater)* (std. masc. *der Vater)* 'then (they) came again, the mother and the father'. The incidence of nonstandard natural gender items is, perhaps, even more frequent than nonstandard grammatical gender, tending to disconfirm the hypotheses that semantic primacy determines the process of second language acquisition (see Pfaff, 1992 and Thiel, forthcoming).

Development of Verbal Morphology

As suggested in the brief contrastive overview of Turkish and German, the systems of the two languages are quite different. In this section we simply summarize some of the major findings with respect to finite and non-finite verbs in both languages.

With respect to the particular finite forms used, we find several differences between the forms used by Turkish and German-dominant children. (see Pfaff et al., 1989 for detailed presentation of quantitative results for both languages; Pfaff, 1992 for a discussion of aspects of German and Pfaff, 1993 for aspects of Turkish). Some of the findings are listed below:

Turkish: The forms which occur are essentially error free for all children, essentially however there is a definite difference with respect to which forms are used, with the German-dominant children like T05 having a much more restricted inventory of forms.

For finite forms, it is striking that the German-dominant T05 the 'evidential', -*mIş* forms very rarely while the Turkish-dominant T16 uses them frequently in narratives. It is not the case that T05 substitutes the wrong suffix where -*mIş* forms would be expected. Instead, as in the narrative excerpts to be discussed below, he describes scenes, from a perspective in which progressive, past or future forms are

---

[6] While Köpcke and Zubin (1984) have pointed out a number of semantic and phonological rules which apply to a large proportion of nouns, there remain many exceptions, some extremely frequent in the lexical inventory of young children.

appropriate. As with the results for case marking, these results for verb morphology are linked to the children's conversational strategies, as we will see in the next section.

Even more striking is the fact that while the Turkish-dominant T16 uses non-finite forms throughout the period of our investigation, the German-dominant T05 uses no finite forms at all. In this respect, as for the types of language mixing discussed above, the Turkish-dominant children we studied in Berlin more nearly approximate the language behaviour of monolinguals than do Turkish children in the Netherlands, whose Turkish is more like that of our German-dominant children[7].

German: We find fewer differences in the type of verbal constructions attempted, but a greater difference in their realization than in Turkish. Agreement inflections for main verbs are frequently nonstandard, despite the fact that the system is similar to Turkish, where almost no nonstandard agreement is observed. Initially, Turkish-dominant children produce zero copula structures, which are not found for German-dominant children. Zero auxiliary forms are much less frequent, but we find overgeneralization of auxiliary *haben* (rather than *sein*) with verbs of motion or change of state.) Finally, there is a tendency for Turkish-dominant, but not German-dominant children to use compound verb structures, with forms *ist+verb* or *mach+verb,* as in *alle Kinder is Jocken anziehen* 'all the children are putting on jogging suits (T16:5;02)' *Elefant komm. die mach hauen* '(the) elephant comes. he is fighting' T12 3;10. It is noteworthy here that the form *is* appears to be invariant and occurs with both singular and plural subjects. This is not the case, however for occurrences of the regular copula, which varies appropriately for person–number agreement with 3sg and 3pl subjects, *is(t), sind.* See Pfaff, 1991, 1992, for further discussion of such forms.

Conversational strategies

In this section we examine two dimensions of conversational strategies employed by the children: (1) global strategies related to the children's interaction with the interlocutors and (2) local strategies related to the perspective taken by the children in producing narratives.

---

[7] Turkish/Dutch bilingual children in the Netherlands show extremely restricted use of gerunds of any type (Verhoeven, 1988: 448-9; Boeschoten, 1990a: 100-120), suggesting stagnation in acquisition of complex structures and possible overgeneralization and reanalysis of the structures.

Global strategies: participation in discourse

From our observations of the KITA children, from informal observations reported by parents and caretakers and from self-reports of language choice by older children[8], it is clear that linguistic dominance correlates with preferred language used in everyday interactions in their families, with friends, etc.

In contrast, in the conversations we recorded with them, the children's language choice was limited; they understood that they were expected to use one language in so far as possible, Turkish with the Turkish interviewers, German with the German interviewers. Our preference for the 'monolingual mode', as Grosjean terms it, in our play sessions enabled us to investigate the relationship between everyday inter-action and the development of the children's linguistic competence in each of their languages.

We approached this question by examining the types of discourse structure cha-racteristic of the conversations we have recorded with the children in their stronger and weaker languages in different elicitation contexts, focused on the 'here and now' in structured interactions, games with toys or looking at picture books, or in conversation drawing on the child's own experience, fantasies or opinions on a variety of topics beyond the 'here and now'. Not surprisingly, the child's willing-ness and ability to engage in such conversations was more likely to take a larger proportion of the interview time in the interactions in the child's preferred, or dominant, language. Even in the more structured 'here-and-now' oriented interacti-ons, children were more able to direct the conversation themselves in their domi-nant language, while in the other language they tended to rely much more on scaf-folding provided by the interviewers.

Table 3 gives a schematic overview of our preliminary findings.

[8] See Pfaff (1991) for discussion.

Table 3. Conversational strategies in Turkish and German.

	Turkish-dominant T16 (3;11 - 5;8)		German-dominant T05 (4;4 - 6;0)	
	Turkish	*German*	*Turkish*	*German*
Reliance on scaffolding	little	much	much	little
Detail	frequent	rare	rare	frequent
Questions	few	few	some (for vocab)	few (for info)
Topic initiations	few	very few	rare	some
Digressions	many (to convers.)	many (back to activity)	many (to diff. act.)	many (to convers.)
Ease of elic. free conv.	easy	difficult	difficult	easy
Delegating turn to another	rare	frequently to sister	whenever possible to interviewer or mother	rare

Local strategies: narrative perspective

We turn now from the children's interactional strategies to their the choice of forms and structures within their linguistic competence in a given language to satisfy the requirements of their communicative 'tasks' in the interviews. For instance, in talking to us about a book, children can adequately participate in the 'task' by producing descriptions of the individual pictures or by producing a connected narrative, or by offering us their opinions and suggestions about how the characters in the story should have acted. This is obviously a matter of individual variation in interactional style, but by comparing the texts elicited by the same book, we can begin to see how the children's productions are in part determined by their linguistic competence. For this reason, we made an effort to elicit parallel conversations in both languages from all the children in our subsample. One set of such parallel conversations was elicited in looking at the book, *Lady and the Tramp*[9].

[9] Walt Disney's *Lady and the Tramp* Ladybird Books. This is a picture book (with text in English - which none of the children in the KITA study could read). The protagonist is the dog, Lady, who lives

In Pfaff 1993, the narrative perspectives and strategies in the Turkish of two children, T05 and T16 are illustrated in detail. Here we examine the other side of the story as well, illustrating some of the striking differences in conversational strategies and forms used in their dominant and weaker languages with parallel examples in both Turkish and German. Some indication of whether the realizations are standard or nonstandard is provided by the glosses, though this is not the primary concern here.

Jim gives his wife a Christmas present

Picture shows Jim giving his wife a the dog, Lady, in front of a Christmas tree

1. T16: *burda Weihnachtsmannbaum yapmışlar*
'here Ø (= they) made a Santa Claus tree'

2. T16: *Tannenbaum*
[Interviewer mentions dog as gift]
''Herzlichen Glückwunsch x Weihnachtsmann.''
'Christmas tree'
'Best wishes x Santa Claus (Christmas man)'

3. T05: *bu Weihnachten diye*
'this (= Christmas tree) (is) for Christmas'

4. T05: *guck mal, der Mann hat ihn (=Darling) als*
Weihnachten ein kleines Hund gekauft.
'look, the man bought her a little dog for Christmas'

Turkish: In (1) and (3) both children focus on the Christmas tree which is in the background. T16, the Turkish-dominant child refers to the presumed prior actions of the couple decorating the tree. She uses a *-mIş* form denoting non-witnessed action. The German-dominant child T05, in contrast, simply identifies the tree's function in a sentence without an overt verb.

German: In (2) and (4) the children's utterances differ maximally. T16 simply gives a name for the tree, and when the interlocutor points out the dog, she provides a formulaic greeting. T05 explicitly addresses the interlocutor and explains the scene, referring not only to what is visible, but to the inferred prior action.

with a young couple, 'Jim dear' and 'Darling'. When they go away, Aunt Sara comes to stay with their baby and chases Lady out. Lady meets another dog, Tramp, with whom she has some adventures before returning home with him to a happy ending.

Aunt Sarah chases Lady

Lady has been looking at the new baby, Aunt Sarah, fearing she will hurt the baby, chases her away with a broom. Lady runs down the stairs.

5.   T16:   *burda da köpek hemen koşturuyo burda da*
           o da köpeğe vurmak istiyo.
           'and here the dog immediately runs here
           and she wants to hit the dog'

6.   T16:   *"Du Hund, geh weg von hier, von die kleine Baby!"*
           '"you, dog, go away from here, from the little baby!"'

7.   T05:   *döwüyo*
           'Ø (=aunt) is hitting Ø (=Lady)'

           INT *neden döwüyo?*
           'why is Ø (=aunt) hitting Ø (=Lady)?'

           bu bu bunu hiç görmedi diye
           'because this (=aunt) has never seen this (=Lady) before'

           bu da korkmuş
           'and this (=Lady) was afraid.

           sonra kaçïyo
           'then Ø (=Lady) runs away'

8.   T05:   *denn kommt seine Tante, und dann hat er schnell Angst, die Lady.*
           'then his aunt comes and he gets scared right away, Lady'

           der kennt sie nich. Der holt sich ein Besenst(iel)
           x wollt er ihn verkloppen.
           'he (=she) doesn't know her. he (=she) takes a broomst(ick) x she
           wants to hit him (=Lady).'

           ich mein aber, der muß das sagen "Ich bin sein Mann, seine Fami-
           lie" Des muß man sagen, sonst schlägt er ihn nich.
           'but I think he should say that: "I'm his (=Lady's) man [owner,
           patron], his family".
           one has to say that otherwise (=so) he (=aunt) won't hit him (=La-
           dy).

Turkish: T16 uses deictic pronouns only with reference to the pictures in the framework of telling the story to the interlocutor. She uses lexical nouns to refer to the participants in the story. T05 uses a sequence of simple sentences, notable for the use of deictic pronominal reference to all story participants.

German: T16 makes up a direct quote to express the situation, using almost a stereotypic 'foreigner talk' German for the aunt to address the strange dog she fears will hurt the baby. T05 provides a not only a full explanation of Aunt Sarah's actions, he offers his opinion about what Jim should have said to her so that she would understand that Lady was part of the household. The forms are quite non-standard, but the point is clear.

> *Lady and Tramp chase chickens*

5. T16:   *burda da köpek xxx istiyomuş bunları*
    'and then here the dog wanted xxx, these'

6. T16:   *will das essen*
    'Ø (= (s)he, they) want(s) to eat that'

7. T05:   *o zaman bu böyle yaptı, bak! bu bunu yicek diye.*
    'then this did like this, look! because this is going to eat this'

8. T05:   *der wollte die Hühner fressen.*
    'he wanted to eat the hens'

Turkish: The picture represents an action. T16's version in (5) expresses the motivation for the action, using a *-mIş* form while T05's version in (7) focuses on the actions itself. Note that T05's use of *-DI* form *yaptı* 'did' is combined with emphasis on witnessing the event, with the imperative *bak* 'look!' directed to the interlocutor. His version of the motivation is expressed by use of the future form, *yicek* 'he is going to eat'.

German: In terms of perspective, these two utterances are almost parallel to the utterances in Turkish, but with reversal of the speakers. Here it is T05 who focuses on the past intention while T16 uses present tense. Structurally, T16 uses deictic reference (with null subject) while T05 uses a pronoun and lexical object.

> *Dogcatcher*

Dogcatcher with a net; the dogs in a cage.

9. T16:   *burda da kafeste kalmıslar;*
    köpekler kafeste kalmış
    'and here Ø (= the dogs) stay (3pl) in the cage

'the dogs stay (3sg/pl) in the cage'

10. T16: *dann hab er (dogcatcher) Ø (=Lady) nehmt*
          "ich wußte nich von wen ist der" die weiß nich x dann hab (Ø=3s)
          hier stellt, die Hund.
          der (=dogcatcher) hab zu ihm (Lady) böse.
          'then Ø (=he) takes Ø (it) "I didn't know who he belonged to" he
          doesn't know [or Ø doesn't know her/it] x
          then Ø (=he) put Ø (=it) here, the dog.
          he is angry at him/it.

11. T05: *o zaman bu ko- bunlar korkuyola.*
          'then this ko- these are afraid.'

12. T05: *dann kommt der Mann und fangt Lady und der Tramp.*
          'then the man comes and catches Lady and the Tramp'

Turkish: Here, T16 refers to the resultant stage using *-mIş* forms as is customary in
storytelling. Note her use of alternative non-redundant plural marking: a marked 3pl
verb form when the subject is null, but an unmarked 3rd person verb form when the
explicit 3pl subject is used. T05 refers to the emotional state of the dogs pictured as
an ongoing process using the progressive *-yor* form.

German: T16 uses two strategies for clarification here: direct quotation to provide
the rationale for the dogcatcher's action and postposed lexical NP, *die Hund,* to
identify referent which is not obvious from the nonstandard pronouns and null
arguments. T05's version, in contrast, is syntactically straightforward, agent and
patient are lexical NPs.

Rat in the garden or in the house

Lady and Tramp confront a rat in the garden, it runs into the house into the baby's
room. They chase it. Aunt Sarah misunderstands and thinks the dogs are attacking
the baby.

13. T16: *burdan da burda da bi bi şey buldu*
          'and from here and here Ø (=Lady) found something'

          ... onu görmüş
          '... Ø (=Lady) saw it'

          eve gelmiş.
          'Ø(=Lady and Tramp) went into the house

> *burda da kïzïyo gene*
> 'and here Ø (=aunt) gets angry again'

> *burda da kïzïyo köpeğe*
> 'and here Ø (=aunt) gets angry at the dog'

14. T16:   *hier xx , in die Babyzimmer liegt was, das, da druff x xx hier hab*
           wiederseht ihn, dann hab immer böse, die Großmutter.
           'here xx, something's lying in the baby's room, that, on top of that
           x xx here Ø (= aunt) saw him again, then Ø is always (=still)
           angry, the grandmother'

15. T05:   *weißt was, wenn er so (wide eyed stare) macht, da fürcht er sich mit*
           eine Ratte.
           'know what, when he (=Lady) does this (stare), he's afraid of a rat'

16. T05:   *bu ne?*
           'what's this?'

Turkish: T05 asks a question, delegating turn to the interlocutor by asking for a lexical item with a simple formula consisting of deictic NP and question word.

German: Here T16's deictic reference, unintelligible syllables and vocabulary gaps are difficult to reconstruct, one of the relatively few such instances in the context of looking at books. T05's question here is of an entirely different sort than in Turkish; this time it is a rhetorical formulaic phrase which allows him to continue to hold the floor, giving commentary.

Puppies

Picture shows that Lady and the Tramp (after a 'marriage ceremony' performed by Jim and 'Darling') have puppies. Two of the puppies look just like Lady, one looks just like Tramp.

17. T16:   *burda da çocuklarï varmïş bunun. bi de bunun çocuklarï varmïş.*
           'and here there are her children, and there are his children.'

> *bunun bi tane, bunun bi tane*
> 'one of hers and one of his'

> *bunun iki tane, bunun bi tane*
> 'two of hers and one of his'

> *bunlarin ikisi de bunun çocuğu, bu da bunun çocuğu.*
> 'and these two are her children and this is his child.'

18. T16:   *hier die (=Lady) hab zwei Baby krieg,*
             die (=Tramp) eine Baby krieg.
             'here she has had two babies, he one baby.'

19. T05:   *o zaman bebek bebekler - bu bu bu iki tane çocuklar bunun, da bu*
             bu çocuk bunun -
             'then the baby, babies - these two children are this one's (=Lady's)
             this child is this one's (=Tramp's)'

20. T05:   *Der Tramp hat ein Baby und der Lady hat zwei Babys ein Junge*
             und ein Mädchen.
             'Tramp has one baby and Lady has two babies, a boy and a girl.'

Turkish and German: Both children attempt to account for the appearance of the puppies as having either Lady or Tramp as parent. It is clear that the confounding lack of grammatical or natural gender marking in German plays no role in this. The answers in Turkish are similar in content in that attribution of parenthood follows appearance.

Conclusions

In the preceding examination of the Turkish and German speech of Turkish/German bilingual children, we have touched on several different aspects of their grammars: lexical and structural inventories, frequency of alternative realizations, and errors. The type of analysis illustrated above attempts to interrelate the use of linguistic forms, structures and systems with discourse-interactional features of communicative competence. We believe that such an integrated approach is particularly appropriate to a study of acquisition and attrition in very heterogeneous bilingual communities such as the Turkish population in Germany.

We have seen that while actual errors in Turkish are relatively infrequent even in German-dominant children's speech, there are clear differences in the inventory of structures used and in the frequencies with which the various alternatives are employed. In German, in contrast, children, such as T05, who are German dominant, make many 'errors'. This is not simply a reflection of the morphological transparency of Turkish vs. opacity of German. It seems to be the case that children growing up in this particular environment have little enough effective contact with German so that their patterns of language acquisition of German are more like L2 than like L1 learners, though, it is clear that they are much closer to the native norms than immigrant adult L2-learners. Nonetheless, all the children whose language we investigated are able to sustain communicative interaction in both languages, an aspect of their linguistic competence which frequently gets lost in studies which focus only on the acquisition of formal norms of monolingual speech.

References

Aksu-Koç, A., 1988. *The acquisition of aspect and modality: The case of past reference in Turkish*. Cambridge: Cambridge University Press.

Aksu-Koç, A. & D. Slobin, 1985. The acquisition of Turkish. In: D. Slobin (ed.), *The Cross-linguistic Study of Language Acquisition, Vol. 1: The Data*. Hillsdale, NJ: Lawrence Erlbaum.

Boeschoten, H., 1990a. *Acquisition of Turkish by Immigrant Children.: A Multiple Case Study of Turkish Children in the Netherlands aged 4 to 6*. Ph.D. Thesis. Tilburg University.

Boeschoten, H. & L. Verhoeven, 1985. Integration niederländischer lexikalischer Elemente ins Türkische: Sprachmischung bei Immigranten der ersten und zweiten Generation. *Linguistische Berichte*, 98, 347-364.

Clahsen, H., 1982. *Spracherwerb in der Kindheit: Eine Untersuchung zur Entwicklung der Syntax bei Kleinkindern*. Tübingen: Gunter Narr.

Clahsen, H., 1988. *Normale und gestörte Kindersprache: linguistische Untersuchungen zum Erwerb von Syntax und Morphologie*. Amsterdam: John Benjamins.

Clahsen, H., J. Meisel & M. Pienemann, 1983. *Deutsch als Zweitsprache: der Spracherwerb ausländischer Arbeiter*. Tübinger Beiträge zur Linguistik. Series A, Language development; 3. Tübingen: Narr.

Ekmekçi, Ö., 1979. *Acquisition of Turkish: a longitudinal study on the early language development of a Turkish child*. Unpublished Ph.D. Thesis. Univ. Texas, Austin.

Ekmekçi, Ö., 1986. The developmental errors in the preschool Turkish children's speech. *Proceedings of the Turkish Linguistics Conference*. Istanbul: Boğaziçi Univ. Publ.

Kardam, F. and C. Pfaff, 1993. Issues in educational policy and language development. In: S. Kroon, D. Pagel und T. Vallen (eds) *Multiethnische Gesellschaft und Schule in Berlin*. Münster / New York: Waxmann.

Klein, W. & N. Dittmar, 1979. *Developing grammars: the acquisition of German syntax by foreign workers*. Springer series in language and communication; vol. 1. Berlin: Springer.

Köpcke, K. & D. Zubin, 1984. Sechs Prinzipien für die Genuszuweisung im Deutschen: Ein Beitrag zur natürlichen Klassifikation. *Linguistische Berichte*, 93, 26-50.

Kuhberg, H., 1987. *Der Erwerb der Temporalität des Deutschen durch zwei elfjähriger Kinder mit Ausgangssprache Türkisch und Polnisch: Eine Longitudinaluntersuchung*. Frankfurt/M.: Peter Lang.

Leopold, W., 1949. *Speech development of a bilingual child: A linguist's record*. Evanston: Northwestern University Press.

Meisel, J., 1989. Early differentiation of languages in bilingual children. In: K. Hyltenstam & L. Obler (eds), *Bilingualism across the lifespan: Aspects of acquisition, maturity and loss*, 13-40. Cambridge: Cambridge University Press.

Meisel, J., 1990. Infl-ection: Subjects and subject-verb agreement. In: J. Meisel (ed.), *Two first languages: Early grammatical development in bilingual children,* 238-298. Dordrecht: Foris.

Meisel, J., 1990. Code-switching and related phenomena in young bilingual children. *Code Switching and Language Contact: Workshop of Concepts, Methodology and Data.* Strasbourg: European Science Foundation Scientific Networks, 143-68.

Mills, A., 1986. *The acquisition of gender: A study of English and German.* Berlin: Springer.

Myers-Scotton, C., 1990. Intersections between social motivations and structural processes in codeswitching. Paper read at the Workshop on constraints, conditions and models, ESF Scientific Network, London.

Myers-Scotton, C., 1992. Comparing borrowing and codeswitching In: C. Eastman (ed.), *Codeswitching,* 19-39. Clevedon: Multilingual Matters.

Pfaff, C., 1990b. Mixing and linguistic convergence in migrant speech communities: linguistic constraints, social conditions and models of acquisition. *Code-switching and language contact: Constraints, conditions and models.* Strasbourg: European Science Foundation Scientific Networks.

Pfaff, C., 1991. Turkish in contact with German: Language maintenance and loss among immigrant children in West Berlin. *International Journal of the Sociology of Language,* 90, 97-129.

Pfaff, C., 1992. The issue of grammaticalization in early German second language. *Studies in Second Language Acquisition,* 14, 273-96.

Pfaff, C., 1993. Turkish language development in Germany. In: G. Extra & L. Verhoeven (eds), *Immigrant Languages in Europe.* Clevedon: Multilingual Matters.

Pfaff, C., F. Kardam, J. Voß, O.Çakarcan, H. MacKerron, T. Savaş & M. Thiel, 1987, 1988, 1989, 1990, 1991. *Bilingualer Spracherwerb.* DFG Projekt Arbeitsberichte I-V.

Pfaff, C. & T. Savaş, 1988. Language development in a bilingual setting: the acquisition of Turkish in Germany. In: S. Koç (ed.), *Studies on Turkish Linguistics.* Ankara: Middle East Technical University.

Romaine, S., 1989. *Bilingualism.* Oxford: Basil Blackwell.

Saunders, G., 1983. *Bilingual children. A guide for the family.* Clevedon, Avon: Multilingual Matters.

Slobin, D., 1985. Cross-linguistic evidence for the language-making capacity. In: D. Slobin (ed.), *The cross-linguistic study of language acquisition (Vol. 2),* 1157-1256. Hillsdale, NJ: Lawrence Erlbaum.

Slobin, D., 1988. The development of clause chaining in Turkish child language. In: S. Koç (ed.), *Studies on Turkish Linguistics.* Ankara: Middle East Technical University.

Statistisches Landesamt Berlin, 1991. *Melderechtlich registrierte Ausländer in Berlin.*

Statistisches Landesamt Berlin, 1991. *Melderechtlich registrierte Einwohner in Berlin.*

Statistisches Landesamt Berlin 1988. *Zum Thema Kinder und Jugendliche in Berlin.*

Statistisches Landesamt Berlin, 1987. *Erfassung der Kinder nach Altersgruppen in den statistischen Gebieten in Kreuzberg.*

Stutterheim, C. v., 1986. *Temporalität in der Zweitsprache.* Berlin: de Gruyter.

Taeschner, T., 1983. *The sun is feminine. A study on language acquisition in bilingual children.* Berlin: Springer.

Thiel, M., forthcoming. *Die Genusmarkierung im Erst- und frühen Zweitspracherwerb des Deutschen.*

Tracy, R., 1991. *Sprachliche Strukturentwicklung: Linguistische und kognitionspsychologische Aspekte einer Theorie des Erstspracherwerbs.* Tübingen: Gunter Narr.

Verhoeven, L., 1988. Acquisition of discourse cohesion in Turkish. In: S. Koç (ed.), *Studies on Turkish Linguistics.* Ankara: Middle East Technical University.

Verhoeven, L. & H. Boeschoten, 1986. First language acquisition in a second language submersion environment. *Applied Psycholinguistics, 7,* 241-55.

Bilingual development of English preschool children in Turkey

Bloomfield (1933: 56) suggested that bilingualism means 'a native-like control of two languages'. Diebold (1968), on the other hand, defined bilingualism as the ability to use or comprehend more than one language. Thus, we can assume that a bilingual is an individual who can demonstrate any skill between these two extremes. Though in the past bilingualism was considered to have negative effects on intelligence and learning ability, case studies of bilingual children conducted since the 1940s supported the efficiency of early bilingualism. Reviews on such case studies come from Hatch (1978) and McLaughlin (1984) (see also McLaughlin, this volume). The study most often cited is that of Leopold (1939-1949). His study was based on Hildegard's learning of English and German. Another well-known study comes from Burling (1959). This study is about Stephen learning Garo (Indian) and English. Although Stephen entered the second language community at the age of 1;4, he quickly acquired Garo. However, he lost his Garo after having left the country. As opposed to the acquisition of English, Stephen acquired the morphology of Garo, not the syntax, due to the fact that Garo was not an Indo-European language where meaning is often conveyed by word order rather than inflections. Mixing of the two languages was also reported. A study with special focus on the acquisition of the bilingual lexicon was conducted by Celce-Murcia (1978). This study was on Caroline learning French and English while being dominant in English. Celce-Murcia divided Caroline's vocabulary into four groups: words known in both languages and used readily (*bird/oiseau*), words with similar pronunciation and causing confusion (*school/école*), words known in one language only (*milk, pipi*), and concepts known in both languages but used in one due to the ease of articulation (*garçon/boy;* 'boy' being easy is utilized). A more recent study comes from Saunders (1983). This study is about Thomas and Frank learning German and English simultaneously. German is not the native language of the parents. They do not live in a German-speaking environment either. It is only that Saunders is fluent in German and wants his sons to learn German from him and English from their mother.

This chapter focuses on the acquisition of Turkish by two pre-school English-speaking children. The aim of the study is to investigate what strategies these bilingual children have adopted in communicating with peers and adults. Children's responses to posed questions are analysed to observe the degree of comprehension as opposed to production. Moreover, attention is paid to strategies for communication in L2 and to patterns of language preference and language transfer.

Design of the study

In the present study the speech samples of two pre-school English-speaking children acquiring Turkish will be analysed (Ölmez, 1984; Bada, 1991). Since the method of data collection was different for each child, the procedure applied will be explained in terms of two separate cases.

Case I

One of the children, named Ian, was monolingual in English and had American parents. He was exposed to Turkish at the age of 2;9 at a day-care centre in Adana, while playing with other Turkish children. He was in Adana because his parents had come to teach at Çukurova University. He was placed at the day-care centre the day after their arrival.

A month after he started attending the day-care centre, he was observed at this setting for a period of four months. He was visited three times a week by the researcher, and each visit lasted about three hours. During the visits he was recorded whenever the conditions permitted. Since there were many children around the subject shouting and making all kinds of noise, the recordings were not very successful. In circumstances of this kind, the research assistant made do by taking notes of the verbal and non-verbal behaviour of the subject. Thus, most of the data consisted of spontaneous speech samples and non-verbal behaviour of the subject during conversations with his peers and his teacher.

Case II

The second child, named Serkan, had a British mother and a Turkish father. He had been brought up in Turkey within the family from the day of his birth. Up to the age of two, he had no contact with English speakers other than his own family consisting of his parents and two elder sisters. When the parents moved to a larger city, the mother had the opportunity to meet some native speakers of English with whom the child also had an opportunity to speak. However, he still did not have anybody from his peer-group to practice his English.

At the age of 2;3, the boy's mother started to work and sent him to a day-care centre. From this period on, the subject seemed to be reluctant to shift to English at home. When the subject got sick, the mother would stay at home with him. During this short period of time, a noticeable shift in language preference towards English could be noted (Ölmez, 1984). The method of data collection for this child was more guided because at the time of the study he was very fluent in Turkish, perhaps primarily due to the longer period of exposure. Thus, in order to observe the instances causing a shift in the language and to determine in which language he was more fluent, a special technique was utilized in collecting data. Four different types of conversations with two variations were recorded between the subject and adults known to the subject (see Table 1).

Table 1. Information on data collection for Case II

Linguistic background of the speaker (type)	Language of conversation	Conversation sessions	Language of the book (variations)
Monolingual (English)	English	One	English
Monolingual (English)	English	One	Turkish
Bilingual (English)	English	Two	English
Bilingual (English)	English	Two	Turkish
Monolingual (Turkish)	Turkish	Three	English
Monolingual (Turkish)	Turkish	Three	Turkish
Bilingual (Turkish)	Turkish	Four	English
Bilingual (Turkish)	Turkish	Four	Turkish

The types of adult speakers varied depending on the adult being monolingual in English or Turkish, or bilingual but dominant in one of the languages. Variations also related to the book utilized to find topics for conversation with the subject. In one context, an English storybook consisting of pictures was made use of; in another context, a Turkish textbook consisting of lots of pictures with related exercises was utilized. The aim of using different books written in different languages, and asking different people of different language backgrounds, was to see how much the subject would be influenced and effected by the linguistic and social environment.

The first conversation was carried out in English between the monolingual English speaker and the subject, using the English book first and then the Turkish one. The second conversation was conducted in a similar fashion but with a bilingual speaker dominant in English. In the third conversation, a monolingual Turkish speaker conversed with the subject using both books. In the forth one, a bilingual dominant in Turkish conversed with the subject in Turkish using the same books.

Data analysis

Case I

Although the language used at home was English, the instruction provided in the kindergarten was Turkish. Therefore, the child started to become bilingual to the extent that the language of the school and community differed from the language of the home (Genesee, 1987). During the time of his stay in Turkey, the subject was observed to have gone through certain stages towards becoming bilingual (Bada, 1991).

Since he started without any knowledge of Turkish, the subject had to go through a silent period trying to familiarize himself with the language and to adjust himself to the social environment.

Then he started to develop an awareness of the target language. One day he came home and told his mother in English that his teachers had asked the pupils to tidy the room in school. Obviously, he had not understood what the teacher had asked them to do. However, seeing the other children tidying the room after the teacher's statement, he joined them in the activity. This way, he guessed the content of the teacher's statement. He mentioned this to his mother as the most important news of the day, because it was the first time that anything said by the teacher had made sense to him.

As a next step, he started to perform required actions in response to given instructions such as 'Take off your shoes', 'Put them under your bed'. Gradually, in order to cope with the other children and to defend himself during play, he learnt certain key words that his friends used to get their basic needs fulfilled. In learning vocabulary, he went through several stages. First he refused to pronounce an introduced vocabulary item and repeated the English version. Eventually he used both versions (Example 1). When he reached a point where he felt comfortable in pronouncing the word, he used the Turkish version only.

1.   Teacher   – Bak bu kuş.
                               (Look this [is a] bird.)
       Subject   – No it's a birdy.
       Teacher   – Kuş. Çocuklar bu ne?
                               (Bird. What's this, kids?)
       Other children   Kuş. (Bird.)
       Teacher   – Bu neymiş?
                               (What do they say this is?)
       Subject   – It's kuş-birdy.

After having learned to respond to imperatives by performing the required actions, he started to comprehend the questions as well, but attempted to respond to them in English (Example 2).

2.   Teacher   – Arabayı ver.
                               (Give me the car.)
       Subject   – It's right there.

At the end of the third month, he started to imitate his peers and to utter the sentences he heard with very slight variation in pronunciation. For instance, he articulated the dental fricative voiceless rather than the voiced counterpart (Example 3).

3.   Children   – Biz yaptık, biz yaptık.
                    (We made [it], we made [it].)
     Subject   – *Bis* yaptık, *bis* yaptık.

In the first week of the fourth month, we observed the occurrence of imperatives such as 'ver' (give), 'at' (throw), 'gel' (come), and 'git' (go) in the speech samples of our subject. These imperatives were composed of two or three sounds that would not cause any problems of articulation, and at the same time help him to participate in activities in which other children were involved. In the second week of the fourth month, he started to use two-and three-word utterances (Example 4).

4.   – Bak burun. (Look, [it's a] nose.)

Case II

The data collected from the four conversations with the second subject were analysed to look into deliberate vs. non-deliberate code-switching and interference phenomena.

The term 'deliberate code-switching' is used to refer to instances where the subject is aware of the code to be used, and deliberately shifts to that language in order to be able to carry on the conversation: for instance, a shift of the language to English while talking to a monolingual speaker of English and to Turkish when talking to a monolingual speaker of Turkish. Non-deliberate code-switching takes place when the speaker unconsciously shifts to the other language. Four possible reasons were considered for this type of shift: the speaker being associated with a particular language, the topic or domain being associated with a particular language, the lack of knowledge of vocabulary of the speaker in one language, and the physical or psychological state of the speaker.

Interference in Selinker's (1969) term is the application of linguistic elements of one language while conversing in another language. Regarding the speech of our subject in Case II, interference phenomena were observed in three main linguistic domains: syntax, lexicon, and semantics. Accordingly, they are categorized as occurrences of syntactic (Example 5), lexical (Example 6), and semantic transfer (Example 7).

5.   – Where are my *shoe?*
                    – It's like *a* scissors.

In English some nouns are used in the plural form only as in 'scissors'. However, these nouns do not necessarily take a plural marker in Turkish.

6.   – I like *dondurma.*
7.   – It's a *water star.* (To mean 'star fish')

The subject knows the Turkish word 'deniz yıldızı' (star fish), and when he is forced to refer to the same concept in English, he tries to translate it. Not knowing what 'deniz' (sea) means in English, he uses 'water' instead. The translated phrase, however, does not refer to any concept in English nor does it help the listener to think of the 'star fish', which the subject had in mind.

Conversation One

In Conversation One, one may assume that the Turkish book triggered the use of Turkish. With a monolingual speaker of English, the child responded 100 percent of the time in English when talking about a storybook written in English. When the topics to be discussed were derived from a Turkish book comprising mainly pictures, the subject shifted 16 percent of the time to Turkish (Table 2).

Table 2. English and Turkish responses in Conversation One.

Responses	English Book		Turkish Book	
	Token	Percentage	Token	Percentage
English	27	100%	42	84%
Turkish	0	0%	8	16%
TOTAL	27	100%	50	100%

One may expect that the percentage would have gone higher if the book had been written in Turkish, and especially if it had been read to him several times. Although the book had no Turkish text but only pictures, and the speaker did not know any Turkish, it triggered Turkish because the subject had been discussing the content of the book in Turkish at school.

As can be seen from the results, the subject used English as his code when conversing with a monolingual speaker of English. While discussing the pictures in the Turkish book, several code-switches of non-deliberate nature could be noted, due to the fact that the subject had not been introduced to the English words corresponding to these vocabulary items. In some cases, the mother kept utilizing Turkish words such as 'dondurma' (ice-cream) and 'kapıcı' (apartment manager) while talking to the subject in English. Thus, the subject might have considered these terms to be cognates. The numbers of these instances of non-deliberate code-switching are indicated according to the type of transfer involved and the book utilized (Table 3).

Table 3. Categories of non-deliberate code-switching in Conversation One (Ölmez, 1984: 51).

	Semantic	Syntactic	Lexical	Total
English book	2	0	0	2
Turkish book	1	1	6	8
TOTAL	3	1	6	10

Conversation Two

Although there was only one instance of code-switching observed in the second conversation while utilizing the English book, thirteen instances could be noted during the utilization of the Turkish book (Table 4); they were all lexical in nature (Table 5). Out of this number, seven were directly associated with the type of the book used. Since the topics in the Turkish text were discussed in Turkish at the day-care centre, the subject had difficulty in talking about these items in English. Even when the conversation was not limited to the topics in the Turkish book but extended to other subjects related to his family life, we observed the subject's reluctance to use English because he was aware of the fact that the speaker also knew Turkish (Example 8).

8.   – Why didn't you go to school yesterday?
            – Çünkü ablam korktu.

Table 4. English and Turkish responses in Conversation Two.

Responses	English book		Turkish book	
	Token	Percentage	Token	Percentage
English	19	98%	17	56.6%
Turkish	1	2%	13	43.3%
TOTAL	20	100%	30	100%

Three main reasons could be identified for instances of non-deliberate code-switching (Ölmez, 1984: 59): association of language with topic or domain, psychological state of the speaker, and lack of vocabulary.

Table 5. Categories of non-deliberate code-switching in Conversation Two.

	Semantic	Syntactic	Lexical	Total
English book	0	0	1	1
Turkish book	0	0	13	13
TOTAL	0	0	14	14

Conversation Three

No instances of code-switching could be noted. The subject carried out the conversation in Turkish with a monolingual speaker using both books without any difficulty at all.

Conversation Four

Although no instances of code switching could be noted during the utilization of the Turkish book, there were instances of code switching comprising 10 percent of the whole conversation while talking about the topics in the English book (Table 6).

Table 6. English and Turkish responses in Conversation Four.

Responses	English book		Turkish book	
	Token	Percentage	Token	Percentage
English	15	10%	0	0%
Turkish	135	90%	70	100%
TOTAL	150	100%	70	100%

Given the number of tokens, a great deal of communication took place during the fourth conversation. The length of the conversation being long reveals that the subject was more comfortable while talking in Turkish.

Overall analysis of the four conversations

When we analyse the results obtained from the four conversations, we can draw the following conclusions. First of all, a subject's choice of language varies according to the language of the interlocutor. The amount of code-switching is greater when a bilingual interlocutor is involved. The subject is aware of the interlocutor's knowledge of more than one language and this gives him the freedom of shifting to the other language whenever he is confronted with a problem. While talking to bilinguals, the subject tends to shift to Turkish rather than to English. Shifting to Turkish is readily made whenever the linguistic background of the interlocutor or the language the topics yield encourages discussion in Turkish. The language in which the topic was discussed, rather than the language of the interlocutor, seems to trigger the shift.

With respect to the acquisition of lexical items, the following observations could be made. The use of the same vocabulary item in both languages seems to give the child the impression that the same word exists in both languages. Lack of vocabulary in one language seems to force the child to retrieve words from the other language.

Teacher and learner strategies

According to Krashen's Input Hypothesis (1985), we can understand what is said to us if we are exposed to an input that is a little beyond our present level of competence, and we can easily acquire the language if this treatment continues. Genesee (1987: 181) suggests five strategies adopted by the teacher and three by the learner in order to make language input comprehensive. The findings of this study will be discussed in relation to these proposed strategies.

Teacher strategies

Modification of talk is the most observed strategy. A teacher tries to use simplified, redundant and slower speech in order to facilitate comprehension by a second language learner. The same technique is applied for first-language learners (Snow and Ferguson, 1978; Ekmekçi, 1979). Most of those who are in contact with foreigners are aware of the fact that native speakers, while talking to non-native speakers in non-school settings, apply the same strategies (Long, 1980).

In the speech of the teacher directed to our subject in Case I, the number of words per utterance does not exceed four. The teacher's statements are generally in the form of a command requiring a change in the behaviour of the subject, or a question inquiring about basic needs, such as food and toilet (Examples 9-10).

9. – Hadi, kahvaltıya.
   (Come on, to breakfast)
10. – Karnın aç mı?
    (Are you hungry?)

Direct questioning of previously presented material is another strategy encountered at schools. Teachers or native speakers involved in communication with a non-native speaker try to reformulate misunderstood messages or try to convey the same message by other means when the non-native speaker does not seem to comprehend the message.

In Case 1, when a nurse sees the subject's finger all bandaged, she asks a general question about the child's health. When she does not get an answer, she formulates her question in a more specific way (Example 11).

11. Nurse – Ne oldu oğlum sana?
(What happened to you, son?)
    Child – [No answer]
    Nurse – Ne oldu eline?
(What happened to your finger?)
    Child – Anne kapı. [He points at the door]
(Mummy, door.)

Defining or clarifying new or unfamiliar concepts that may cause confusion is another strategy adopted by teachers. In Case 2, the adult asks the subject what the picture is about. When the subject says that he does not know, the adult gives assurance that he does, and tries to clarify that it is a little animal, and asks him to name it (Example 12).

12. Adult – What is this?
    Child – I don't know.
    Adult – You do. It is a little animal. What do we call it?
    Child – Frog.

In Genesee's words, 'meaning can also be made comprehensible through the provision of contextual support, that is, the use of nonverbal frames of reference, such as physical objects or realia, or experiences familiar to the students' (1987: 181).
    In Case 2, the adult, realizing the reluctance of the subject in answering her questions, tries to draw the subject's attention by explaining the content of the pictures, and asks for a response that has already been cited (Example 13).

13. Adult – What is this?
    Child – [No answer]
    Adult – Here are the elves and the shoemaker.
    – Who is this? [Pointing at the picture of the shoemaker]
    Child – The shoemaker.

Teachers are also sensitive to nonverbal feedback they get from their learners, because some nonverbal behaviour may lead to different denotations depending on the culture of the learner. Other qualifications or strategies of the adult affect the learner in adjusting himself to the environment and to start working on his second language. For instance, in Case 1, one of the boys at the day-care centre who usually led the other children around him has decided to include our subject into the group. When one of the children was opposed to this, he said, 'N (initial of the American boy) is just a baby, he doesn't know how to speak. My little brother can't speak properly either'. From that day on, our subject has been included into the group, and from then on, there has been a great improvement in the speech of our subject because he had felt the security of being a part of the group. In this instance, the leader of the group, having a small brother at home, has shown sensitivity to the subject's extraordinary situation.

One more strategy is observed as adopted by the Turkish teacher at the daycare centre while communicating with the American boy and teaching him certain vocabulary items. The teacher introduced a vocabulary item in relation to a picture or an item in the room, but the subject refused to 'admit' it. Then she asked the other children in the day-care centre to tell her the name of the object and turned back to our subject to ask the very same question. Finally, she managed elicit the requested answer.

Another strategy adopted by most mothers involved in mixed marriages is to pretend not to understand (Example 14) or to misunderstand (Example 15) the child's utterances in the other language (Ölmez, 1984: 31).

14. Child — Su istiyorum.
    (I want [some] water.)
    Mother — What?
    Child — Bana su ver.
    (Give me [some] water.
    Mother — I don't understand.
    Child — I want a drink of water.

15. Child — Bak! Yüzümü yıkadım.
    ['Yüz' means 'face' or 'a hundred']
    (Look! I washed my face.)
    Mother — What was that?
    Child — [impatient] Yüzümü yıkadım.
    Mother — You washed a hundred what?
    Child — [laughing] No! I did wash my face mummy!

Learner strategies

Learners may question the teacher demanding clarification, simplification or repetition. No instance of this strategy could be observed in our two cases. In Case 1, the subject did not know enough to ask for explanation. Being the only American child among all the other Turkish children, he might not have the courage to demand clarification. In Case 2, the recorded speech samples were not spontaneous; therefore, they did not yield much information regarding this type of a strategy.

Moreover, learners try to indicate the fact that they have not understood the teacher by nonverbal gestures. In Case 1, whenever the subject did not understand the teacher's question or command, he would usually put his hand up and look at her with a puzzled face. Learners also shift to their own native language especially if they know that the teacher or the adult they speak to is bilingual. This is one of the most common strategies encountered in both cases.

When the subjects realized that they lacked native-like proficiency, they were afraid of being marked as non-native speakers. Thus, they refused to speak or get involved in any conversation in the second language. A feeling of this kind, as Ryan (1983) states, has negative social connotations. As in Case 1, children in the day-care centre tried to approach the American boy, but, at initial stages, he would always refuse to play with them, and preferred to play by himself.

The subjects are successful in utilizing some key words that help them in controlling the behaviour of others. For instance, in Case 1, the American boy was very successful in acquiring certain words such as 'anne' (mummy) and 'yapma' (don't) that proved to be beneficial in defending him against other children's mischievous behaviour. Thus whenever he was in trouble, he used to get away from it with this limited number of words. Other words, such as 'çiş' (pipi) and 'su' (water) were useful to get his essential needs fulfilled.

While talking with a monolingual speaker, and not being able to find the name of the object they would like to express their need or opinion about, the subjects imitate an aspect of it, point at it, or demonstrate its function (Examples 16-18). This is also true when they are asked to name the location of an object. They either point at the object only or, along with the nonverbal behaviour, they utter demonstrative adverbials (Example 19).

16. Child   – Dondurma.
                    (ice-cream)
    Adult   – What do you do with it?
    Child   – [imitates licking]

17. Child   – Makas gibi.
                    (Like scissors.)
    Adult   – Uh?
    Child   – It's like this.
    Adult   – It's like a fork?
    Child   – No, it's like a ...[demonstrates using scissors]

18. Adult   – Have you seen a penguin?
    Child   – Yes, kanatları yokmuş.
                    ([It] hasn't got wings.)
                    It can't ...[swings his arms up and down.]
    Adult   – Fly?
    Child   – Yes. It can't fly.

19. Adult   – Uçak nerede?
                    (Where is the plane?)
    Child   – [Points at it in the book] işte.
                    (Here.)

When they are forced to use a suffix in the second language that they have not acquired yet, they apply the corresponding morpheme in their first language. Our subject in Case I applied English suffixes on the acquired Turkish words when he did not know how to express them in Turkish (Example 20).

20.   – kuş+es
                      (bird+s)

Perspective

Most of the strategies uncovered, have also been observed in children acquiring Turkish in a monolingual setting (Ekmekçi, 1979). Since our subjects have been exposed to Turkish at very early ages, the adaptation of similar strategies seems to be natural. However, it is difficult to make generalizations at this point due to the small number of subjects and observations. Further research on this matter should shed light on the issue.

References

Bada, T., 1991. *Second language acquisition: A case study of American and Turkish children*. Unpublished M.A. Thesis. Çukurova University, Adana, Turkey.

Bloomfield, L., 1933. *Language*. New York: Holt.

Burling, R., 1959. Language development of a Garo and English speaking child. *World*, 15, 45-68.

Celce-Murcia, M., 1978. Simultaneous acquisition of English and French in a two-year old. In: E. Hatch (ed.), *Second language acquisition: A book of readings*. Rowley, Mass.: Newbury House.

Cummins, J., 1981. The role of primary language development in promoting educational success for language minority students. In: *Schooling and language minority students: a theoretical framework*, 1-50. Los Angeles: Evaluation, Dissemination, and Assessment Centre.

Diebold, A., 1968. The consequences of early bilingualism in cognitive development and personality formation. In: E. Norbeck, et al. (eds), *The study of personality*. New York: Holt, Rinehart and Winston.

Ekmekçi, Ö., 1979. *Acquisition of Turkish: A longitudinal study on the early language development of a Turkish child*. Unpublished Ph.D. Thesis. The University of Texas at Austin, Austin, Texas.

Genesee, F., 1987. *Learning through two languages*. New York: Newbury House.

Hatch, E., (ed.), 1978. *Second language acquisition: A book of readings*. Rowley, Mass.: Newbury House.

Krashen, S., 1985. *The input hypothesis*. London: Longman.

Leopold, W., 1954. *Speech development of a bilingual child: A linguist's record*

(1939-1949). 4 vols. Evanston, Illinois: Northwestern University Press.

Long, M., 1980. Linguistic and conversational adjustments to non-native speakers. *Studies in Second Language Acquisition, 2*, 177-193.

McLaughlin, B., 1984. *Second-language acquisition in childhood.* Volume 1: Pre-school children. Hillsdale, N. J.: Lawrence Erlbaum Associates.

Ölmez, C., 1984. *Code-switching in a pre-school bilingual child.* Unpublished M.A. Thesis. The Middle East Technical University, Ankara, Turkey.

Ryan, E., 1983. Social psychological mechanisms underlying native speaker evaluations of non-native speech. *Studies in Second Language Acquisition, 5*, 148-161.

Saunders, G., 1983. *Bilingual children: Guidance for the family.* Cleveland, England: Multilingual Matters.

Selinker, L., 1969. Language transfer. *General Linguistics, 9*, 67-92.

Snow, C. & C. Ferguson, 1978. *Talking to children: Language input and acquisition.* Cambridge, England: Cambridge University Press.

Abdelâli Bentahila and Eirlys Davies

Two languages, three varieties:
codeswitching patterns of bilingual children

In discussions of childhood bilingualism, it seems important to recognise that a bilingual child may in fact be the outcome of a number of rather different situations; bilingualism may be achieved for different reasons and in different ways. The children we describe as bilingual may differ with regard to the timing of their acquisition of each language (simultaneous or consecutive), the extent to which they master them (whether they become balanced or dominant bilinguals), the sources from which they encounter each language (whether, for instance, they encounter both languages in the home, one in the home and one outside, or some other configuration) and the nature of their exposure to each (whether each person uses only one language to them, or different languages on different occasions, or mixes the two through frequent code-switching) and in other ways as well. However, not all these various combinations of factors are equally represented in the literature on early bilingualism. In fact, among the most well-known and often quoted studies certain configurations seem to be particularly common.

In the first place, the majority of published studies seem to have dealt with cases of what might be termed 'exceptional' bilingualism, where a child acquires two or more languages while living in a community which is nevertheless basically monolingual. The exceptional situation of the child is usually due to the fact that one or both of the parents use a language other than the dominant community language, generally because this is their native language, though sometimes a parent may deliberately choose to adopt a non-native language which is not the community language either (as in the case of Saunders, 1982). Moreover, a large number of the publications seem to be based on linguists' studies of their own children. As Romaine (1989: 169) points out, such children will tend to exhibit what she calls 'elitist or additive bilingualism', and we may add to this the possibility that such linguistically sophisticated parents may also take particular care over the amount and type of exposure to each language that their child receives, at any rate in the early stages when the child's social interactions are within the parents' control. The bilingualism of such children may thus often be a carefully planned enterprise which is not only monitored but also nurtured by the parents, who may take steps to provide balanced and distinct input in each language.

For instance, among published case-studies the 'one person, one language' principle seems to be adhered to in the vast majority of cases. Indeed Grosjean (1982:

198) seems to imply that this 'person-language bond' is a universal feature of childhood bilingualism, when he states that 'anyone who interacts for some time with a young bilingual child will notice the strong bond that exists between a person and a language. In the eyes of the child a person is tagged with a particular language'. However, this is certainly not true of the large numbers of bilingual children who live in communities where people use both languages interchangeably.

Moreover, a relatively large number of studies seem to claim that the child's exposure to each language was separate, in the sense that they were not exposed to much discourse involving code-switching, and in some cases at least it would seem that special efforts were made to maintain this clear separation. For instance, both Ronjat (1913) and Leopold (1970) claim that if their children asked them for vocabulary items in the language they did not habitually use with them, they refused to provide then. Even when it is admitted that code-switching is to be heard in the child's home environment, linguist parents may seek to impose special restrictions on how this is done; Bergman (1976: 92), for instance, reporting on her bilingual daughter, states that 'at our house we follow a rule which permits switching only at sentence boundaries'. Again, the imposition of such rigid separations or specific limitations on mixing may not be at all representative of the environment of the majority of bilingual children. It therefore seems important to recognise that the literature on early bilingualism does not necessarily reflect the diversity of ways in which children become bilingual.

Arabic-French bilingualism in Morocco

In this paper we should like to focus our attention on language acquisition in a bilingual setting which is in a number of ways different from those which seem to have attracted most attention so far. The children we shall look at are Moroccan, as are both their parents, and they have spent all their life so far in Morocco. Thus their bilingualism is not traceable to the fact that their parents are of different nationalities, or to the fact that travel or migration has exposed them to two different speech communities. Their parents, grandparents and indeed the vast majority of people in their entourage share the same native language, Moroccan Arabic. Nevertheless, at the age of four or five, these children can be considered relatively fluent speakers not only of Arabic but also of French, despite the fact that they have had relatively little contact with native speakers of French. To understand how this situation comes about, a little information about the Moroccan language situation is required.

While Arabic is the native language of the majority of Moroccans, as well as being the official language of Morocco, the country was assigned the status of a French protectorate during the period from 1912 to 1956. During this time, French became the language of administration and education, and even after independence the French language continued to assume an important role in these and other domains. Accordingly, the majority of Moroccans receiving more than a minimal education, either during the protectorate or in the decade or two that followed it, developed a relatively high proficiency in French as well as Arabic. There is thus in Morocco today a large group of educated people, now in their thirties, forties and fifties, who are perfectly at ease in French as well as Arabic, and who continue to use both in their everyday interactions. More recently, the government's policy of progressive Arabisation of the education system and administrations has meant that those in younger age-groups, such as those now in their teens or early twenties, are often less at ease in French and use it less than the older group. Thus while Arabic-French bilingualism is quite widespread in Morocco today, the patterns of language use and language dominance differ from one section of the community to another.

We have elsewhere (Bentahila and Davies, 1991 and forthcoming) attempted to compare the code-switching patterns of these older and younger adult bilinguals. In this paper we are concerned with a third group, the offspring of these older balanced bilinguals. The parent and child generations can be sharply contrasted with regard to the way in which they became bilingual. The parents' generation typically came from homes where French was rarely if ever heard, their own parents being monolingual Arabic speakers; they learned French only at the age of six or seven when they went to school and were suddenly immersed in a French-speaking environment. Their bilingualism was thus clearly successive, and for them the languages were at least initially associated with the separate domains of home and school. However, by adulthood many of this generation acquired the habit of using both languages in the same domains, such as work, entertainment and everyday transactions in a variety of context. More particularly, they developed what might be considered a separate, mixed variety involving frequent code-switching between Arabic and French, and for many of this age-group this is the variety they use most for informal interaction with others of similar background.

When the members of this group became parents, then, a number of choices were available to them with regard to the language(s) they could use with their children and expose them to. Some of them, while maintaining the use of both French and Arabic within the circle of their contemporaries, have tended to retain Arabic as the traditional home language. Just as their own parents addressed them only in Arabic, they have tended to adopt Arabic as the language they use to their own children. In these cases, although the children will certainly hear a certain amount of French used around them, they will not tend to have it systematically addressed to them, or be expected to use it themselves, until they encounter it within the education system. Other parents tend to use both languages in the home, and address their children in the same way as they address their spouse, using sometimes Arabic, sometimes French, and very often a mixture involving much code-switching. They may not make any particular effort to expose the child to each language in a balanced way, or to keep the two languages separate. However, there are some parents who do take a particular interest in their children's language development and these may attempt to control it by, for instance, increasing the amount of French they use to the children as they grow older, setting aside periods for using one language or the other, and attempting to keep the two languages separate as they speak to the children.

The other important way in which these parents influence their children's language development is through the kind of education they choose to offer them. In the present curriculum of the state education system, French is not introduced as a subject until the third year of primary school, i.e., around the age of 8 or 9, and it is no longer used as a medium of instruction for any other subject, but merely taught as a foreign language. Clearly this programme is not conducive to the development of balanced bilinguals, and children whose main exposure to French is through public education will not be likely to reach anything like fluency for quite a number of years. Thus, while the older generation, born of monolingual parents, nevertheless became balanced bilinguals as a direct result of the French-medium education they received, we can now see children of these balanced bilinguals who, if their parents do not take other measures to develop their proficiency in French, may end up being less than fluent in this language. However, many parents, perhaps most of those who can afford it, do not rely solely on the state system for their children's education. In particular, large numbers send their children to private nursery schools or kindergartens between the ages of three and six. Most of these provide systematic exposure to French as well as Arabic, often with the morning being devoted to one language and the afternoon to the other. Following this nursery education, the parents may choose to place their child in a state school or have them continue in a private institution, in which case, again, they may use French far more than they would have done in the public system. The extreme case is that of parents who send their children to the French-run schools of the *Mission Universitaire et Culturelle Française,* where the programmes are those used in France; Arabic is taught as a subject but the medium for all other subjects is French.

Accordingly, in Morocco today the older bilingual generation is producing children with very different degrees of bilingualism. At one extreme we find children who hear mainly or almost exclusively Arabic at home, and who receive a state education; these may effectively remain monolingual up to the age of 9 or 10, and even after this may achieve only a limited proficiency in French. At the other extreme are children whose parents may use French more than Arabic at home and who are given a French-dominant private education; some of these may grow up more at ease in French than in Arabic, at least in certain domains. Between these two extremes are to be found a wide variety of individual cases, which leads us to reiterate our initial observation that bilingual children spring from diverse circumstances and cannot always be conveniently lumped together for the purpose of discussion.

Informant characteristics

The present paper draws on a study we have made of the language use of four Moroccan children ranging in age from 4 years 5 months to 5 years, though we shall here look closely at the langauge of only two of these children. Our observations are based on audio-recordings of interactions between each child and an adult who was a friend of the family or an aunt; the conversations took place in the children's homes, and sometimes the mother or older siblings were also present and took some part in the conversation. In the recorded conversations the investigators varied their own choice of language, addressing the child sometimes in French, sometimes in Arabic, and sometimes themselves code-switching within an utterance. This variation does not appear artificial to a Moroccan listener, but seems typical of the language patterns used by bilinguals in informal discourse. The data are rather limited, consisting of an average of 1 1/2 hours interaction per child, recorded over a couple of weeks; however, we hope that they may serve to give a general impression of some of the features of these children's discourse.

Details of the four children are as follows (though their names have been changed for the sake of anonymity);

- *Oussama* (4;5), with a one older sister, whose parents both work in a bank;
- *Amine* (4;6), with a one older sister, whose parents are both teachers;
- *Miriam* (4;9), an only child, whose father is a lecturer and whose mother teaches French;
- *Sara* (5;0), an only child, whose father is a doctor and whose mother teaches French.

Miriam attends one of the French Mission schools, while the other three attend private bilingual schools.

On the face of it, these are the type of children one might expect to achieve a relatively high degree of bilingualism. Their parents are all well-educated and hold jobs where they are bound to use a lot of French; in all four cases French is used in the home as well as Arabic. Moreover, all four children are exposed to French, and to some attempt at formal teaching of French, in their schools.

In fact, however, even though the four children might seem to have relatively similar backgrounds, the data suggest that there are very considerable differences between them with regard to their ability to use French.

At one extreme we have Sara, who at 5,0 displays a good comprehension of spoken French, but seems reluctant to use it and hesitant when she does sol In the vast majority of cases where the interviewer asks her a question in French, she replies appropriately, but in Arabic, as in the following exchanges;

1. Interviewer: *Qu'est-ce que tu fais le dimanche?* 'What do you do on Sundays?'
   Sara: tanlℂ?ab 'I play'

2. Interviewer: *Et après, qu'est-ce que tu fais?* 'And after that what do you do?
   Sara: tijdek l?aras w mama tat?i 'The bell rings, and Mummy comes'

3. Interviewer: *Ton oncle Mostapha, combien d'enfant il a?* 'How many chil-

Sara: tlata 'Three'

When she does reply in French, her replies are brief, often simply *oui* or *non*, and when she produces more complex structures, these are often marked by hesitations. When invited to tell a story she naturally tells one in Arabic, and at no time in the recordings does she actually initiate discourse in French. When she does speak French, it seems to be in order to please the interlocutor. In fact, then, though Sara's ability to understand French is clearly demonstrated by her replies, she does not seem to be very comfortable in speaking it.

Oussama, in contrast, manages to sustain a conversation almost exclusively in French when the interlocutor keeps to this language. His responses to questions are often limited and sometimes hesitant, but he is clearly willing and able to keep going in French alone when the interlocutor asks him to do so. When he apparently finds it difficult to express himself in French, he tends to fall back on one of a few recurrent expressions, such as *ca y est* or *je ne sais pas*. Occasionally he responds to a French utterance in Arabic, or switches within an utterance; when he does this it usually seems to be because he cannot find the word he wants in French, as in the following examples:

4.   Oussama (listing the types of fish in the market):
           Il y a le rouget, il y a ftun, *il y a sardines, sole... et... c'est tout.* 'There is red mullet, there are anchovies, *there are sardines, sole...and... that's all'*

5.   Interviewer: *Et le mouton, tu le connais?* 'And the sheep, do you know what it is?'
       Oussama: *Oui, il est blanc,* ɛandu lqrun 'Yes, it's white, it has horns'

Amine and Miriam contrast with the other two children with regard to the fluency and spontaneity with which they use French. They seem to be quite happy to chat in either language about everyday topics, and clearly have the necessary skills to be able to do this, although their Arabic seems rather more fluent and accurate than their French. There is the occasional mistake of vocabulary in both languages (for instance, Amine wrongly uses the Arabic word /ferx/ instead of /faxer/ and on another occasion uses the French word *moutarde* when he means *tarte!*), but deviations from adult usage are certainly much more frequent in their French than in their Arabic. Some of these deviations might be interpreted as the result of applying Arabic rules to French structures. For instance, Miriam places all French attributive adjectives after their nouns, even ones like *petit* and *grand* which should precede the noun, and she also frequently produces sentences with a pronominal subject and a dislocated NP following the verb, instead of using the NP as a preverbal subject; thus she produces forms like *il joue Toutou* and *il vient papa*, which are reminiscent of the Arabic Verb-subject ordering, rather than *Toutou joue* and *papa vient..*

However, quite a number of other deviations from adult norms, such as problems with verb forms (wrong person for auxiliary, or wrongly formed past participle), gender (wrong choice of article, pronoun or agreement of adjective) or choice of prepositions could well be found in the speech of monolingual French-speaking children as well. Both children seem quite aware of the distinction between the two languages, and are able to respond in a particular language when asked to.

However, they also spontaneously code-switch quite frequently. In the course of one and a half hours of conversation Amine produced 61 code-switches (where these are defined as a change of language either within an utterance or between one utterance and the next), while an hour of recorded conversation yielded a total of 71 switches by Miriam. In the rest of this paper we should like to concentrate on the code-switching patterns used by these two children.

Code-switching patterns of kernel informants

In the first place we may draw a major distinction between utterance-internal switches and switches across turns. The latter, which can be seen as instances of divergence, where the child fails to respond in the language of the preceding section of the communication, are relatively infrequent; Miriam produced 9 such inter-turn switches while Amine produce 18. In the majority of these, the child addressed in French chooses to respond in Arabic.

A second distinction to which many code-switching studies have paid particular attention is that between single-word switches and those extending over more than one word. If we classify the utterance-internal switches into these two types, we find a very clear preponderance of the longer type; Miriam uses only 4 single word switches, Amine 13. In addition we may note the occurrence of seven word-internal switches in Miriam's speech, though Amine does not use this pattern at all. The proportions of these various categories of switch in each child's discourse are summarised in Table 1.

Table 1. Major categories of switch in two children's discourse.

	Miriam		Amine		Total	
Inter-turn switches	9	(12.6%)	18	(29.5%)	27	(20.4%)
Intra-turn switches	62	(87.3%)	43	(70.5%)	105	(79.5%)
of which:						
single-word	4	(5.6%)	13	(21.3%)	17	(12.8%)
multi-word	51	(71.8%)	30	(49.1%)	81	(61.3%)
word-internal	7	(9.8%)	0		7	(5.3%)
Totals	71		61		132	

The intra-turn switches can also be classified in structural terms, with regard to the boundary at which the switch occurs. Table 2 shows the distribution of the various types in the speech of each child.

Table 2. Intra-turn switches in two children's discourse.

	Miriam	Amine	Total
1) For a whole clause	18 (29%)	6 (13.9%)	24 (22.8%)
2) For a whole NP	21 (33.8%)	26 (60.4%)	47 (44.7%)
including: subjects NPs	4	2	6
objects NPs	7	8	15
NPs within PPs	8	9	17
coordinated NPs	0	2	2
independent NPs	2	5	7
3) Within NP	15 (24.1%)	9 (20.9%)	24 (22.8%)
including: between Det and Det	7	2	9
between Det and N	1	6	7
between N and Adj	4	0	4
between N and poss	3	1	4
4) For verb alone	0	1 (2.3%)	1 (0.9%)
5) Within verb (word-internal)	7	0	7 (6.6%)
6) For adverb	1	1 (2.3%)	2 (1.9%)
Totals	62	43	105

It should be noted that the first category listed in Table 2, switches for a whole clause, subsumes both switches between two independent or coordinated clauses and those between a main clause and a subordinate clause, i.e., some switches which other researchers might label intersentential and others which might be termed intrasentential. We do not find this distinction a convincing one to draw in spoken discourse where it is often not at all clear whether a particular string should be segmented into one multiclause unit or two separate units, and where the traditional concept of a sentence does not prove particularly useful as a unit of analysis.

Finally, Table 3 shows the categories represented among the small number of single word intra-turn switches.

Table 3. Single-word intra-turn switches used by two children.

	Miriam	Amine	Total
Nouns	1	11	12
Verbs	1	1	2
Adjectives	1	0	1
Adverbs	1	1	2
Totals	4	13	17

Two languages, three varieties

There are some noticeable differences between the two children with regard to the types of switch they appear to prefer.

The first point which seems to us noteworthy is the relative paucity of single-word switches in both children's discourse, which might seem surprising given that single-word switches have repeatedly been found to be predominant in young children's discourse. To mention only a couple of studies where the informants seem comparable to our own in age, Linholm and Padilla (1978) found that among their Spanish-English bilingual informants aged between 2;0 and 6;4 the vast majority of switches were for single words, mainly nouns, and Boeschoten and Verhoeven (1987) similarly found single item switches to predominate in the speech of Dutch-turkish bilinguals aged between 4 and 7. Among younger children the tendency to favour single-word switches seems even more pronounced, as is attested by, among others, Redlinger and Park (1980), Arnberg and Arnberg (1985) and De Houwer (1990).

In contrast, our two Moroccan informants show a strong preference to switch for more complex structures. Two patterns clearly predominate in their intra-turn switches; most frequent, by far, are switches for entire NPs or multi-word parts of larger NPs, while in second place come switches for whole clauses, whether dependent or independent. The majority of the NP switches consist of a determiner plus noun, and most of them involve a switch from Arabic for a French NP, as in the examples given below:

6.   Miriam: msaħtla *la a maîtresse* fumha '*the teacher* wiped her face'

7.   Amine: ana tangulek ɛt ini *des cotelettes* 'i tell you give me *some chops*'

8.   Amine: tanlɛab mɛa *les garçons* 'I play with *the boys*'

9.   Miriam: tandir *les bougies* hna 'I put *the candles* here'

10. Miriam: iwa w *les bébés* djal džaža mhit takbar tajxurž 'well, and *the babies* of the hen when they grow big, come out'

Even where the switch is for only part of an NP it often involves the use of a French determiner plus noun in an Arabic context. In particular, we find a pattern where the switch occurs between one determiner in Arabic and a second one in French, the entire structure (Det Det N) conforming to the rules of Arabic but not of French.

11. Miriam: kanu ɛandhum haduk *les pailles* baʃ fajʃerbu lma 'they had those-*the straws* to drink water with'

12. Amine: w f dak *les bonbons* w dakʃi kajna msika 'and in those-*the sweets* there is chewing gum'

13. Miriam: ɛtatni waħed *la feuille* xra 'she gave me one-*the paper* other (i.e., another paper)'

As for the switches involving an entire clause, they include switches between two coordinated clauses, ones for a relative clause and one between two clauses loosely linked by an adverbial:

14. Amine: *J'ai couru avec Soufiane* w sufjan tɛaleq f ʃi fežra aɛlija '*I ran with Soufiane* and Soufiane climbed up into a big tree

15. Amine: *C'est un langage* ħafdu f ddar '*it's some language* I learnt at home'

16. Miriam: tutu bda tajlɛab *alors Toutou il joue avec le chien* 'Toutou started to play, *so Toutou plays with the dog*'

Finally, Miriam's word-internal switches all involve a French verb stem to which Arabic inflections and/or clitics are attached, as in the following:

17. Miriam: w huda *pouss*atni w dert hakda 'and Houda *push*ed me and did like that'

This pattern is in fact one which we have previously found to be very characteristic of adult bilinguals who are dominant in Arabic (see Bentahila and Davies, 1991; forthcoming).

   Indeed, while the code-switching patterns favoured by these two children may contrast with those found in other studies of young bilinguals, their switches are all of types considered normal in the discourse of adult Moroccans, as attested in our previous studies (Bentahila and Davies, 1983; 1991; forthcoming). They do not produce any cases which violate the conventions which seem to govern adult French-Arabic code-switching. Some of the patterns used by these children and their parent do, however, appear to violate some of the syntactic constraints proposed by others, such as Poplack's (1980) Equivalence Constraint (violated, for instance, by examples like (6), (11)-(13), and (15)) and Free Morpheme Constraint (violated by examples like (17)). The tendency to switch between an Arabic and a French determiner, in particular, has attracted quite a lot of discussion (see, for instance, Nait M'Barek and Sankoff, 1988; Nortier, 1989; Muysken, 1991), because it poses a problem for some other theories. the ubiquity of this pattern in Moroccans' code-switching is reflected in the fact that it is exploited even by these four-year olds.

Motivations for code-switching

Having tried briefly to point out some of the interesting structural features of the children's switches, we may now attempt to comment on the functions of or motivations for them. It has often been suggested that switches in young children's discourse are frequently motivated by their finding it difficult or impossible to express certain things in one of their languages – what Meisel (1990:147) has termed the 'relief strategy'. As Meisel notes, adult bilinguals also resort to this strategy. While it is of course difficult to be sure of whether switches in naturally occurring discourse are motivated in this way, there are a number of examples in our corpus which we can be fairly sure are or this type. For instance, Amine's switches to Arabic in the following two examples seem likely to be prompted by ignorance of the equivalent items in French:

18. Interviewer: *Dis-moi, qu'est-ce que tu aimes manger? 'Tell me, what do you like to eat?'*
    Amine: *Des côtelettes 'Chops'.*
    Interviewer: *Et puis? 'And what else?'*
    Amine: zzaɛtar 'Thyme'

19. (in the course of a conversation in French about what Amine saw on a visit to a farm)
    Interviewer: *Et puis, tu as vu autre chose? Des chiens? 'And did you see anything else? Dogs?*
    Amine: bibi '*A turkey*'

Similarly, the recourse to French in the following examples is probably due to ignorance of the Arabic words for spinach and crocodile:

20. Amine (telling a story about Popeye):
    Popeye tajakul *les épinards* 'Popeye eats *spinach*'

21. Miriam (telling a story about Robin Hood):
    Robin des Bois ža ɛandu hadak *le crocodile* w derbu b ssif derbu b hadak ssif '*That crocodile* came up to Robin Hood and he hit it with the sword, he hit it with that sword'

Even where it seems likely that the child has met a term in both languages, one may remain much more available to him or her, if for instance this has been learnt first or used most. For instance, when the children are talking in Arabic about activities at school, they switch to French for what might be considered school jargon, terms like *la maîtresse, les dessins libres, la dictée.*

Among the inter-turn switches, there are quite a number of cases where Amine moves to Arabic to express an explanation for some previous statement in French, and these too might be considered instances of the relief strategy, in the sense that where the child feels under a certain amount of pressure to justify a claim or point of view, he falls back on the language he is most at ease with.

22. Interviewer: *Tu n'aimes pas Miriam? Pourquoi? 'Don't you like Miriam? Why not?*

    Amine: tatdrabni w bɛad merrat tatɣuwat 'She hits me and sometimes she shouts'

23. Amine: *Non, les garçons ne pleurent pas. 'No, boys don't cry'*

    Interviewer: *Pourquoi? Dis-moi. 'Why not? Tell me'*

    Amine: mħit huma maʃi bnat baʃ jbkiw. walakin *les garçons* la kanu sɣiwrin daba jqedru jbkiw 'Because they are not girls, for them to cry. But *boys*, if they are small, then they can cry'

Sometimes a switch is clearly for an aside which appeals for help in continuing in the original language:

24. Miriam (listening what there is in her garden):

    On a la balançoire, la balançoire et la maison de Toutou... de arbres et des fleurs et... comment s'appellent...comment on appelle... kifaʃ kifaʃ kensimmiw nmilat? *'We have the swing, the swing and Toutou's house...trees and flowers and...what are they called...what are they call...what do they call ants?'*

    Interviewer: *Des fourmis 'Ants'*

    Miriam: *Il y a des fourmis dans le jardin 'there are ants in the garden'*

25. Miriam (recounting a story of Robin Hood):

    hadak txebɛa f dak lmariju w tajgul *'Donne-moi, donne-moi, donne-moi'* – smiʃtu hadak lli tajaxud Robin des Bois? 'That one is hiding in that wardrobe and he says, "*Give me, give me, give me*" – what do you call the thing that Robin Hood has?'

    Interviewer: *L'épée 'The sword'*

    Miriam: *L'épée.* w txbaɛ mur hadak ssenduq w gal *'Donne-moi l'épée, donne-moi l'épée* "The sword. And he was hiding behind that box and he said 'Give me the sword, give me the sword' "

There are other instances too where a child seems to exploit a switch to mark an aside as such before continuing the main discussion in the original language:

26. Interviewer (chatting to Miriam about what makes her frightened, while the latter is engaged in drawing a picture):

    Tu as peur des serpents? 'Are you afraid of snakes?'

    Miriam: *Non 'No'*

    Interviewer: *Et la sauterelle? 'And of the tortoise'*

    Miriam: *Non 'No'*

    Interviewer: *Et la sauterelle? 'And of the locust?'*

Miriam:	*Non 'No'*
Interviewer:	*Tu as peur de quoi alors? 'What are you afraid of, then?'*
Miriam:	ana zidni waħed l crayon. *Qui, j'ai peur à le robot, et à le chien...* 'Give me another pencil. *Yes, I am afraid of the robot, and of the dog...'*

Another way in which both children exploit switching to structure their discourse is through the use of a switch for a quotation. In most of the examples in our recordings it seems clear that the switch is to the language in which the quotation was originally uttered.

27. Miriam (telling a story which she has originally heard in French):
bacε da tajgulu *'Le roi Richard qu'il est méchant! Le roi Richard qu'il est méchant!'* iwa w hadak *le roi Richard* bqa tajnqez hakda bqa tajnqez w tajgul *'Moi je suis le roi! Moi je suis le roi'* bqa tajuγwwet w huma tajgulu *'Bravo, bravo, Robin des Bois, bravo!'* ''Then he was saying *'How evil King Richard is How evil King Richard is!'* Well, that *King Richard* kept twisting like that, he kept twisting and saying *'I am the king! I am the king!'* he kept shouting and they were saying *'Bravo, bravo, Robin Hood, bravo!'* ''

28. Amine: tajgul *'à droite et à gauche'* ''he says *'on the right and left'* ''

29. Miriam: *la maîtresse...* xdatlhum haduk *les pailles,* kulhum xdatlhum w galtlhum *'ne porte pas les pailles dans l'école'* ''the teacher... took *those straws* away from them, she took them all and she said to them *'don't bring straws to school'* ''

One other tendency seems to be for the children to switch from French to Arabic when they want to insist on something or make some kind of urgent appeal. This could be compared to the switches for emphasis or in assuming authority which are noted by McClure and Wentz (1975) in the speech of Spanish-English bilingual children. For instance, in (30) Miriam moves to watch television, while in (31) Amine likewise switches to Arabic to insist that he has had enough of the discussion.

30. Interviewer: *Mais regarde! 'But look!'*
      Miriam: xellini ntferž 'Let me watch!'

31. Interviewer: *Tu n'aimes pas jouer avec elle? 'Don't you like playing with her?'*
      Amine: *J'aime,* barak εalija *'I like it.* I've had enough!'

Thus we see that as well as using switching as a relief strategy when they find it easier to express something in one language than in the other, the children are already, before the age of five, exploiting some of the rhetorical functions of switching in structuring their discourse. There remain, however, numerous switches which do not seem to be motivated in either of these ways. In particular, this seems true of most of the intra-turn switches, especially those for NPs or parts of NPs. Here we find the children switching to French even for items for which the Arabic equivalent is well-known to them, as in utterance like the following:

32. Amine: klina lḥelwa *et de la limonade* 'we ate cake *and lemonade*'

33. Amine: daba *l'arabe* 'now a Arabic'

34. Amine: mima tatfrili wahed lksar *chocolat* 'Grandma buys me a castle made of *chocolate*'

There are many such examples in the following extract from Miriam, who could just as well have used the Arabic words for garden, house and doll instead of switching to French; indeed, sometimes we find the corresponding Arabic term being used in the same stretch of speech, as here where Miriam uses both *sa maison* and later, /ddaru/.

35. Miriam: ndiruha f had *la balançoire* w rfre *la maison de Toutou* w hadik *la maison* thattiha f fi blasa w Toutou tajtxul f *sa maison* w illa ɛtitih jakul thatti ḥda *sa maison* bla ma tdiri f *le jardin* baf ma tawessexf *le jardin*...mnin sali lmakla tɛtih *la poupée* djalu w txeržu f *le jardin* w jlɛab f *le jardin* fwija, men bɛad jmfi jnɛas w jakul w jmfi jnɛas f ddaru 'we put it on this *swing* and you buy *Toutou's house* and that *house* you put it down in a place and Toutou goes into *his house* and if you give him something to eat you put it near *his house* without putting it in *the garden,* so that you don't dirty *the garden*...when he has finished his food you give him his *doll* and you take him out in *the garden* and he plays in *the garden* a bit. Afterwards he goes to sleep and he eats and he goes to sleep in his house'

In fact, while we can see no obvious need for such switches, the resulting pattern is very similar to that adopted by adult French-Arabic bilinguals when using their code-switching mode in casual conversation. It would seem, in fact, that these four-year-old children are modelling their alternation of the two languages on the patterns they regularly hear from their parents and other adults. We might go so far as to say that as well as acquiring Arabic and French, they are also acquiring a third variety which consists of mixing the two according to certain well-established patterns.

Conclusions

The striking differences between the patterns of switching found in the speech of these four-year-old Moroccans and those attested in many other studies of young bilinguals – notably the Moroccans' strong preference for phrasal and clausal switches as opposed to single-word switches, and the tendency to switch for a French noun accompanied by its determiner rather than for a noun alone – may be traced to differences in the types of language use to which the children are exposed. For the children in many of the reported case studies, code-switching is something rarely heard in adult speech and possibly regarded as an aberration from the norms; there are several reports in the literature of such children being disturbed by or critical of those who code-switch (see for instance Ronjat, 1913: 83-4; Saunders, 1982: 131; Fantini, 1985: 62). For our informants, in contrast, code-switching is a commonplace strategy of communication, the norms of which they therefore seem to have picked up as readily as they have acquired the rules of each separate language. Whereas in the literature children's code-switching is often regarded as evidence that they have not achieved an adult-like grasp of the two systems, or, as Gardner-Chloros (1991: 280) puts it, 'that they have not yet mastered the normatively influenced adult control/deactivation principles', this interpretation is not equally appropriate for children of all backgrounds. In the case of children like these Moroccans, their code-switching behaviour can on the contrary be seen as evidence of their quire considerable mastery of adult norms of usage.

Our present observations are of course based on only a small amount of data, and we therefore do not presume to draw any general conclusions about the code-switching behaviour of Moroccan children. However, we hope to have achieved our aim, which was to show that the environments in which children become bilingual vary considerably, and that their use of code-switching may have very different implications depending on this environment. If code-switching can sometimes be perceived as a failure to master norms, it may in other cases be seen as a successfully acquired skill.

References

Arnberg, L. & P. Arnberg, 1985. The relation between code differentiation and language mixing in bilingual three to four year old children. *Bilingual Review*, 12, 20-32.

Bentahila, A. & E. Davies, 1983. The syntax of Arabic-French code-switching. *Lingua*, 59, 301-330.

Bentahila, A. & E. Davies, 1991. Constraints on code-switching: a look beyond grammar. In: *Papers for the symposium on code-switching in bilingual studies: Theory, significance and perspectives* (Barcelona, March 1991). Strasbourg: European Science Foundation.

Bentahila, A. & E. Davies, forthcoming. Code-switching and language dominance. To appear in: R. Harris (ed.), *Cognitive processing in bilinguals*. Amsterdam: North Holland/Elsevier.

Bergman, C., 1976. Interference vs. independent development in infant bilingualism. In: G. Keller, R. Teschner & S. Viera (eds), *Bilingualism in the bicentennial and beyond*. New York: Bilingual Press.

Boeschoten, H. & L. Verhoeven, 1987. Language mixing in children's speech: Dutch language use in Turkish discourse. *Language Learning, 37*, 191-215.

De Houwer, A., 1990. *The acquisition of two languages from birth: A case study*. Cambridge: Cambridge University Press.

Fantini, A., 1985. *Language acquisition of a bilingual child: A sociolinguistic perspective*. Clevedon: Multilingual Matters.

Grosjean, F., 1982. *Life with two languages: An introduction to bilingualism*. Cambridge and London: Harvard University Press.

Gardner-Chloros, P., 1991. Children's code-switching: a review of the evidence and a comparison of child and adult mechanisms. In: *Papers for the symposium on code-switching in bilingual studies: Theory, significance and perspectives* (Barcelona, March 1991). Strasbourg: European Science Foundation.

Leopold, W., 1970. *Speech development of a bilingual child*. New York: AMS Press.

Lindholm, K. & A. Padilla, 1978. Child bilingualism: report on language mixing, switching and translations. *Linguistics, 211*, 23-44.

McClure, E. & J. Wentz, 1975. Functions of code switching among Mexican-America children. In: R. Grossman, L. San & T. Vance (eds), *Papers from the parasession on functionalism*. Chicago: Chicago Linguistics Society.

Meisel, J., 1990. Code-switching and related phenomena in young children. In: *Papers for the workshop on concepts, methodology and data* (Basel, January 1990). Strasbourg: European Science Foundation.

Muysken, P., 1991. Needed: A comparative approach. In: *Papers for the symposium on code-switching in bilingual studies: Theory, significance and perspectives* (Barcelona, March 1991). Strasbourg: European Science Foundation.

Nait M'Barek, M. & D. Sankoff, 1988. Le discours mixte arabe/français: Emprunts ou alternances de langue? *Canadian Journal of Linguistics, 33*, 143-154.

Nortier, J., 1989. *Dutch and Moroccan Arabic in contact: Code switching among Moroccans in the Netherlands*. Ph.D. Thesis, University of Amsterdam.

Poplack, S., 1980. Sometimes I'll start a sentence in English y termino en espanol: toward a typology of code-switching. *Linguistics, 18*, 581-618.

Redlinger, W. & T. Park, 1980. Language mixing in young bilinguals. *Journal of Child Language 7*, 337-352.

Romaine, S., 1989. *Bilingualism*. Oxford: Basil Blackwell.

Ronjat, J., 1913. *Le développement du langage observé chez un enfant bilingue*. Paris: Champion.

Saunders, G., 1982. *Bilingual children: Guidance for the family*. Clevedon: Multilingual Matters.

Kathleen A. Wodala

The development of initial reading in a bilingual child

A great deal has been written on the subject of bilingualism and many studies of the speech acquisition of bilingual children have been made, but literature dealing with the acquisition of reading skills by individual children is extremely sparse. Söderbergh (1971) wrote an interesting account of how her daughter learnt to read Swedish at the age of about two-and-a-half years following the method set forward by Doman (1964) in his book 'How to Teach your Baby to Read'. He proposed that all the words from a story should be written in really large letters, later smaller letters, on flash cards and the book only introduced when the child knows all the words. Söderbergh considers the use of such large letters as being rather like the way one speaks more clearly to a small child.

Studies of bilingual reading mainly present the situation in schools attended by bilingual children. American studies by Andersson (1976), Cohen (1979) and Kaminsky (1976) dealt with bilinguals (mainly Hispanics) who are put at a disadvantage on starting school because they have to learn to read, not in their dominant language first, but in English. In several other studies the acquisition of biliteracy was explored. Hanson (1980) investigated the process of learning to read of three Spanish-English speaking children from the age of two through the third grade at primary school. All children learned to break the code in the two languages with minimal interference. Deemer (1978) tested groups of Spanish-English bilinguals to measure their reading ability and to look for evidence of transfer. Her main conclusion was that 'reading for meaning is a skill which is non-language-specific and is thus transferable to a foreign language learned. As was expected, the correlation between first and second language reading skills becomes stronger as the student gains proficiency in the second language'. In other words she makes a case for positive transfer, as opposed to the findings of Cowan and Sarmed (1976) who studied bilingual children's performance in reading English and Persian and found that their achievements were below those of the monolingual English and Persian groups they observed. Kupinsky (1983) reported a study of kindergarten classes with Hebrew-English bilinguals who received simultaneous reading instruction in both languages. She found that all children successfully acquired reading skills in the two languages. Moreover, the reading skills in the two languages turned out to be related. Finally, in some studies the initial biliteracy outcomes of bilingual children in school have been studied. Mace-Matluck, Hoover and Calfee (1984) carried out a longitudinal study on the processes of learning to read in two langua-ges by Spanish-English speaking children at primary school in the United States. There was evidence for interdependency taking place in the acquisition of biliteracy. Verhoeven (1991) compared the literacy outcomes of Turkish children in the Netherlands in L2 submersion classes vs. transitional classes. He found that a transitional literacy approach may have beneficial effects. A strong emphasis on instruction in L1 does lead to better literacy results in L1 with no retardation of literacy results in L2. Moreover, the transitional approach tended to develop a more positive orientation toward literacy in both L1 and L2. Verhoeven also found empirical evidence for the interdependency hypothesis in biliteracy learning.

The present chapter is an outline of the study made by the author of her son's early reading acquisition in English and Hungarian. Aspects of the various processes he used in reading are covered. My findings back up the implications which Goodman (1989) and Goodman and Goodman (1978) drew from their study of the reading process from a psycholinguistic point of view. Their main claims are that it will be easier for someone who can already read to learn to read a second language and that it will be easier for someone to learn to read a language he already speaks. Particular mention is made of the kinds of positive and negative transfer the author was aware of in both languages and their importance in the acquisition of reading skills. Finally, there are some remarks on the wider bearing of this study on the teaching of reading and of languages in general.

The study of Mark's reading

As a practising linguist I fully appreciate the value of fluency in several languages. Although I was born and brought up in Britain and the languages I had studied were French and German, I ended up living in Hungary. My husband, a Hungarian teacher of English, shared my views on multilingualism and so, when our first child, Mark, was born in 1976 we deliberately set out to make him bilingual. Mark's home environment was kept exclusively English-speaking and the first language he learnt was English. Contact with Hungarian was rather limited until he started nursery school at the age of three but he made rapid progress from that time. By the time I started to teach Mark to read (about 22 months later) he was a natural, well-balanced bilingual child with the fluency and range of vocabulary of an intelligent 5-year-old from an above average socio-economic background.

Mark had expressed an interest in reading and, since I agree with Andersson (1976: 73) who said, with reference to bilinguals in the United States, 'that a non-English-speaking child has the right to learn to read his or her mother tongue and then has the duty to learn to read English', I wanted to help Mark to learn to read in English. The teaching of Hungarian reading would in any case take place at school.

Although some children do learn to read without any help from their elders, I thought it better to teach Mark to read. Living in Hungary he was not likely to 'pick up' the ability to read English! Finally, I decided to study how Mark was to acquire his initial reading skills, first in English alone and then in the two languages in an attempt to see how they affected each other in the written form. This study was presented as a Ph.D. Thesis which I defended in 1984 and which was later published (Wodala, 1985).

I started teaching Mark to read on 29th July, 1981, when he was 5 years 2 months 18 days (5;2,18), 13 months before the start of school. The choice of starting date was influenced by the fact that English is more difficult to read because of its peculiar spelling and by the concept of reading readiness. Mark had a good command of English, he was interested in the printed word and his memory was retentive. The method I used was basically Look-and-Say where whole words are learnt and I introduced very little deliberate phonic practice. The main books read during the period of study, including the period between 2nd September and 18th December, 1982, after Mark had started school, were Books 1, 2 and 3 in the Ladybird Sunstart Reading Scheme and Books 2, 3 and 4 in the b series of the Ladybird Key Words Series, all by Murray (1969).

Altogether 300 English vocabulary items occurred in Mark's reading material, the overwhelming majority of which were nouns (128) and verbs (64). Furthermore, 22 prepositions and/or adverbial particles, 3 forms of the articles, 5 interrogatives, 4 conjunctions, 2 demonstratives and 4 interjections were introduced. With the exception of the articles and the conjunction 'and', Mark learnt nouns (particularly proper nouns with their capital letters) and verbs more quickly than function words even though some of the latter are shorter.

Pre-school reading in English

In general Mark's progress in reading English prior to starting school was slow. His environment contained very little in English outwith the reading scheme to attract his eye. He had no feeling of competition with his peer group, one of the factors encouraging reading at school. Our reading sessions were short and usually took place after 4 p.m. after a full day at nursery school. While Mark was still reading relatively little at each session, I relied entirely on my own notes made during or immediately after each reading session in order to collect data. Later I made audio recordings as well of some reading sessions which were useful also in monitoring Mark's speed of reading and gradual mastery of phrasing and intonation.

Mark's way of reading during the first eight months (when Mark's age was 5;2,18 to 5;10,20) was typical of any child learning to read using a Look-and-Say method, which encourages the child to look for a distinctive feature and then guess. Consequently, Mark frequently substituted for a printed word another word containing the same letter or letters, e.g., *came* for 'can', *boy* for 'big' and vice versa where there may have been a confusion of 'o' and 'a', 'y' and 'g'. In these misreadings the initial letter was common far more frequently than the final letter: the ratio was 6:1.

Kathleen A. Wodala

The initial letter is all-important for the child at this stage and the fact that confusions often involved words of different lengths indicates that the length of a word is of less importance in a child's eye than an adult, used to reading, might think. Söderbergh (1971) also found that the length of the written word and the word it was supposed to be frequently did not correspond. In late November, 1981, Mark remarked that 'fish' and 'for' looked similar. There is no question here of similar length or overall shape, so he must have based his remark solely on the common initial letter 'f'.

At this stage Mark made 38 unaided successful first readings of words as opposed to only 1 unsuccessful first reading – in some cases he was helped by the picture or he extrapolated from a previously read form of the word. However, successful first readings occurring at a rate of about 5 a month and a total of 1 unsuccessful first reading in 8 months only underline Mark's lack of confidence in reading and his unwillingness to try unless he was sure that he was right. At the same time he appeared to be aware that what he read in his book should make sense: his substitution of *ladies* for 'women' makes perfect grammatical and semantic sense.

Eight months after he had started reading, Mark read 'please' as [p#l#ɛ#a], I supplied the correct phoneme for the digraph and Mark completed the word, adding a query about the mute 'e'. Thus he had spontaneously introduced analysis as a form of working out how to read words. This seemed an important milestone in his progress and led me to divide his pre-school reading into two sections at this point.

During the next five months (when Mark's age was 5;10,21 to 6;3,21) many of the tendencies already mentioned continued. It was obvious that to some extent Mark was still looking for a distinctive feature and guessing. This feature was usually the initial letter, e.g., he read *boat* for 'but', but not always: he read *kite* for 'asks'. At this stage of reading there were more confusions of letters so probably Mark was beginning to consider individual letters in his segmentation, but he did not always look at them with close enough attention. Confusions were most often of letters with a round body, e.g., 'a' and 'o', or a round body and a tail, e.g., 'b' and 'd'.

Mark obviously now considered analysis a good way of decoding new or forgotten words. His analysis usually started with the first letter and more often than not he scanned from left to right. Sometimes he completed the word immediately, at other times he failed to do so. When he continued to analyse sometimes he could re-synthesise the word from the elements, but in many cases he was unable to modify the elements he had read out to make the word he knew orally. Compared with the first eight months of reading the number of misreadings rose considerably indicating that Mark had more courage to try to read words even at the risk of being wrong. It also reflects the fact that he was relying more on his analysis in reading which was still far from perfect.

Clark and Clark (1977) described how listeners use various strategies to make speech intelligible, in other words, when they hear a particular 'cue' word they 'expect' a certain grammatical structure to follow. Some of Mark's misreadings indicate that he was using such strategies to interpret the written text. In the sentence 'They find that one letter is from an old man who is at sea on his boat' he misread the last clause as *who is doing*.... Although the present continuous had not been used in his reading material at that point, obviously he commonly applied it in speech and therefore assumed that 'is' was the first element of the present continuous.

By the end of 13 months of reading practice in English, Mark had read 5 books from the selected reading material and attained a certain level of competence, although his progress was slower than would be expected of a child of his socio-economic level in Britain. He was displaying various techniques, notably analysis, to assist with recognising or de-coding words in a written text. Eleven of the words he had read showed some Hungarian influence and eight of these reflected mistakes in pronunciation such as also occurred in his speech at that time.

Mark starts school

Mark started school at the age of 6;3,22. During the first term at school (a period of less than 4 months, when Mark was aged 6;7,7) one more book from the Key Word Series was read and an additional book from the Cat in the Hat Series – Dr. Seuss's Hop on Pop (1963). It was only at this stage that I introduced writing, using Workbook 2 of the Keyword Series and Workbooks 1 and 2 of the Sunstart Series. I do not think that their use had much influence on Mark's reading progress at this stage. Introducing them sooner, however, might have speeded up his progress in the earlier stages. In school Hungarian reading was taught using the books Olvasni tanulok (I learn to read) and Irni tanulok (I learn to write) by Romankovics, Tóth and Meixner (1981). This reading method uses global reading (Look-and-Say) initially but phonic practice is introduced quickly and intensively.

The types of mistakes Mark made in his English reading showed little change, except where influence from Hungarian could be observed. Where he misread the written word as another word containing the same letter or letters the letter overlap improved, so it was not enough for the first letter only to be the same: Mark considered other letters, too, thus he read *them* for 'then' and *bell* for 'ball'.

In general Mark's English reading improved. He made 82 unaided successful first readings (although this total is inflated by 18 words which he probably remembered from having Hop on Pop by Dr. Seuss (1963) read to him on previous occasions), while unaided unsuccessful first readings numbered only 25, a figure boosted by 12 attempts at analysis which failed. Grammatically unacceptable misreadings continued to occur at a rate of about half of those which were grammatically acceptable. Failed analyses accounted for more than half of the unacceptable misreadings, indicating that Mark was beginning to rely more heavily on this method of decoding which was actively encouraged in Hungarian reading.

At the same time there was a drop in the overall number of instances of analytical reading recorded. Very likely Mark's analysis was internalised: he no longer sounded out what he read, but analysed silently and read out only his final version.

Kaminsky (1976: 158) describes how 'in the early stages of reading, children may recode graphic sequences into aural input, from which they derive meaning. At a point when he achieves relative fluency in reading, the reader probably collapses the process, simultaneously supplying the aural input with the recoding of the graphic unit. Compression of these processes takes place at the most efficient level of fluency, where the reader decodes meaning directly from the graphic sequences.'

Confusions of letters with a round body decreased, confusions of letters with a round body and a tail disappeared or decreased, except in the case of 'g' and 'y' which may have been influenced by Mark's confusion in Hungarian reading of 'g' and 'gy'. He also confused capital 'I' with small case 'l' after this confusion had arisen in Hungarian.

During Mark's first term at school six times as many instances of direct Hungarian interference in individual words in English were observed as in the previous five months. To begin with they still reflected mistakes in pronunciation which occurred in his speech but, mainly from October on, when Hungarian reading had become established, interference could be found in words which previously had been read quite correctly. Here are some examples: he read 'all' as [a:l] and possibly confused it with the Hungarian verb 'àll' (stand) which had occurred a month previously in his Hungarian reading material. For 'fun' he read [fun] after the introduction of the Hungarian letters 'u' and 'ù', for 'keep' he read [kɛp] and for 'her' [her] after the introduction of the Hungarian letters 'e' and 'é' had been practised intensively, 'Jim' was read as [jim] and even when I corrected the 'j' he retained the Hungarian phoneme (i), [d im].

Hungarian influence could be noticed when he tried to read new words, too. Although Mark sometimes mispronounced 'w' in speech, his reading of 'new' as [nav] and insisting that [v] should be added to my correction to make [njuv] indicates that he was influenced by the printed letter which occurs only in loan words in Hungarian, notably his own surname, and is pronounced [v] as is the letter 'v'.

The Hungarian letter 'c' is pronounced [ts] and an additional confusion for Mark was the variation between [s] and [k] for English 'c'. For 'cakes' he suggested [tʃ k] and refused to accept that the word began with (k). For 'Police' he read [p ltsɛ] and for 'cats' [tsæt], all after the Hungarian letter 'c' had been introduced. The Hungarian letter 's' is pronounced [ʃ] and Mark himself observed the difference with English: in the word 'star' he said that 's' is *like [ʃ] in Hungarian.* He read 'us' as [uʃ] and 'só' as [ʃo], possibly further confused by the Hungarian word 'só' (salt). Mark had difficulty with the English digraph 'sh' sometimes confusing it with 'th'. Towards the end of this period he read 'shop' as [ʃh p] and 'shops' as [ʃh pʃ], then overcorrected to [s]. Although he was more familiar with the English digraph 'th', on the day that the letter 't' was practised in school Mark read 'then' correctly, afterwards changing it to [tɛn] and refusing to accept my correction. He even used the value of a Hungarian doubled consonant when he read 'we'll' as [wil:].

Many of these rather striking misreadings were corrected by Mark himself, either after I reminded him he was reading English or spontaneously, and at the end of the period of close observation of Mark's reading they were on the decline and soon afterwards disappeared. Besides an increasing monitoring of the reading process, the exactness of Mark's reading was improving as was his visual perception of the words themselves. This is shown by the rising letter overlap between the actual and the supposed words. Because of the intensive letter-phoneme correspondence practised in Hungarian Mark was paying closer attention to the letters which made up the words instead of just 'guessing'. Another indication of his progress in reading was the gradual increase in tempo and the improvement in intonation.

Reading in Hungarian

Mark's Hungarian reading was carried out in very different circumstances and with a different method from his English reading. He was being taught in a class of 34 children, all of whom were over the age of 6. Thirteen of them had already had their 7th birthday by mid-December, 1982, which put Mark among the younger children. Three of the children could read Hungarian fluently on starting school.

The reading scheme by Romankovics, Tóth and Meixner (1981) is a decidedly phonic method, using elements of Look-and-Say only in the initial stages. Each letter or digraph is practised as it is introduced in four ways: practice in pronouncing correctly and clearly the phoneme it represents, recognising the phoneme it represents, recognising the letter in print (both small case and capital forms) and writing the letter, using the cursive form almost from the outset.

Children are actively encouraged to analyse words: lists of three or four words appear in which the child has to indicate the common element. This also meant that Mark read a large number of Hungarian lexical items in isolation, whereas in English almost all of the words read were contextualized. The number of lexical items read in less than four months of school was over 1200, almost six times as many as the English words read in 17 months. As in English most of the words introduced were content words (667 nouns, including 92 proper nouns, 275 verbs and 173 adjectives and adverbs) and, since Hungarian is a synthetic language, the number of function words amounted to only about one-twelfth of the total.

Most of Mark's Hungarian reading took place in school, but for the purposes of the study I asked Mark to read pages from his reading book that he had not yet read in school and from two supplementary books written for children using a different reading scheme called A Maci olvas (Teddy reads) by Sahin-Tóth and Ligeti (1980). The books, Piroska és a farkas (Little Red Riding Hood) and Hüvelyk Matyi (Tom Thumb), adaptations by Sahin-Tóth and Ligeti (1981a; 1981b) of well-known stories, were of a similar standard to his school book. As with English reading I made notes on the reading sessions I held with Mark and asked my husband to make audio recordings all in Hungarian of Mark reading which I could then play back.

Mark's Hungarian reading followed roughly the same pattern as his English reading: firstly a global stage where he looked for a distinctive feature and guessed, e.g., he read 'ùjsàg' (newspaper) as *juhàsz* (shepherd); a second stage where analysis played a part, but was not perfect, and a third stage where Mark's reading was much more accurate. He reached roughly the same standard in Hungarian reading in about one-fifth of the time. His misreadings were more often grammatically acceptable than otherwise and he misread words as others which contained the same letters, but the letter overlap was higher than in English.

Confusions of letters rarely involved those which he had formerly confused in English reading. Hungarian uses a variety of diacritic marks on the vowels to indicate quality and length and these caused some problems, as well as some of the Hungarian digraphs. He confused 'é' and 'ö' when he said *körd* (* signifies a non-existant word) for 'kérdezte' (he asked), although when he read 'gyenge' (weak) as [œngɛ] he may merely have been pronouncing it according to the dialect used in his home town. He confused the digraph 'gy' with 'g': for 'gonosz' (evil) he read [n s] then *gonosz* correctly. He divided the digraph 'sz' into two separate phonemes when he read 'szólt' (she said) as [soz]. He also confused small case 'i' and 'í' and capital 'I' with small case 'l', this last mainly because the same symbol was used for both in his reading books.

Naturally there were plenty of examples of analytical reading and the fact that analysis had already become established in English reading probably helped Mark. Of course it is fairly easy to reassemble a word such as 'cimbalom' (the musical instrument) from the elements *cim-ba-lom*. Mark's analysis was logical from about the end of October, beginning with the first sound (or sounds) or reading syllable by syllable and leading to the whole word with little help from me. Where he divided a word his division conformed with Hungarian rules for word division: he read first the prefix *be* (in) then the whole word *beugrott* (he jumped in). Of course Hungarian children acquire a grasp of the grammatical function of the various morphemes as their speech develops so recognising these different elements in writing is an extension of this skill. There were exceptions in Mark's reading, e.g., for the compound word 'diótortàt' (walnut cake) Mark began with *diót,* but perhaps he was putting the accusative marker '-t', which occurs at the end of the word, on to the first syllable.

Each Hungarian letter or digraph always corresponds to the same phoneme, except in cases where assimilation occurs. Lotz (1972) described this phenomenon very well: briefly it is a switch in the voicing of an element to conform with the voicing of the following morpheme (a stop, affricate or fricative) and a modification of (n) to (m) before (p), (b), (f) and (v). Although Hungarian children apply these modifications naturally in speech, when confronted with reading and they are told, for instance, that the letter 'd' has the sound [d], they are so much influenced by the physical presence of the 'd' that they often read a word like 'mondta' (he said) as [m ndtå] instead of [m nt:å]. Mark also went through this phase but by the end of the period of study he appeared to be perfect in this respect, reading 'dobozt' (box), for instance, correctly as [d b st], whereas children in the second year of primary school still tend to make mistakes with assimilation. The speed with which Mark overcame these problems can perhaps be attributed to his already realising that since writing reflects speech it is often necessary to modify the pronunciation of the graphic elements to make a word sound the way it should!

The ratio of successful to unsuccessful first readings of words in Hungarian (at home) was about 5:1, compared with ratios of 20:1, 1:1 and 4:1 in the three stages of English reading. In December the ratio was 7:1 and the overall ratio was probably lower than it might have been because Mark was more confident in reading Hungarian and tried to read words even at the risk of reading them incorrectly. Direct influence from English was negligible in his Hungarian reading. The letters 'j' and 's' confused him and he made mistakes, such as reading 'menj' (go) as [mɛnd] and 'sietek' (I hurry) as [sɛ].

Conclusions

I have already mentioned Goodman's (1989) claim that it will be easier for someone to learn to read a language he already speaks. This is important in the case of monolingual children, too, and books should be designed which provide opportunities to develop listening and speaking skills and range of vocabulary. Children should be encouraged to talk about the pictures and situations shown in them. Pictures, especially coloured ones, make books more attractive for children. My father has told me that as a boy he refused to read books with no pictures. They are also a source of pragmatical help in reading the related text. Meek (1982) and Stanovich (1986) warned against excluding techniques such as guessing from the context and using 'strategies', i.e., completing phrases in accordance with familiar syntactical constructions.

Chall (1983) claimed that reading programmes which emphasised the alphabetical code produced better readers than those with a meaning emphasis. The Hungarian reading scheme Mark used was firmly based on the alphabetic code and was much more effective than the method used in English reading. The way of printing reading books for beginners is also important. In the first instance letters should be fairly big. Söderbergh (1971) used letters 12.5 cm high in teaching her daughter of two-and-a-half years to read. My own daughter, Mairi, at the age of three liked to read letters one metre tall painted on a wall. Since most children start school at 5 or 6 probably letters of about 1 cm (size of lower case 'l') are best for beginner readers. Mark's claim that he could not read the words grouped at the end of his first English reading book in small print, although he could read them all in the book or on flash cards, underlines the importance of this. He made no complaint about the size of letters in his Hungarian reading book (5 mm) but then he already had experience of letters even smaller in his English reading series. Perhaps larger letters might have made reading easier for others in his class.

The lay-out of the text can also play a part in the ease with which a child reads. Most books one looks at have lines of the same length neatly arranged in a rectangular block on the page. The result of this is that very often a clause, a phrase or even a word is divided in two. Carpenter and Just (1981) showed that interpretation

Kathleen A. Wodala

immediately follows recognition in reading, and that fixations tend to be longer at clause endings. The latter finding indicates that integrative comprehension processes must particularly take place at clause boundaries. Thus, it will be easier to remember a text set out so that a printed line finishes at a constituent break in the syntax. When a child is starting to read he has difficulty remembering the beginning of the sentence because his short-term memory fades quickly. I often had to re-read to Mark what he had already read so that he was able to use the context as a clue to a word which was causing problems. It is obviously easier for a child to recapitulate in this way if the sentence or phrase is all on the same line.

The presence or absence of inverted commas seemed to make less difference than the spacing between words and Mark even ignored full stops sometimes. Once he omitted the word 'says' because it occurred after a larger space than usual because of the presence of inverted commas. These Mark ignored, and the fact that 'says' and its subject were on different lines probably added to Mark's confusion. When I pointed the word out to him he complained *I don't know why they have to put it a metre over there!*

I can see that there are many ways in which I could have helped Mark to progress more quickly with his English reading. Earlier introduction of writing practice would have helped him to remember words and letters better. The importance of an early connection between writing and reading is emphasized in recent studies by Ferreiro and Teberosky (1982) and Teale and Sulzby (1986).

Reading skills certainly seem to be transferable, so it would probably have turned the negative transfer to Mark's advantage if I had clearly emphasised the different phonemes represented by the same grapheme in English and Hungarian, instead of trying to keep the two languages strictly apart. Mark himself noticed the contrast between English 's' and Hungarian 's', so such observations could have been built on to bring out the similarities and differences of English and Hungarian in phoneme-letter correlation, in pronunciation of sounds and possibly in intonation, too. This is the view held by Cohen (1979): 'For example, two days after a class of Spanish [-English] bilingual children is introduced to the triple blend *str* in a medial position, such as in the word *estrella,* the experienced teacher will introduce the blend in English, using the initial position, as in *street* or *straight.*' (5) In Mark's case this extra help could only have been given in English reading, not in his Hungarian class, where he was the only English-Hungarian bilingual. However, where all the children in a class are learning a second language, transfer can be assisted in both directions in this way.

Mark is a fluent speaker of English but he lives in a Hungarian-speaking environment very different from the cultural background depicted in his reading books. Although I did my best to compensate there were times when he could not understand the text because of a gap in his cultural knowledge. Certainly when languages are taught in school I feel teachers should make every effort to acquire posters and everyday objects with writing on them, not just so that the names of the things can be learnt, but also to spark off discussion about how scenes and objects fit into the everyday life of the country whose language is being taught. Perhaps in this way it might be easier to explain cultural differences which children may find puzzling.

Perhaps some of these remarks will prove to be of assistance in helping backward readers to improve, in particular those whose 'backwardness' is said to be caused by bilingualism. As Cohen (1979: 100) claimed, 'even a poor reader equipped with two sets of tools or languages tends to have an advantage over a monolingual reader.'

Appendix: a guide to the pronunciation of Hungarian

The following list gives all the letters of the Hungarian alphabet with an indication of how each is normally pronounced and the phonetic symbol used for each. Unless otherwise indicated the words are English and Received Pronunciation is intended to be used:

letter	approximate pronunciation	phonetic symbol	letter	approximate pronunciation	phonetic symbol
a	between 'far' and 'hot' [å]		o	'not'	[ ]
à	'tralala'	[aː]	o	Scots 'oat'	[o]
b	'big'	[b]	ö	German 'zwölf'	[œ]
c	'rats'	[ts]	o	'third' – long	[œː]
cs	'chin'	[tʃ]	p	'pin'	[p]
d	'din'	[d]	q	German 'Quarz'	[kv]
dz	'lids'	[dz]	r	Scots 'run' – rolled 'r'	[r]
dzs	'jam'	[d]	s	'sure'	[ʃ]
e	'bet'	[ɛ]	sz	'sun'	[s]
é	Scots 'mane'	[e]	t	'ten'	[t]
f	'fin'	[f]	ty	palatalised 't' – 'I'll beat you'	[tj]
g	'game'	[g]	u	'moot'	[u]
gy	palatalised 'd' – 'He hid your book'	[ ]	ù	'rude' – long	[uː]
h	'hit'	[h]	ü	French 'lune'	[y]
i	'beat'	[i]	ű	same sound, but long	[yː]
í	'me' – long	[iː]	v	'vane'	[v]
j	'yes'	[j]	w	same sound	[v]
k	'kite'	[k]	x	'Max'	[ks]
l	'light'	[l]	y	'feet'	[i]
m	'milk'	[m]	z	'zebra'	[z]
n	'nine'	[n]	zs	'pleasure'	[ ]
ny	Spanish 'señor'	[ŋ]			

References

Andersson, T., 1976. The bilingual child's right to read. *Georgetown University Working Papers on Languages and Linguistics,* 12, 63-72.

Carpenter, P., & M. Just, 1981. Cognitive processes in reading: Models based on readers' eye fixations. In: M. Lesgold & C. Perfetti (eds), *Interactive processes in reading.* Hillsdale, NJ: LEA.

Chall, J., 1983. *Learning to Read: The great debate.* New York: McGraw Hill.

Clark, H., and E. Clark, 1977. *Psychology and Language.* New York: Harcourt Brace Jovanovich, Inc.

Cohen, B., 1979. *Models and methods for bilingual education.* Hingham, USA: Teaching Resources Corporation.

Cowan, J. and Z. Sarmed, (1976), Reading Performance of Bilingual Children According to Type of School and Home Language, *Working Papers in Bilingualism,* No. 11, August.

Deemer, H., 1978. *The transfer of reading skills from first to second language. The report of an experiment with Spanish speakers learning English.* ERIC ED 172532.

Doman, G., 1964. *How to Teach your Baby to Read.* New York.

Ferreiro, E. & A. Teberosky, 1982. *Literacy before schooling.* London: Heinemann.

Goodman, K., 1989. Whole language research: Foundations and development. *Elementary School Journal,* 90, 207-221.

Goodman, K. & Y. Goodman, 1978. Reading of American children whose language is a stable rural dialect of a language other than English. *ERIC ED,* 173-754.

Hanson, I., 1980. *An inquiry how three preschool children acquired literacy in two languages.* Georgetown University, Unpublished Ph.D. Thesis.

Kaminsky, S., 1976. Bilingualism and Learning to Read. In: A. Simoes, Jr. (ed.), *The Bilingual Child: Research and Analysis of existing educational Themes.* New York: Academic Press.

Kupinsky, B., 1983. Bilingual reading instruction in kindergarten. *Reading Teacher,* 37, 132-137.

Lotz, J., 1972. Script, Grammar and the Hungarian Writing System. *The Hungarian-English Contrastive Linguistics Project, Working Papers.* Budapest: Linguistics Institute of the Hungarian Academy of Sciences and Center for Applied Linguistics.

Mace-Matluck, B., W. Hoover & R. Calfee, 1984. *Teaching reading to bilingual children study: A final report.* Austin, Texas: SEDL.

Meek, M., 1982. *Learning to Read.* London: The Bodley Head.

Murray, W., 1969. *Teaching Reading.* Loughborough: Ladybird Books Ltd.

Romankovics, A., J. Tóth, & J. Meixner, 1981. *Olvasni tanulok (I learn to red), Irni tanulok (I learn to write).* Budapest: Tankönyvkiadó.

Sahin-Tóth, K. & R. Ligeti, 1980. *Olvasàs- és iràstanulàs az I. osztàlybanhe (The learning of reading and writing in Primary 1).* Budapest: Tankönyvkiadó.

Sahin-Tóth, K. & R. Ligeti, 1981a. *Piroska és a farkas (Little Red Riding Hood).*

Budapest: Tankönyvkiado.

Sahin-Tóth, K. & R. Ligeti, 1981b. *Hüvelyk Matyi (Tom Thumb)*. Budapest: Tan-könyvkiado.

Seuss, Dr., 1963. *Hop on Pop*. New York: Collins.

Söderbergh, R., 1971. *Reading in Early Childhood: A Linguistic Study of a Swedish Preschool Child's Gradual Acquisition of Reading Ability*. Stockholm: Almqvist and Wiksell.

Stanovich, K., 1986. Matthew effects in reading: Some consequences of individual differences in the acquisition of reading. *Reading Research Quarterly,* 21, 360-407.

Teale, W. & E. Sulzby, 1986. *Emergent literacy: Writing and reading*. Norwood, NJ: Ablex.

Verhoeven, L., 1991. Acquisition of biliteracy. *AILA Review,* 8, 61-74.

Wodala, K., 1985. *The Development of Reading Skills in an English-Hungarian Bilingual Child:* Hungarian Studies in Psycholinguistics III; Szeged.

Part 2

Bilingual development at school age and beyond

Kenji Hakuta and Lucinda Pease-Alvarez

Proficiency, choice and attitudes in bilingual Mexican-American children[1]

The United States is home to native speakers of practically every major language of the world, yet the rate at which immigrants have shifted from their native language to English has given it the reputation of a monolingual English-speaking country with severely limited competence in other languages. In many ways, California, where this study was conducted, is an intensified version of the language minority picture of the United States (most language minority students are concentrated in just five large states: New York, Texas, California, Illinois, and Florida).

[1] Assistants to the project include: Carola Cabrejos, Yuri Kuwahara, James Rodriguez, Griselda Silva, David Whitenack and Adam Winsler.

Table 1. Number of limited and fluent-English-proficient students in California Public Schools, by Language, 1990. Source: California State Department of Education.

Language	Limited-English-proficient students	Fluent-English-proficient students	Total
Spanish	655,097	408,280	1,063,377
Vietnamese	34,934	27,681	62,615
Pilipino	16,338	35,135	51,473
Cantonese	21,154	23,113	44,267
Korean	13,389	20,178	33,567
Cambodian	19,234	5,243	24,477
Hmong	18,091	3,824	21,915
Mandarin	7,201	13,257	20,458
Lao	12,177	4,275	16,452
Armenian	9,046	3,021	12,067
Japanese	5,505	6,541	12,046
Farsi	4,875	7,041	11,916
Other Chinese	3,293	4,220	7,513
Portuguese	2,830	4,601	7,431
Arabic	2,771	3,248	6,019
Punjabi	2,093	2,161	4,254
Hindi	1,754	1,892	3,646
Mien	2,834	508	3,342
Samoan	1,490	1,842	3,332
Ilocano	1,041	1,468	2,509
Hebrew	904	1,399	2,303
Russian	1,510	669	2,179
Thai	852	985	1,837
Tongan	956	610	1,566
Taiwanese	560	899	1,459
Other Filipino	584	853	1,437
Rumanian	820	504	1,324
German	307	956	1,263
Gujarati	501	705	1,206
Urdu	396	413	809
French	265	539	804
Assyrian	415	384	799
Italian	153	443	596
Pashto	375	128	503
Polish	247	201	448
Indonesian	295	152	447
Greek	103	310	413
Visayan	148	130	278
Hungarian	99	103	202
Dutch	58	122	180
Guamanian	48	123	171
Burmese	79	85	164
Croatian	30	125	155
Native American	61	85	146
Turkish	27	41	68
Serbian	13	22	35
All other languages	16,578	32,990	49,568
State totals	861,531	621,505	1,483,036
Percent	58.0%	42.0%	100.0%

The robustness of linguistic diversity in the United States is captured quite well in some recent statistics compiled in the State of California by the Department of Education. Table 1 makes three points. First, there is a very large number (1,483,036 to be exact) of language minority students, defined as those in whose home a language other than English is spoken. Second, there is a large range of languages represented. And third, Spanish represents by far the largest group, accounting for about 72 per cent of the total language minority population.

The magnitude of the language minority population has intensified the politicization of language issues, as witnessed in the 'English-only movement' as well as the backlash against bilingual education programs (Crawford, 1992). Some have charged that unlike previous immigrant groups, Hispanics have refused to assimilate and have hung on to their ethnic language and heritage (Epstein, 1977). In countering such charges, some Hispanic leaders have pointed to demographic data showing that Spanish-speaking immigrants shift to English at a rapid rate, for example, that 'more than half the immigrants who arrived in the United States before they were fourteen have made English their usual, everyday language, relegating Spanish to the status of a second language' (Nicolau & Valdivieso, 1992: 319).

Indeed, ethnographic information (e.g., Mallory, 1971; Ortiz, 1975) as well as large-scale demographic studies (Fishman, 1966; Lopez, 1978; Veltman, 1983, 1988) suggest that bilingual individuals show a strong preference for English in many conversational situations, and that this preference is translated into a monolingual English upbringing for their offspring.

The shift from the non-English language to English that occurs may be both *intra-individual* and *inter-generational* in nature, i.e., individuals during the course of their lifetime shift their choice of primary language use from their native ethnic language to English, and ethnolinguistic communities in successive generations will likewise shift in their linguistic preference.

Although there is widespread agreement about the fact that this shift occurs rapidly, our understanding of the process is quite limited. This weakness is due to the fact that most of the studies of language shift have been inter-generational studies using available archival and census data on self-reported language preference. At present, our understanding of language shift is hampered by a number of problems.

First, most studies refer to a shift in language *choice* and do not directly address its relationship to language *proficiency*. Individuals may indeed choose not to use their native language, but that does not necessarily mean that they have lost proficiency in the language. In the limit, of course, the choice not to use the ethnic language by individuals translates into the loss of the language through its non-acquisition by their offspring. However, an important piece of information on how choice and proficiency are interrelated within an individual is missing.

Second, there are few detailed studies of the psycholinguistic nature of language attrition in language minority populations. Most studies have focused almost exclusively on the loss of a foreign language (e.g., Bahrick, 1984; Cohen, 1975; Gardner, Lalonde & MacPherson, 1985; Lett & O'Mara (forthcoming); Lett, personal communication; Weltens, van Els & Schils, 1989). Where loss of the native language has been investigated, the subjects have been young children where it is difficult to distinguish between *language attrition* and *incomplete acquisition* (Kaufman & Aronoff (forthcoming) a, b; Merino, 1983; Smith, 1983; Weltens, de Bot & van Els, 1986).

Third, the studies conducted with large samples have based their findings on self-reported measures of language choice and language proficiency. (Gumperz, 1982; Blom & Gumperz, 1972) points out the limitations of self-reported data in matters of language *choice,* especially when the questions are phrased in general terms, such as asking what language is typically used in the home or at church. Self-reported language *proficiency* data also carry obvious measurement problems.

Measurement of language shift[2] has at least three components that should be measured separately: (1) an individual's actual proficiency in the two languages, (2) an individual's choice to use differential amounts of the languages (in different discourse settings) given threshold proficiency in the languages, and (3) an individual's attitudes toward the languages. These components are in principle separable (i.e., there may be an individual with high proficiency in both English and Spanish who chooses to use mostly English, but maintains an identity that is primarily Mexican), but in reality they are probably related. For example, Veltman focuses on language choice over language proficiency, not just because the census bureau questions have tended to ask the question on usual language practice (e.g., 'What language does (this person) usually speak?' in the Survey of Income and Education, 1976), but also because he considers it a logical outcome that if a language is not usually spoken in the home, the children will not develop proficiency in it.

In addition to distinguishing between these components of language shift, it is important to ask whether the data are based on self-report or on direct observation. For example, the High School and Beyond survey asked 'How well do you speak *that* language?' with response choices *very well, pretty well, not very well,* and *not at all.* How accurate would this self-report be when compared with direct observation of proficiency in the language? Obviously, self-reported data are the easiest to obtain, but they sacrifice objectivity; however, in some cases, direct observation may be extremely difficult or impractical, such as in the case of language identification.

The rough measurement model in the study of language shift, then, can be thought of as a 2x3 table as follows:

---

[2] The empirical basis for these claims are explored further in Hakuta (forthcoming).

Table 2. Constructs and data types used to study language shift.

	Type of Data	
Aspect of Bilingualism	Self-Report	Observation
Language Proficiency	1	2
Language Choice	3	4
Language Attitudes	5	6

In an ideal situation, one would look at the correlations between 2, 4, and 6 based on actual observations. However, we are often dependent on self-report and other indirect means of inference.

With this picture about measurement in mind, we would like to offer a characterization of pilot work we have been conducting over the past few years looking at language maintenance and shift among Mexican background minority school-aged children and youths in two communities in the northern part of California near San Francisco.

One community, Watsonville, is located in an agricultural area known as the Central Coast. The subjects in this study were students at a single, four-year, high school, of which 65 per cent (about 1500) are of Mexican descent. Having arrived from other areas of California, other states in the US and directly from different states of Mexico, the vast majority of the Mexican-descent population have settled in this area in the last 20 years (Donato, 1988).

The second community is located in the suburban area of San Francisco, to which we have given the pseudonym Eastside. Like many communities in Northern California, Eastside has become increasingly more diverse with regards to income and ethnicity. In the mid 1960s, the community was populated mostly by working class Anglos; now it is home to immigrants from southern Europe, the Pacific Islands, and Latin America. Among these groups, immigrants from Mexico are the most numerous and along with other Latinos represent more than 80 per cent of the school age population in the four Eastside elementary schools. Figure 1 shows the increase in Hispanic students in Eastside schools over the years 1964-1990.

The Watsonville study

The study of high school students was conducted primarily using paper-and-pencil instruments. The major goal of the study was to look at language proficiency (both observed and self-reported), language attitude (self-report), and language choice (self-report) as a function of immigration background. Since the results have already been published in Applied Linguistics (1992, Vol. 13), only a brief outline of the findings will be provided here.

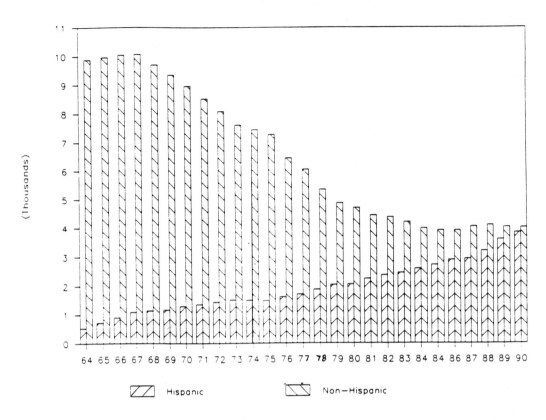

Figure 1. Changes in percentages of Hispanic and Non-Hispanic students in East-side, California Public Schools, over the years 1964-1990.

Subjects in the study were divided into six groups:

1. Born in Mexico, arrived in the USA older than 10 years old.
2. Born in Mexico, arrived in the USA between the ages of 6 and 10 years old inclusively.
3. Born in Mexico, arrived in the USA when 5 years old or younger.
4. Born in the USA, both parents born in Mexico.
5. Born in the USA, at least one parent born in the USA.
6. Born in the USA, at least one parent and associated grandparents born in the USA.

One major result of the analysis was the importance of distinguishing between language proficiency from language choice – in many ways as different a set of realities as the worlds of psycholinguists from sociolinguists – for very different pictures of language shift emerged.

With respect to proficiency, the main findings for English and Spanish proficiency can be seen in Figure 2. For English, it shows that the only notable difference is between groups 1 and 2, i.e., the most recent arrivals have not yet mastered English as well as the other groups; for Spanish it shows that maintenance of Spanish is strong until the drop at Group 5.

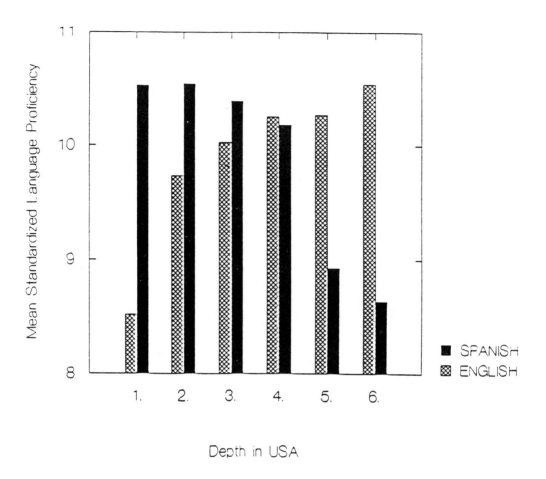

Figure 2. Mean Standardized Spanish and English language proficiency measures for six Depth cohorts. (Depth 1: Born in Mexico, arrived in the USA > 10 years old; Depth 2: Born in Mexico, arrived in the USA between the ages of 6 and 10 years old inclusively; Depth 3: Born in Mexico, arrived in the USA when 5 years old or younger; Depth 4: Born in the USA, both parents born in Mexico; Depth 5: Born in the USA, at least one parent born in the USA, at least one parent and associated grandparents born in the USA).

On the other hand, with respect to language choice, rather than the discontinuous appearances that characterized English and Spanish proficiencies, the shift was more of a gradual one, as seen in Figure 3.

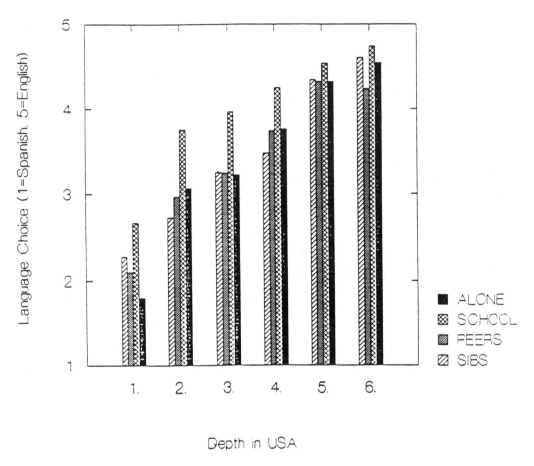

Figure 3. Language choice with siblings, with peers, for academic purposes at school, and when alone, by Depth cohorts.

Different views of shift that emerge from language proficiency and language choice are underscored in analyses of correlates of between-group and within-group diffe-rences as well. For Spanish, *maintenance of proficiency in Spanish is principally associated with adult language practice in the home, rather than the subject's language attitude or language choice outside the home*. That is to say, once the adults shifted into using English at home, there was little chance for Spanish to be passed on to their offspring. English proficiency is related to language usage with peers, and is not associated with language practice in the home.

Finally, a major methodological point to emerge from the study was the importance of taking direct measurements in language proficiency rather than relying on self-report. We found that although there were sizeable correlations between actual measured proficiency and self-reported proficiency ($r=.61$ for Spanish, $r=.46$ for English), there was an almost equal contribution of the attitudinal variance component to the self-report measures. Thus, one view of self-reported proficiency measures is that they are just as good a measure of language attitude as they are of language proficiency[3].

Eastside study

The Watsonville study was what might be considered a one-shot study with few provisions for in-depth exploration of the issues. We decided to collect further descriptive data, but in a different community – in which Lucinda Pease-Alvarez had conducted her dissertation research in language socialization. The study is also given character by the fact that we are focusing on both quantitative and qualitative measurements – for example, in addition to asking individuals to report their language choice, we also ask them to explain their choices. Finally, we have gone through an extensive process of sample selection by first surveying the community, defining a sampling frame, and recruiting the final sample.

Sampling

A survey of the students in the bilingual programs in the Eastside City School District was conducted starting in December, 1990. Based on the continuing work of Lucinda Pease-Alvarez in understanding the sociolinguistics of bilingualism in the schools and the Mexican-descent community in the area of Eastside (Vasquez, Pease-Alvarez & Shannon (forthcoming)), as well as data on the proportion of Hispanic students in the different schools from the district records, we identified four schools within a three-mile radius area from which to obtain our sample. The survey had two purposes. First, we wanted to identify the sample for the main study in a systematic way. And second, we wanted to obtain a broadly representative picture of language use in the community.

The survey asked for the following information: language used among adults,

---

[3] This claim would of course be limited by the extent to which the sociolinguistic circumstances of language learning, maintenance and loss are related to attitudes and symbolism around language. In the United States, language, and especially Spanish, is charged with political symbolism.

between adults and children and among children in the house; place and date of birth for the mother, father, and all children in the house; age of immigration to the United States for the mother and father. The forms were bilingual and printed on opposite sides of a single legal size paper.

The surveys were distributed with the cooperation of all third-grade teachers in the four schools. All students in these classes with Hispanic surnames were given a survey form to take home to the parents, with instructions to return them the following day. A total of approximately 344 survey forms were distributed, of which 184 (53 per cent) were returned with completed information. About a month later, we sent a second wave of surveys to approximately 158 non-respondents, and received 49 responses. In total, then we received 233 out of an original 344 targeted respondents, for a response rate of 68 per cent. The following results are based on analyses of responses from the first wave of responses.

Grouping by immigration background

In this study, several modifications were made from the Watsonville grouping criteria, as follows:

– Group MM: Born in Mexico; parents born in Mexico.
– Group MU/A: Born in USA; parents born in Mexico, mother immigrated at age 15 or older.
– Group MU/C: Born in USA; parents born in Mexico, mother immigrated at age 10 or younger.
– Group UU: Born in USA; at least one parent born in USA.

Reported language use in the home is broken down by the Groups and appears in Figure 4. There are two notable features in the data. First, as early as by Group MU-A, there is an evident shift among the children towards a preference for English. And second, by Group UU, the shift to preference of English is complete, with both the adults and the children demonstrating a preference for English. This pattern is consistent with our findings from Watsonville, and also consistent with the macro-sociolinguistic picture of language shift among Hispanic students suggested by demographers (e.g., Veltmann, 1983).

Siblings

In the survey, we were encouraged by a small but statistically reliable effect of sibling birth order on reported language use, t (175)=2.41, p = .017. Because this variable could represent the effect of sibling language exposure controlling for fa-

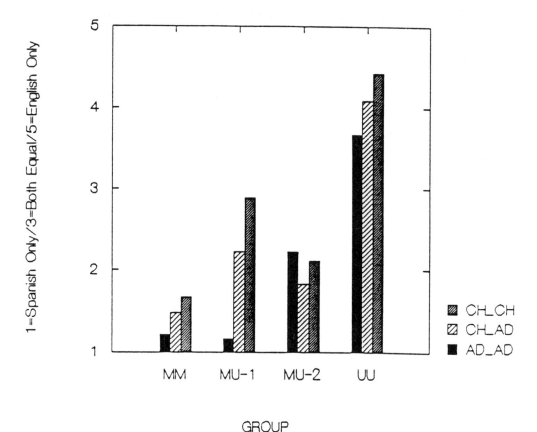

Figure 4. Reported language choice among children (CH-CH), between children and adults (CH-AD), and among adults (AD-AD) for the four different Groups.

mily, we decided to incorporate it into our sampling frame. In our sampling, we have been selecting our sample in pairs of siblings, which consist of a target child, and the sibling counterpart. The target sample will all be in the third grade, and on average be eight years old; the sibling counterparts will vary. In half of our cases, the target child is the first born, and therefore the sibling counterparts is younger. In the other half, the target child is the second born, and therefore the sibling counterparts is older. Additionally, we have constrained the sampling such that the chronological separation in each pair will be less than three years.

We can then pursue two kinds of comparisons. First, there will be a straightforward independent-samples comparison between the target first born and target second born children. The next set of comparisons will involve waiting for our subjects to mature chronologically until they can be compared with their own sibling. Thus, for the target children who are first born, we will wait until their younger sibling counterpart reaches the same age as when they (the target children) were assessed, and then they (the younger sibling counterpart) will be assessed, and the pairs will be compared. In this comparison, the pairs will be on average 8 years old. For the target children who are second born, we will immediately assess their first-born sibling counterpart, and then wait for the target children to reach the same age as the sibling counterparts, at which time they will be assessed again. In this comparison, the pairs will be on average 10 years old. We believe that this method will provide an accurate assessment of the effect of birth order on language maintenance and shift.

Sampling for the main study

Broadly speaking, we based our data collection strategy upon two distinctions. The first is a distinction between language proficiency and language choice, as was illustrated earlier with the Watsonville data. The second distinction in our data collection process is one between bilingual performance/behaviour and bilingual knowledge/awareness.

We find it useful to cross these two distinctions as illustrated in the following table:

Table 3. Summary of data collection strategy.

	observation/ behaviour	self-report/ awareness
language proficiency	1	2
language choice	3	4

Our most systematic data collection is concentrated in Cells 1, 2, and 4.

Language proficiency/behaviour (Cell 1)

We decided to utilize both standardized language proficiency measures as well as somewhat more naturalistic elicited narratives. While neither of us are great fans of standardized language tests, we felt it necessary in order to establish comparability with other studies. For this measure, we decided on the English and Spanish versions of the Peabody Picture Vocabulary Test, which measures receptive vocabulary. There were several reasons for our choice. First, it is available in both languages in comparable form. Second, the technical manual was satisfactory. Third, it provides a wide range of possible scores since it is appropriate from ages 3 to adulthood. And fourth, it is easy to administer. Our previous experience suggests that receptive vocabulary correlates well with other types of standardized language proficiency measures.

The elicited narratives task was more engaging and involved. We introduced children to a board on which two Ninja turtles were mounted. When the child would speak to one of the turtles, the other turtle (via a sound-activated motor) would rock back and forth. Once the child became comfortable with the setup, s/he was told that the turtle (Michelangelo) had many friends in Mexico, and that they are always curious about children in the United States, in Eastside, and in their school. A green canister was then introduced, and s/he was told that the task now was to make a tape recording of some stories to put in the can and send to Michelangelo's friends in Mexico. To make it more realistic as well as entertaining, we took a polaroid picture of the child, watched it develop, and placed it in the canister.

Four Spanish prompts and one English prompt were used to elicit narratives. The Spanish prompts consisted of an autobiography, a narrative of a book about a bear, a narrative about a magnitude 7.1 earthquake that occurred in October, 1989 (or if they were not here for that exciting event, a story about the most scary thing that happened to them), and a description of a surrealistic picture of a floating bed (taken from a book by Chris van Allsburg). In the English narrative, we asked them to tell a story from a book about a mouse.

One of the reasons we chose narratives was because they would by necessity contain references to the past. Silva-Corvalán (1989) has documented temporal reference as a major feature in the shift in east Los Angeles Mexican Spanish. Thus, reference to the past is a major part of our structural analysis. We will also be looking for other grammatical and narrative features, as well as conducting analyses of lexical variety and overall proficiency.

Language proficiency/awareness (Cell 2)

An interview was constructed to assess how much the children knew about their own bilingual proficiency, and also how well they could reason and talk about specific linguistic contrasts between English and Spanish. We begin by asking them to estimate the number of words that they know in English and in Spanish. (To stimulate this, they are shown a head of a popular movie monster character, Beetlejuice, containing yellow and white ping pong balls, with English words written on the yellow and Spanish on the white balls.) They are then introduced to a game in which they are asked to think of as many words as possible that are appropriate translations of an English word. For example, starting with the word CRY, they might come up with LLORAR and GRITAR, and then from GRITAR, they would come up with SHOUT and YELL. This warm-up is intended to help them think about connections between English and Spanish.

They are then given a series of word and sentence translation tasks targeting specific English to Spanish translations in which Spanish makes finer distinctions. These include FISH = PEZ (a live fish), PESCADO (fish to be eaten); WAS = FUE (expressing temporary state), ERA (expressing enduring state); YOU = TÚ (familiar), USTED (formal); PLAYED = JUGÓ (preterite), JUGABA (imperfect). The children are asked to reason about the appropriateness of the translations.

Choice/behaviour (Cell 3)

We will not be observing the language choices of all of our subjects explicitly. However, we are obtaining estimates of their choice from their parents as well as their teachers to validate the self-reports obtained from the children. Further, we are conducting systematic observations of six subjects targeted for intensive study in both the classrooms and homes.

Choice/awareness (Cell 4)

This interview is structured to address the following questions:
- What languages do children use with their everyday interlocutors at home and school?
- What sorts of macro- and micro-sociolinguistic factors are related to their language choices?
- What kinds of attributions do children make about their language choices? What do they feel motivates their language choices with their different interlocutors at home and school?
- What sorts of attitudes do the children have towards bilingualism?
- Do they prefer one language over the other? Why?
- Do they feel that one language is more important than another? Why?

The format of the interview is quite straightforward, with the first half concentrating on language choice, and the second half on language attitudes.

Parents

The parent (usually the mother) of each subject is being interviewed. The following questions guide our interview:
- What language do parents and their children use at home?
- What factors do parents feel influence these choices?
- Do parents have a theory about bilingualism for their children?
- What is the nature of their theory?
- Do they feel that bilingualism will benefit their children?
- Are they committed to the maintenance of bilingualism in their children? Why?
- Do they feel that there is a trade-off between native-language maintenance and second language acquisition?
- Who do they feel should be responsible for their children's development of their native language?
- Who do they feel should be responsible for their children's development of their English?
- What should be the nature of this responsibility?
- Where do these theories come from?

- Have schools and teachers influenced the development of these theories? How?
- Have community and family members influenced the development of these theories? How?
- Have parents' own life experiences contributed to these theories?
- Are parents' theories consistent with the way in which they use language with their children?
- Do parents consciously act to influence the language choices and language development of their children? How?

Preliminary results

Due to the preliminary nature of our data collection and analysis efforts, the following results should still be seen as tentative at best. Our best single measure at this point for English and Spanish proficiency remains the PPVT scores, for example, and we are still in the process of validating these scores against the other interview measures. In addition, we are just beginning an exhaustive content analysis of the text data, so at this point, we can only rely on interesting examples without being able to say anything about how they are related to a broader sampling framework. The preliminary conclusions we have are as follows:

- There are increases in English proficiency and decreases in Spanish proficiency across groups. It should be noted that the sample sizes are only adequate for Groups 1 (MM) and 2 (MU/A), but the trends are already evident in the other groups as well. The difference in means between the two groups achieves statistical significance for Spanish ($F[1,32]=5.58$, $p<.05$), but not for English ($F[1,32]=2.09$, $p=.16$). This result is due to the higher variability in English for the MM group, where individual children seem to have attained a higher proficiency in English than in any other group.
- The effect of birth order appears minimal for English and Spanish proficiencies. An analysis of variance reveals a marginal effect of birth order on English proficiency ($F[1,36]=2.05$, $p=.16$) and no effect on Spanish ($F <1$).
- The relationship between Spanish and English proficiency interacts with Group. There is a strong and positive relationship for Group MM, but no relationship for Group MU/A. One interpretation for this differential interlingual dependency is that they are related to the nature of the 'native language' – in the case of the MM group, it is a native language both in the home and the cultural context, while in the MU/A group, it is a native language in the home, but its status is less secure in the larger cultural context (Lambert, 1975). Since English proficiency is primarily an indicator of the learning of academic language skills at school for these groups, the lack of correlation for the MU/A group may signal that variance in native language in this group is not picking up on the more academic uses of Spanish.
- Language choice as reported by both parents and by the children shows a consis-

tent shift toward English, with an almost complete shift to English for the MU/C children.
- There is a birth order effect for language choice, second borns using more English than first borns. This effect is statistically reliable, $F(1,32)=5.03$, $p<.05$.
- Language choice among siblings is correlated with English proficiency, but not with Spanish proficiency. This suggests that language choice is limited by the availability of English, and that once available, shift occurs in choice.
- Both children and their parents successfully predict the child's proficiency in English, but not their proficiency in Spanish. In addition, the children and parents agree with each other in predicting English, but not in predicting Spanish. The data suggest that members of the community monitor proficiency in English, perhaps using feedback such as school success and degree of usage of English as indicators of proficiency. On the other hand, Spanish proficiency may be defined on a more sociolinguistic basis, with passive participation in the speech community being sufficient in some cases for proficiency in Spanish (see Dorian, 1981).

Reasons for language choice

When we ask children to provide a reason for their language choices with their different interlocutors, they usually tell us that the interlocutor's proficiency or choice of language influenced their language choices. However, some children also refer to ethnicity and culture as factors that influence their language choices (e.g., 'Hablo español con él porque es Mexicano', 'Hablamos ingles porque ella es Americana'), thus giving the impression that languages are to a certain extent delineated by people's cultural affiliations. Sometimes though very rarely, this kind of talk leads to more intriguing discussions about the scope of these cultural affiliations. For example, one child felt that the negative attitudes that some Anglo children have toward Mexicanos would be diminished if Anglo children learned Spanish:

> Como dijo la niña, como aquella niña guera, a ella no le importaba los mexicanos, no le importaba ninguno. . . Pero si ella supiera en español y sabía como muchas cosas bonitas que puede aprender uno en el mundo entonces ella no diciera eso de los Mexicanos.
> [Like what that girl said, that Anglo girl. She doesn't care about Mexicans. But if she knew Spanish and knew about many nice things that one can learn about the world, then she wouldn't say that about Mexicans.]

Attitudes towards bilingualism and native language maintenance

During our interviews children and parents across immigration groups voiced very positive attitudes toward bilingualism and native language maintenance. As they see it, bilingualism will lead to economic security in this country and in Mexico, the ability to communicate and interact with a wide range of people, and access to knowledge sources both inside and outside of their immediate community. Many parents describe the immediate advantages of having a child who is bilingual as having someone who can help them communicate with monolingual English speakers. Moreover, our interviews reveal that parents are committed to the maintenance of Spanish and advocate its use to varying degrees in their homes. Most are confident that their children will not lose Spanish though they can provide examples of other children who are no longer proficient in Spanish or who no longer want to use Spanish. Interestingly enough, the one parent who feels that her child is losing her ability to speak Spanish also tells about how the school has influenced language choice patterns in her home:

> Mi esposo habla inglés con lon niños ahora porque las maestras le han dicho a él que tiene que ayudarlos para que no atrasen en su ciclo escolar. Cuando los niños no entienden bien no pueden aprender. Entonces le decía la maestra que le hablara más a él en inglés y para las tareas.
> [My husband speaks English with the children now because the teachers told him that he has to help them so that they don't fall behind in school. When children don't understand well they can't learn. So the teacher told him to speak with him (their son) in English and when helping him with homework.]

When asked to consider how they would feel if they had a child who no longer spoke Spanish, many parents display strong emotional reactions that reveal the depth of their commitment to their Mexican roots and, in some cases, the difficulties that they have had adjusting to life in the US. For example, Mrs. Carroza spoke about how the loss of Spanish on the part of her children or their refusal to use it would eliminate her hope that they return to Mexico or maintain ties with her family.

> Pues sería dificil en mi familia si ellos agarran el inglés ajeno y olvidar el español. Será dificil en mi familia . . . Tal vez pasará porque cuando yo les digo . . . cuando ustedes estan grandes yo voy a regresar a mi pais. Luego me dicen, 'Te vas a ir tú mamá porque nosotras no nos vamos.' Es dificil porque ellas se criaron en otro ambiente y no quieren regresar.
> [Well it would be difficult in my family if they learn English and forget Spanish. It would be difficult in my family . . . Perhaps it will happen because when I tell them ,'When you are grown I'm going to go back to my country.' They tell me, 'you're going to go (alone) mama because we aren't' going.' It's difficult because they were raised in another environment and don't want to return.]

Despite their commitment to Spanish at home, parents do not agree about the role of Spanish in the school. Most are grateful to have their children enroled in bilingual classes where teachers use Spanish when giving directions and explanations. One parent expressed the less common opinion that Latino children should have access to Spanish instruction throughout their elementary school careers to combat the loss of that language. As she reasoned:

> El inglés lo van a ir aprendiendo. Me preocupa más el español – que se les olvide. O sea que lo practican bien en escritura, en dictado, y en lectura porque cuando pasan a quinto, sexto grado casi no le van a dejar en español. Entonces yo quiero que adquieran muy buenas bases en español como están haciendo allí (at school).
> [Here they'll learn English. I'm more worried about Spanish – that they don't forget it. That is, that they practice writing, dictation and reading because when they go on to fifth, sixth grade there won't be much Spanish (in school). So I want them to acquire a strong foundation in Spanish like they're doing there (at school).]

Some parents worry that the use of Spanish in the classroom will jeopardize their children's acquisition of English. Others worry about the education their children are receiving in the bilingual programs and bilingual schools that they attend. They are concerned that their children are being taught by teachers who are, in most cases, non-native speakers of Spanish and who aren't proficient in that language or, to use their words, speak 'un español mocho'. These parents would rather have their children's Anglo teachers use English and not Spanish, a language that they feel teachers should speak well or not at all. Some parents feel that they, not their children's Anglo teachers, should be responsible for making sure that their children maintain Spanish. For them, schools should be places where teachers use English to instruct students in the various content areas.

Overall, these findings are consistent with the attitudinal data toward language and schooling obtained from Mexican-American (and other ethnic minority) adults in the Detroit area (Lambert & Taylor, 1990), who find strong support for the maintenance of home language and culture, but some hesitation when it comes to the role to be played by the schools.

Conclusions

The model of language shift suggested by the Watsonville and Eastside studies might be forwarded as a set of propositions to be tested against future analyses and new studies:

- The community's loss of individuals with Spanish proficiency is due to the incomplete acquisition of the language or to the acquisition of a contact variety (or some combination of these two), rather than to an individual's loss of profi-

ciency during the course of his/her lifetime.
- Proficient Spanish speakers' shift from Spanish to English is principally a sociolinguistic phenomenon. Having once attained adult-like levels of proficiency in Spanish, individuals who use mostly or exclusively English in all domains may not experience subsequent loss of Spanish proficiency.
- Incomplete acquisition results from the sociolinguistic rather than the psycholinguistic circumstances of the home. That is to say, even though the parents may be proficient in Spanish, once they acquire proficiency in English and start to use English in the home, the children are unlikely to develop proficiency in Spanish. This model is something like an irreversible seepage model of English proficiency, and predicts that once English proficiency is established, there is a strong tendency to use it, and once this happens, there is minimal learning of Spanish.
- Sociolinguistic variation is attributable to social psychological (language attitude, ethnic identity, etc.) as well as sociological factors (social network, rootedness in the United States, social mobility, etc.). This has both between-group (generation level) as well as within-group variance components.
- Proficiency in English and Spanish have very different meanings for members of the community. English is defined in psycholinguistic terms, while Spanish is defined in sociolinguistic terms.

References

Bahrick, H., 1984. Semantic memory content in permastore: Fifty years of memory for Spanish learned in school. *Journal of Experimental Psychology: General, 113*, 1-29.

Blom, J. & J. Gumperz, 1972. Social meaning in linguistic structures: Code switching in Norway. In J. Gumperz & D. Hymes (eds), *Directions in sociolinguistics*. New York: Holt, Rinehart & Winston.

Cohen, A., 1975. Forgetting a second language. *Language Learning, 25*, 127-138.

Crawford, J., 1992. *Hold your tongue: Bilingualism and the politics of 'English Only'*. Reading, Mass.: Addison Wesley.

Donato, R., 1988. *In Struggle: Mexican-Americans in the Pajaro Valley Schools, 1900-1979*. Unpublished Ph.D. Thesis, Stanford University, 1979.

Dorian, N., 1981. *Language death: The life cycle of a Scottish Gaelic dialect*. Philadelphia: Univ. of Pennsylvania Press.

Epstein, N., 1977. *Language, ethnicity, and the schools: Policy alternatives for bilingual-bicultural education*. Washington, DC: Institute for Educational Leadership.

Fishman, J., V. Nahirny, J. Hofman & R. Hayden, 1966. *Language Loyalty in the United States*. The Hague: Mouton and Company.

Gardner, R., R. Lalonde & J. MacPherson, 1985. Social factors in second language attrition. *Language Learning, 5*, 519-540.

Gumperz, J., 1982. *Discourse strategies.* New York: Cambridge University Press.

Kaufman, D. & M. Aronoff, (forthcoming). Morphological disintegration and reconstruction in first language attrition. In H. Seliger & R. Vago (eds), *First language attrition: Structural and theoretical perspectives.* New York and Cambridge: Cambridge University Press.

Lambert, W., 1975. Culture and language as factors in learning and education. In A. Wolfgang (ed.), *Education of immigrant children.* Toronto: Ontario Institute for Studies in Education.

Lambert, W. & D. Taylor, 1990. *Coping with cultural and racial diversity in urban America.* New York: Praeger.

Lett, J. & F. O'Mara, (forthcoming). Predictors of success in an intensive foreign language learning context: Models of language learning at the Defense Language Institute Foreign Language Center. To be published by the Center for Applied Linguistics, Washington, DC.

Lopez, D., 1978. Chicano language loyalty in an urban setting. *Sociology and Social Research,* 62, 267-278.

Mallory, G., 1971. *Sociolinguistic considerations for bilingual education in an Albuquerque community undergoing language shift.* LC3733.A6M2 1971a: Green Stacks.

Merino, B., 1983. Language loss in bilingual Chicano children. *Journal of Applied Developmental Psychology,* 4, 277-294.

Nicolau, S. & R. Valdivieso, 1992. The Veltman Report: What it says, what it means. Introduction to C. Veltman, *The future of the Spanish language in the United States.* New York: Hispanic Policy Development Project. Reprinted in: J. Crawford (ed.), *Language loyalties: A source book on the official English controversy.* Chicago: University of Chicago Press.

Ortiz, L., 1975. *A sociolinguistic study of language maintenance in the northern New Mexico community of Arroyo Seco.* P115.5.N5077 1983: Green Stacks.

Silva-Corvalán, C., 1989. Subject expression and placement in Mexican-American Spanish. In: J. Amastae & L. Elías-Olivares (eds), *Spanish in the United States: Sociolinguistic aspects.* Cambridge: Cambridge University Press.

Smith, M., 1983. On first language loss in the second language acquirer: Problems of Transfer. In: S. Gass & L. Selinker (eds), *Language Transfer and Language Learning.* Rowley, MA: Newbury House.

Vasquez, Pease-Alvarez & Shannon, forthcoming.

Veltman, C., 1983. *Language shift in the United States.* New York: Mouton.

Veltman, C., 1988. *The Future of the Spanish Language in the United States.* Hispanic Policy Development Project: New York City and Washington, DC.

Weltens, B., K. de Bot & T. van Els (eds), 1986. *Language Attrition in Progress.* Providence, RI: Foris Publications.

Weltens, B., T. van Els & E. Schils, 1989. The long-term retention of French by Dutch students. *Studies in Second Language Acquisition,* 11, 205-216.

Wilkinson, Leland. *SYGRAPH.* Evanston, Illinois: SYSTAT, INC. 1988.

Jeroen Aarssen, Petra Bos and Ludo Verhoeven

Turkish and Moroccan children in the Netherlands: acquisition of complex syntax in a first and second language

Language development in children at school age can be characterized by a growing command of discourse. Gradually, developmental shifts take place from intra- to intersentential devices, from basic structures to additional functions and from extra- to intralinguistic abilities. With respect to bilingual development at school age, it is still unclear what sort of operating principles children use. It is also unclear under what conditions processes of language transfer occur. Moreover, the studies that have been conducted so far were limited in their scope, given the fact that the languages under consideration were highly related (cf. Grosjean, 1982; McLaughlin, 1985). The analysis of children's data in two typologically unrelated languages will give new perspectives on the role of structural properties of these languages in the process of acquisition. In this paper some preliminary data of a research project on first and second language acquisition by ethnic minority groups in the Netherlands will be presented[1]. The proposed research project aims at a scientific interpretation of the narrative development among Dutch, Turkish and Moroccan children in the Netherlands at school age. For an overview of the project see Verhoeven (1993). In the present paper two linguistic domains will be explored: anaphoric reference and relativization.

In the domain of anaphoric reference the developmental patterns of bound and free anaphora in the children's first and second language will be compared. The distinction between the two types of anaphora refers back to different principles in the standard binding theory of Chomsky (1981). In a variety of studies the acquisition of lexical anaphors and pronouns have been studied in languages such as English and Dutch. With respect to bound anaphors, a fast pattern of acquisition could be evidenced, while the development of free anaphor resolution showed a much more irregular and delayed development. However, the outcomes of studies referring to languages that are typologically very different from English seem to challenge Chomsky's claims. More recently, the acquisition of anaphoric reference

[1] This research is supported by the Foundation for Linguistic Research, which is funded by the Netherlands organization for research, NWO. We thank Hayat El Koun and Fazilet Okuducu for their assistance in collecting the data.

was explored in a bilingual context. On the basis of empirical data on L2 acquisition of anaphora among Japanese and Spanish learners of English, Flynn (1987) concluded a primacy of the head-initial/head-final parameter's role. In the present study the acquisition of anaphoric reference in Turkish and Moroccan children in L1 and L2 will be studied by means of a series of experiments. The experimental set-up involves a one sentence/four pictures multiple choice task that is similar to the one used by Deutsch, Koster & Koster (1986).

The second domain under consideration is relativization. With respect to relativization there is a large body of literature on the processing of relative clauses in various unrelated languages. From such reviews as Hakuta (1981), Clancy, Lee & Zoh (1986) and MacWhinney & Pléh (1988) it is clear that several intricately interacting factors determine the processing of relative clauses: (1) the grammatical role played by the head of the relative clause, (2) the use of word order configurations in surface structure, (3) the interruption of processing units, and (4) the use of grammatical markers as cues to processing. From studies across Indo-European languages the general finding is that for children at school age subject-subject sentences are relatively easy, subject-object sentences relatively complex, while object-object and object-subject sentences take an intermediate position. Data on the acquisition of relative clauses in typologically different languages have proved to be rather scarce: Hakuta (1981) on Japanese, Clancy, Lee & Zoh (1986) on Japanese, Korean and English, Slobin (1986) on Turkish and English, and MacWhinney & Pléh on Hungarian (1988). The attempts so far to relate typological differences to sentence processing difficulties underscore the need for cross-linguistic studies on the acquisition of relative clauses. In the present study the acquisition of relative clauses in Turkish, Moroccan Arabic and Dutch will be examined in bilingual subjects at school age level. It will be determined in what order the various types of grammatical relations in relative clauses are acquired and which determining factors do account for difficulty in the processing of relative clauses in the three languages.

Design of the study

Informants

The present study has a pseudolongitudinal design, based on first and second language data collection with groups of 45 Turkish, 45 Moroccan and 45 Dutch children of 8 years old. For the sake of control only informants have been selected with parents of a low socio-economic and educational level. All Turkish and Moroccan children visit a Dutch primary school and have been living in the Netherlands for at least two years. A total of 20 schools participates in the project. Most of these schools have a high percentage of L2-learners of Dutch, mainly Turks and Moroccans. The Turkish children come from families in which Turkish is the preferred language, the Moroccan children originate from primarily Moroccan Arabic-speaking families. The minority children in the present project belong to a third generation of immigrants who initially moved from rural sites in Turkey and Morocco to industrialized areas in the Netherlands.

Instruments

The anaphoric reference task consists of 24 short sentences, either with a bound, reflexive anaphor or with a free, non-reflexive anaphor. The test sentences each contain one of these six verbs: (the Dutch, Turkish, and Moroccan Arabic equivalents of) *to wash, to scratch, to defend, to pinch, to tie up* and *to release*. Two friends, named *Martijn* (a typically Dutch boy's name) and *Karim* (a Turkish/ Moroccan boy's name), served as potential antecedents for the anaphoric pronouns. Thus, three factors were varied in the test sentences:

(1) type of anaphor, 3rd person singular masculine:

	Dutch	Turkish	Moroccan Arabic	English
reflexive	zich	kendini reflexive suffix	raṣu	himself
pronoun	hem	onu	-u	him

Turkish has two types of reflexives. First there is the reflexive suffix -(İ)n-, which can be placed after the stem of the verb. The verb *yıkamak* means *to wash (someone or something)* and *yıkanmak* means *to wash oneself.* A second type is verb + *kendini (himself)* in direct object position.

In Moroccan Arabic the noun *ras* (literally: *head)* + possessive suffix indicates a reflexive action (sometimes *nefs* (literally: *soul, spirit)* + possessive suffix). In the case of third person singular masculine this is *raṣu (his head).* Thus, *ka-yerbet ras-u* means *he ties himself up* (literally: *he ties his head up).* The suffix for the direct object third person singular masculine is *-u.* Thus, *ka-yrebt-u* means *he ties him up.*

(2) verbs:

Dutch	Turkish	Moroccan Arabic	English
wassen	yıka(n)mak	ka-yeġsel	to wash
krabben	kaşı(n)mak	ka-yxebbeš	to scratch
verdedigen	koru(n)mak	ka-ydafeᶜ ᶜla	to defend
knijpen	çimdiklemek	ka-yeqreṣ	to pinch
vastbinden	bağlamak	ka-yerbet	to tie up
bevrijden	kurtarmak	ka-yfekk	to release

In Moroccan Arabic the durative aspect of the verb is characterized by prefixing the particle *ka-* (sometimes *-ta*) to the imperfect tense of the verb. The prefix for the third person singular masculine imperfect tense is *y-*. *ᶜla* is a preposition meaning *on, upon, over, against, to, about*, etc. and stands in collocation with *ka-ydafeᶜ* in order to express the meaning *to defend*.

(3) antecedents: *Martijn* and *Karim*. Each test sentence contains a proper noun (Martijn or Karim) and the relationship term *de vriend van* (*the friend of*). In Turkish the noun *arkadaş* is used and in Moroccan Arabic *saheb*.

(i) and (ii) are examples of test sentences that are being used in the experiment.

(i)	Dutch:	de vriend van Karim knijpt zich
	Turkish:	Karim'in arkadaşı kendini çimdikliyor
	Moroccan Arabic:	saheb Karim ka-yeqres rasu
	English:	the friend of Karim pinches himself
(ii)	Dutch:	de vriend van Karim knijpt hem
	Turkish:	Karim'in arkadaşı onu çimdikliyor
	Moroccan Arabic:	saheb Karim ka-yqersu
	English:	the friend of Karim pinches him

Four pictures are assigned to each sentence. The task is administered to the child in two languages (in different sessions): either Turkish and Dutch or Moroccan Arabic and Dutch. The interviewer (native speaker of the language in question) reads aloud the test sentence and the child is asked to point to the picture that matches the sentence. Only one of the four pictures shows the situation described in the test sentence. The other three pictures show actions that differ systematically from the 'right' picture: one shows the right actor but the wrong action (anaphoric error), another one shows the wrong actor but the right action (antecedent error) and the third one shows the wrong actor and the wrong action (anaphoric and antecedent error).

The relativization task has also been administered in the first language of the children as well as in Dutch and by native speakers of the languages in question. In each of the three languages 32 relative clauses were constructed, involving several nouns as actors and several action verbs. The nouns were all animals:

Dutch	Turkish	Moroccan Arabic	English
beer	ayı	debb	bear
leeuw	arslan	sbeᶜ	lion
aap	maymun	qerd	monkey
poes	kedi	mišš	cat
hond	köpek	kelb	dog
muis	fare	far	mouse

The verbs were four different action verbs:

Dutch	Turkish	Moroccan Arabic	English
slaan	dövmek	ka-yedreb	to hit
aaien	okşamak	ka-yemseh	to stroke
kussen	öpmek	ka-ybus	to kiss
knijpen	çimdiklemek	ka-yeqres	to squeeze

There are four logically possible sentence types: SS, SO, OS and OO (where the first letter refers to the grammatical role (**S**ubject or **O**bject) of the complex noun in the main clause, and the second letter refers to the role of the head noun within the relative clause). For example, in the English SS-sentence in (iii) *the bear* is both subject of the main clause and of the relative clause. In (iv) *the bear* is subject of the main clause and object of the relative clause. In (v) *the lion* is object of the main clause and subject of the relative clause. In (vi) *the lion* is object of both clauses.

(iii)   SS   the bear that kisses the monkey, strokes the lion
main clause   [S   V   O]
relative clause   [S   V   O   ]

(iv)   SO   the bear that the monkey kisses, strokes the lion
main clause   [S   V   O]
relative clause   [O   S   V   ]

(v)   OS   the bear strokes the lion that kisses the monkey
main clause   [S   V   O   ]
relative clause   [S   V   O   ]

(vi)   OO   the bear strokes the lion that the monkey kisses
main clause   [S   V   O   ]
relative clause   [O   S   V   ]

In Dutch relative clauses a postnominal pronoun precedes the verb and only one word order occurs: SVO. A problem arises in SO and OO sentences where use of agreement is required to avoid ambiguity:

SS   de beren die de aap kussen, aaien de leeuw
      the bears that kiss the monkey, stroke the lion
SO   de beren die de aap kust, aaien de leeuw
      the bears that the monkey kisses, stroke the lion
OS   de beer aait de leeuwen die de aap kussen
      the bear strokes the lions that kiss the monkey

Jeroen Aarssen, Petra Bos and Ludo Verhoeven   169

OO   de beer aait de leeuwen die de aap kust
the bear strokes the lions that the monkey kisses

Turkish relative clauses are prenominal. Two suffixes can be attached to the verb stem to make non-finite verb forms: (1) -An (present participle) to make SS and OS sentences, as in:

> ayı-yı / döv-en / maymun
> bear-OBJ / hit-PART / monkey
> *the monkey that hits the bear*

(2) -DİG- (personal or possessed participle) to make SO and OO sentences. The subject is expressed by an obligatory possessive suffix attached to the -DİG-form and an optional preceding noun + genitive case, as in:

> ayı-nın / döv-düğ-ü / maymun
> bear-GEN / hit-PART-POSS / monkey
> *the monkey that the bear hits*

In Turkish four types of word order are possible: SOV (being the unmarked word order), SVO, OSV and OVS. Turkish has clear grammatical markers for subject and object to be used as cues in the processing of sentences. In total there are 16 configurations of relative clauses:

SOV SS	ayıyı döven maymun arslanı öpsün
SOV SO	arslanın okşadığı ayı maymunu çimdiklesin
SOV OS	arslan ayıyı okşayan maymunu dövsün
SOV OO	maymun arslanın çimdiklediği ayıyı öpsün
SVO SS	arslanı okşayan ayı çimdiklesin maymunu
SVO SO	maymunun öptüğü arslan dövsün ayıyı
SVO OS	maymun okşasın arslanı öpen ayıyı
SVO OO	ayı çimdiklesin maymunun dövdüğü arslanı
OSV SS	arslanı maymunu çimdikleyen ayı dövsün
OSV SO	ayıyı arslanın okşadığı maymun öpsün
OSV OS	maymunu okşayan ayıyı arslan çimdiklesin
OSV OO	arslan ayıyı okşayan maymunu dövsün
OVS SS	maymunu okşasın ayıyı öpen arslan
OVS SO	arslanı çimdiklesin maymunun dövdüğü ayı
OVS OS	ayıyı döven arslanı öpsün maymun
OVS OO	maymunun çimdiklediği ayıyı okşasın arslan

In Moroccan Arabic, which has postnominal relative clauses, the same four sentence types are possible. Although the unmarked word order in complex sentences (such as relative clauses) in Moroccan Arabic is SVO, OVS word order is also possible, but requires a prestated object and a coreferential pronoun suffixed to the verb (in the main clause):

SVO OS   s-sbe^{c} / ka-yedreb / l-qerd / lli / ka-yemseh / d-debb
         the lion (S) / hits / the monkey (O/S) / that / strokes / the bear (O)
         the lion hits the monkey that strokes the bear

OVS SS   s-sbe^{c}, / ka-yderb-u / l-qerd / lli / ka-yemseh / d-debb
         the lion (O) / hits-him / the monkey (S/S) / that / strokes / the bear (O)
         the monkey that strokes the bear hits the lion

In order to construct SO and OO sentences (either in SVO or in OVS word order) a prestated object and a coreferential pronoun suffixed to the verb are required in the relative clause. This leads to 8 configurations of relative clauses:

SVO SS   d-debb lli ka-ybus l-qerd, ka-yemseh s-sbe^{c}
SVO SO   s-sbe^{c} lli ka-ybus-u l-qerd, ka-yedreb d-debb
SVO OS   s-sbe^{c} ka-yedreb l-qerd lli ka-yemseh d-debb
SVO OO   d-debb ka-yeqres s-sbe^{c} lli ka-yderb-u l-qerd

OVS SS   l-qerd, ka-ymesh-u s-sbe^{c} lli ka-ybus d-debb
OVS SO   d-debb, ka-ybus-u l-qerd lli ka-ymesh-u s-sbe^{c}
OVS OS   d-debb lli ka-yemseh l-qerd, ka-yqers-u s-sbe^{c}
OVS OO   s-sbe^{c} lli ka-ybus-u l-qerd, ka-ymesh-u d-debb

For each sentence the child is asked to act out the action with toy animals. The interviewer writes down the actions performed by the child.

Procedure

The experimental tasks for anaphora and relativization were administered by a researcher in a separate room in the school in two sessions with an interval of at least one week. Half of the anaphora task and half of the relativization task were administered in the first session and the other two halves in the second session.

     Afterwards, the subscores on the two tasks which were distinguished in advance were computed. The question was whether the different types of subscores do indeed represent different levels of difficulty. In order to test temporal and structural aspects of the acquisition of anaphora and relativization in a bilingual context, for the Turkish and Moroccan group separate multivariate analyses of variance on the mean number of correct subscores of each informant were conducted. The within-subject factors were language and type of subscore. On the anaphora task, the latter factor concerned the distinction between principle A and principle B sentences. On the relativization task, this factor referred to the distinction between subject-subject, subject-object, object-subject and object-object sentences.

For the Dutch versions of the tasks, a relevant question was whether the order of difficulty of subscores on each task is similar for each ethnic group. To test these assumptions, for each task a two-way analysis of variance was computed on the mean number of correct subscores of each informant. The between-subjects factor was ethnic group, and the within-subject factor was type of subscore.

Results

Anaphoric reference

The means and standard deviations for the subscores on the anaphora task in both L1 and L2 are given in Table 1. It can be seen that for the two minority languages the scores on principle A items tend to be higher than on principle B items. For the Dutch language, there appears to be no uniform pattern. The mean subscores on the anaphora task (principle A vs. principle B) for Turkish, Moroccan and Dutch children are graphically displayed in Figure 1, 2 and 3 respectively.

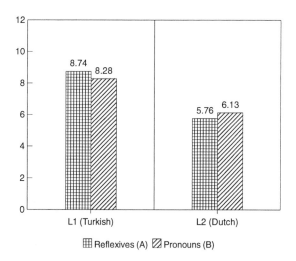

Figure 1. Mean subscores on the anaphora task for Turkish children.

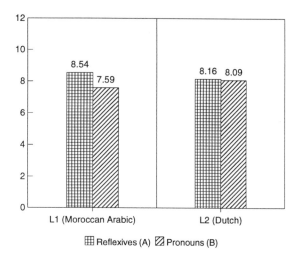

Figure 2. Mean subscores on the anaphora task for Moroccan children.

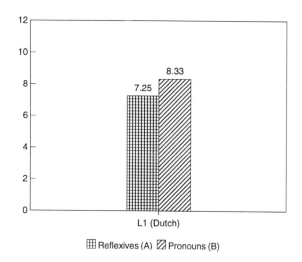

Figure 3. Mean subscores on the anaphora task for Dutch children.

Table 1. Means and standard deviations for the subscores on the anaphora task: principle A vs. principle B

	Minority language				Dutch			
	A		B		A		B	
	Mean	Sd	Mean	Sd	Mean	Sd	Mean	Sd
Turks	8.74	2.13	8.28	2.59	5.65	3.27	6.21	2.89
Moroccans	8.54	2.74	7.59	2.73	8.16	2.96	8.09	2.26
Dutch	–	–	–	–	7.25	3.64	8.33	2.57

Multivariate analysis of variance was conducted with Ethnic Group (Turkish vs. Moroccan), Principle (A vs. B) and Language (L1 vs. L2) as factors. The Group factor turned out to be significant ($F(85,1)=4.39$, $p<.05$), indicating that Moroccan children generally obtained higher scores than Turkish children. The factor of Language was also significant ($F(85,1)=26.89$, $p<.001$), as was the Group by Language interaction ($F(85,1)=29.37$, $p<.001$). The factor of Principle was not significant, nor was the interaction between Principle and Group.
However, there was a significant interaction between Principle and Language ($F(85,1)=5.68$, $p<.05$). The latter results seem to indicate that the scores on principle A items tend to be higher than on principle B items, in the first language.

Separate multivariate analyses of variance for Turkish and Moroccan children were carried out with the factors Principle and Language. For the Turkish children Language was a significant factor ($F(42,1)=48.05$, $p<.001$), but the factor of Principle was not significant. Some, though not significant, interaction between Principle and Language was found. For the Moroccan children the only significant factor was Language ($F(43,1)=145.53$, $p<.001$).

Multivariate analysis of variance was also conducted on the minority languages with Principle and Group as factors. A significant effect was found for Principle ($F(85,1)=6.53$, $p<.05$).

Another multivariate analysis of variance was conducted on the Dutch language subscores with Ethnic Group (Turkish vs. Moroccan vs. Dutch) and Principle (A vs. B) as main factors. A significant effect was found for Ethnic Group ($F(136,2)=11.61$, $p<.001$), showing that Moroccan and Dutch children obtained higher scores than their Turkish peers. No significant effect was found for Principle, nor for the interaction between Principle and Ethnic Group. Thus, we may conclude that there is no principle effect in anaphoric reference in Dutch as a first and second language.

Relativization

Table 2 presents the means and standard deviations for the subscores of Turkish and Moroccan children on the relativization task in L1. It can be seen that the scores for Turkish tend to be much higher than those for Moroccan Arabic.

Table 2. Means and standard deviations for the subscores of Turkish and Moroccan children on the L1 version of the relativization task.

| | SS | | SO | | OS | | OO | |
	Mean	Sd	Mean	Sd	Mean	Sd	Mean	Sd
Turks	5.05	1.79	5.30	1.21	4.88	1.98	5.12	1.72
Moroccans	3.21	1.88	1.58	1.38	3.42	1.58	1.61	1.50

In Table 3 the means and standard deviations for the subscores of Turkish, Moroccan and Dutch children on the Dutch version of the relativization task are given. It can be seen that the subscore patterns are highly comparable, while in general the scores for the Turkish children are somewhat lower than those for the other ethnic groups. In Figures 4, 5 and 6 the mean subscores on the relativization task are graphically displayed.

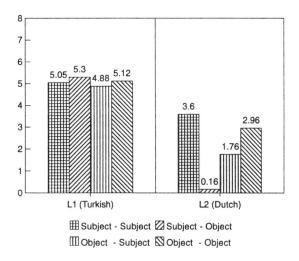

Figure 4. Mean subscores on the relativization task for Turkish children.

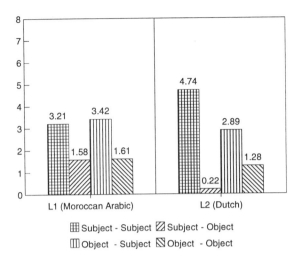

Figure 5. Mean subscores on the relativization task for Moroccan children.

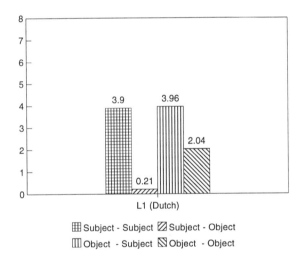

Figure 6. Mean subscores on the relativization task for Dutch children.

Table 3. Means and standard deviations for the subscores of Turkish, Moroccan and Dutch children on the Dutch version of the relativization task.

	SS		SO		OS		OO	
	Mean	Sd	Mean	Sd	Mean	Sd	Mean	Sd
Turks	3.60	2.83	.16	.37	1.76	2.22	2.96	2.79
Moroccans	4.74	2.92	.22	.47	2.89	2.88	1.28	1.75
Dutch	3.90	3.16	.21	.50	3.96	2.93	2.04	2.64

Separate multivariate analyses were carried out with Sentence Type (SS vs SO vs OS vs OO), Order (SOV vs SVO vs OSV vs OVS for Turkish and SVO vs OVS for Moroccan Arabic) and Language (L1 vs L2) as main factors, in order to test the differences in L1 and L2 subscores for Turkish and Moroccan children. For the Turkish group there was a significant effect for Sentence Type (F(126,3)=8.22, p<.001), Language (F(42,1)=254,61 p<.001) and for the interaction between Language and Sentence Type (F(126,3)=27.56, p<.001). For the Moroccan group there was no significant effect for Language. However, the effect of Sentence Type (F(126,3)=32.56, p<.001) and the interaction between Language and Sentence Type were significant (F(126,3)=16.38, p<.001).

Two additional multivariate analyses of variance were conducted with Sentence Type and Order. For the Turkish group the effect of Order turned out to be significant (F(126,3)=4.27, p<.01), while the effect of Sentence Type was not significant. However, the interaction between Sentence Type and Order was significant (F(378,9)=9.98, p<.001). For the Moroccan group both the effect of Sentence Type (F(126,3)=21.24, p<.001) and Order (F(42,1)=27,67, p<.001), as well as the interaction between the two factors (F(126,3)=14.94, p<.001) turned out to be significant.

Thus, it can be concluded that there is a striking effect of order in L1 for both ethnic groups. With respect to sentence type there is only a significant effect for Moroccan Arabic.

Another multivariate analysis of variance was conducted on the Dutch data with Ethnic Group (Turkish vs Moroccan vs Dutch) and Sentence Type as main factors. A significant effect was found for Group (F(136,2)=3.43, p<.05), Sentence Type (F(408,3)=55.27, p<.001) and the interaction between Group and Sentence Type (F(408,6)=4.82, p<.001). However, from Figure 2 it can be seen that the patterns of subscore types for Moroccan and Dutch children are highly similar, while the only deviation for the Turkish group is a relatively high correct score for OO-sentences.

Conclusions

Dutch data

A preliminary analysis of the results on the experimental tasks involving the understanding of anaphora and the processing of relative clauses shows that Turkish and Moroccan children do not fall behind their monolingual Dutch peers. It seems that the pace of development of receptive skills in complex syntax of Dutch is more or less similar in first and second language learners.

From a structural point of view there was evidence that the two groups of L2-learners rely on highly comparable intralingual strategies. With respect to anaphora there was no significant difference in scores on items with free anaphora vs items with bound anaphora. The same result was found in the Dutch children. This is contrary to what Deutsch, Koster and Koster (1986) found. In 6-year-old Dutch monolingual children they found no significant effect for type of anaphora, but they did find a significant effect in the 8-year-olds. A possible explanation for this difference could be that the Dutch children in our project come from lower-class families and seem to lag behind in their development of the comprehension of the reflexive anaphor *zich*.

As regards relativization, it was found that for all children subject-subject sentences were relatively easy, subject-object sentences relatively complex, object-object and object-subject sentences taking an intermediate position. This finding corresponds with findings from earlier studies across Indo-European languages.

Turkish and Moroccan Arabic data

The proficiency scores of Turkish and Moroccan children on both anaphora and relativization tasks turned out to be higher in L1 than in L2. For anaphora, it was found that the understanding of principle A was not easier than the understanding of principle B in both Turkish and Moroccan Arabic. For relativization, no substantial difference in scores on the four types of sentences was evidenced in Turkish. All patterns turned out to be relatively easy. This finding can be explained from the fact that the nonfinite verb forms used to relativize nouns in Turkish are highly transparent. The effect for word order turned out to be significant. In Moroccan Arabic subject-subject sentences and object-subject sentences turned out to be relatively easy, subject-object sentences and object-object sentences relatively difficult. This can be explained from the fact that subject-object and object-object sentences require use of the prestated object and the coreferential pronoun in the relative clause. The unmarked word order (SVO) turned out to be significantly easier than the marked word order (OVS). This can be explained from the fact that in the OVS word order use of the prestated object and the coreferential pronoun is required in the main clause.

The results of the present study furnish new insights into the process of acquisition of complex syntax. For the linguistic domains of anaphora and relativization there is clear evidence that there is cross-linguistic variation in the patterns of acquisition. For such unrelated languages as Dutch, Moroccan Arabic and Turkish both universal and particular characteristics in the understanding of anaphora and relativization could be evidenced. Moreover, it is shown that the strategies first and second language learners use in understanding complex syntax are highly comparable. In a follow-up study we will elaborate the present study in two ways. First of all, the present groups of informants will be tested at three additional moments with intervals of one year. Moreover, a second cohort of 4-year-old informants of the same ethnic origin will be tested over four moments, again with one-year intervals.

References

Chomsky, N., 1981. *Lectures on Government and Binding.* Dordrecht: Foris.

Clancy, P., H. Lee & M. Zoh, 1986. Processing strategies in the acquisition of relative clauses: Universal principles and language specific realizations. *Cognition,* 24, 225-262.

Deutsch, W., C. Koster & J. Koster, 1986. What can we learn from children's errors in understanding anaphora? *Linguistics,* 24, 203-225.

Flynn, S., 1987. *A Parameter-Setting Model of L2 Acquisition.* Dordrecht: Reidel.

Grosjean, F., 1982. *Life with two languages.* Cambridge: Harvard University Press.

Hakuta, K., 1981. Grammatical description versus configurational arrangement in language acquisition. *Cognition,* 9, 197-236.

MacWhinney, B. & C. Pléh, 1988. Relative clauses in Hungarian. *Cognition,* 29, 95-141.

McLaughlin, B., 1985. *Second Language Acquisition in Childhood.* Hillsdale, NJ: LEA.

Slobin, D., 1986. The acquisition and use of relative clauses. In: D. Slobin & K. Zimmer (eds), *Studies in Turkish Linguistics.* Amsterdam: Benjamins.

Verhoeven, L., 1993. Acquisition of narrative skills in a bilingual context. In: B. Kettemann & W. Wieden (eds), *Current Issues in European Second Language Acquisition Research.* Tübingen: Gunter Narr Verlag.

Åke Viberg

Bilingual development of school-age students in Sweden

In northwestern Europe, the number of ethnic minority children has been estimated at seven million, a figure which is rapidly growing. The educational needs of these children have attracted an increasing interest in recent years (see the contributions to Eldering & Kloprogge (eds.) 1989). This paper will account for the situation in Sweden focusing on the bilingual development of Finnish children in so-called home-language classes, a type of bilingual education which aims at maintaining the minority language in addition to teaching the second language and in which children are even able to study subject matter in their first language.

Immigrant children in Swedish schools

In 1991, 12% (102 400) of all children in the Swedish compulsory comprehensive school (grade 1-9) had another home language than Swedish (i.e. another language than Swedish was actively used at home). Totally 130 languages were represented but five home languages account for half of the students: Finnish 22%, Spanish 10%, Arabic 8%, Persian 7% and Polish 6%. (Unless otherwise noted, the figures in section 1 apply to the situation in the autumn 1991 and are taken from Statistics Sweden 1992.)

The official goal of the language instruction for immigrant children is 'active bilingualism,' which means that the aim is both to maintain the home language and to acquire a good command of Swedish. In actual practice, however, greater importance is attached to Swedish. For students who are judged to have an inadequate knowledge of Swedish, lessons in Swedish as a second language are compulsory. Totally 72% of the home language students required such instruction and the majority (82%) of these also received it - in general in the form of pull-out instruction from regular Swedish classes. For recently arrived students, special preparatory classes can be temporarily arranged consisting of students with various home languages other than Swedish. In recent years, Arabic and Persian students have dominated in such classes.

Instruction in the home language is regarded as a right but not as an obligation. In 1991, 59% of the students who were entitled to it attended home language instruction. According to the Home Language Reform passed by the Swedish

Parliament in 1976, home language instruction should be adapted to the individual needs of students, but the school authorities to a great extent have stuck to a rule of thumb that says that each student should have two hours of such instruction a week (Municio 1987). Last year (1991), severe cutbacks were effected in the appropiations to home language instruction. Although it is too early to assess the full impact of this, students still receive two hours a week on the average, according to a questionnaire answered by the municipalities responsible for the instruction (Nilsson 1992). What has changed is that the average size of the groups has increased, even if it is still quite small (3,5 students on the average). Earlier, it was quite common that the teachers taught single students in such lessons. Another consequence is that the number of students has decreased, even if the reduction in this respect has been moderate so far (spring 1992). In addition to home language instruction proper, which aims at supporting the language, students can also receive home language study guidance as a support for subject matter education. In conclusion then, the 'typical' immigrant student attends a regular Swedish medium class, receives two hours of home language instruction a week and various amounts of supportive instruction in Swedish as a second language. Even if home language instruction according to the two-hours-a-week model makes a valuable contribution to the maintenance of the home language, it is obvious that the ultimate result will be very variable, to a large extent will depend on factors outside school and, at least for children born in Sweden, will tend to result in a shift towards Swedish as the dominant language.

There is, however, one type of program, the so-called home language class, where all students share another home language than Swedish and where most of the instruction in early grades is given in the home language (including content areas). In early grades, Swedish is used primarily in lessons in Swedish as a second language, but the proportion of instruction in Swedish increases successively so that the proportion is approximately 50% by grade 6. In general, home language classes can only be organized from grade 1 to 6, but for Finnish students such classes can be organized also in grade 7-9 in many municipalities. Home language classes at present exist in eleven languages but the majority has always been in Finnish (around 70% of the classes). Actually, the number of such classes has decreased substantially in recent years (from 600 home language classes in 1981 to 313 in 1991). The major reason is probably a general decrease in the number of Finnish students due to return migration. In 1981, there were 39 000 Finnish students in comprehensive school as opposed to 23 000 in 1991. Even if only a relatively small proportion of the immigrant students (around 4 000 in 1991) attend home language classes, this type of instruction is of particular theoretical interest since it is a clear example of maintenance bilingual education. After a brief theoretical overview in the next section, this paper will describe a study designed to follow the parallel bilingual development of the home language and Swedish in such classes.

Towards a general model of bilingual development at school.

The development of bilingual proficiency in school-age children is the result of a complex interaction of a number of factors. In Figure 1[1], a schematic model is presented showing some of the major groups of factors represented in seven separate boxes. The arrows are meant to indicate the principal direction of the causal relations but this should not be taken as conclusive, since there are obviously weaker or stronger casusal relations between all the 'boxes' (acting in both directions but with various strengths).

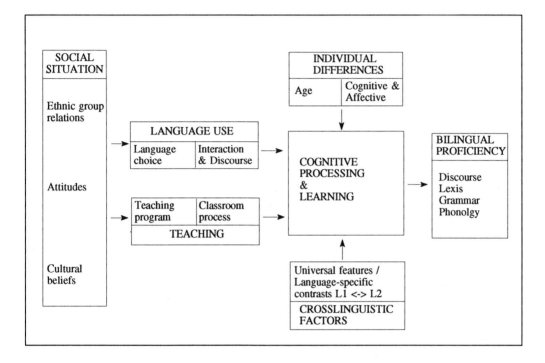

Figure 1. A schematic model of the development of bilingual proficiency at school.

[1] This is a condensed version of a model presented at greater length (in Swedish) in Viberg (1990). The original model was concerned with second language development and has been slightly adapted here to cover bilingual development.

The social (or *sociocultural*) *situation* covers ethnic group relations (Giles, Bourhis & Taylor 1977) such as the economic and social status of the group to which the bilingual student belongs as well as institutional support (media, immigrant organizations, churches). Demographic factors such as group size and settlement patterns are important both for the opportunities to use L1 and L2 out of school and for the opportunities to organize home language classes or for the proportion of native speakers of the majority language in regular classes. In areas with high concentrations of immigrants, hardly any input from native Swedish peers may be available at school or in the neighbourhood. Another important aspect of the sociocultural situation are the various cultural beliefs, especially of the parents, regarding child rearing, the perception of school and the value of formal education. In the USA, sociocultural patterns of various types have been used to explain the relative success of certain groups such as Chinese-Americans and the relative academic failure of others such as Mexican-Americans (Ogbu & Matute-Bianchi 1986, Heath 1986).

For students in bilingual education, input for language learning is provided by language use (outside school) and teaching, which also comprises more or less spontaneous language use in addition to different kinds of metalinguistic input such as explanations of the meanings of unfamiliar words or grammatical rules of thumb. Primarily from a methodological point of view, a distinction is drawn between a more global and a more fine-grained analysis. At a global level, the amount and type of exposure to L1 and L2 can be estimated by examining which languages are used in different domains (Fishman 1971) such as home, neighbourhood and school and with different persons such as parents, siblings, best friend(s) etc. Using a questionnarie, Boyd (1985) showed that immigrant youth in Swedish junior high schools (age around 15-16) tended to use their home language (L1) with parents and older relatives, while they had a strong tendency to use Swedish with their siblings and with their peers, which implied a shift towards Swedish as the dominant language for the second generation. Students in home language classes were not included in Boyd's study (see below). Language distribution at school can be roughly estimated by studying the program, even if a simple measure such as the number of hours alotted to each language is complicated by such factors as the availability of teaching materials (e.g. a Swedish book used to teach subject matter in the home language) and the code-switching behaviour of bilingual teachers.

To get a more exact picture, representative samples of authentic discourse must be recorded and analyzed both in domains outside and within school. The study of discourse and interaction outside school should cover i.a. norms of code switching in the specific community and the amount and type of adapted speech available in the weaker language. Language use outside school and Teaching serve as input for cognitive processing and learning (see e.g. McLaughlin 1987, ch. 6 or O'Malley & Chamot 1990). The model also recognizes the importance of individual differences, which can be divided into age (Harley 1986, Long 1990) and cognitive & affective factors such as intelligence, language aptitude and motivation (see Skehan 1989). Crosslinguistic factors refer to universal features and language specific contrasts between L1 and L2. The latter determine the typological distance between L1 and L2, which is decisive for the amount and type of transfer between the languages and the amount of time required to reach a high level in the weaker language (unless the student has acquired two languages as a first language). In Swedish schools, there is a continuum from very closely related languages such as Norwegian and Danish, to relatively close languages such as German and English and to relatively remote such as Finnish or very remote such as Vietnamese and Cantonese.

Bilingual proficiency can be described along a number of dimensions. An important contribution to the research methodology in this area is the large scale study of the nature of bilingual proficiency which is presented in Harley, Allen, Cummins & Swain (eds. 1990). In this study, a three-way distinction was made between discourse, sociolinguistic and grammatical competence based on the model of communicative competence presented in Canale & Swain (1980) and Canale (1983). The model did not, however, receive any clear support from the results. The major reason for this, in my opinion, is that it is still an open question what the functionally relevant systems are. (I will return to this in the next section.) The subcomponents of bilingual proficiency shown in figure 1 are only meant to serve as a general orientation stressing that proficiency should be conceived of in a broad way covering units of various size from discourse to phonology (or orthography).

Most directly, development can be observed in a longitudinal study as change through actual time. Change involves all of the components in Figure 1 and does not necessarily have a specific direction. Primarily, however, development refers to changes in (bilingual) linguistic proficiency, which is often conceived of in terms of progression and regression (Hyltenstam & Viberg, in press). L1 and L2 gain or lose in expressive potential, complexity, and flexibility. Development can also be related to different kinds of norms which learners approach or deviate from, such as adultness, nativeness or standardness.

The general design of the project 'Bilingualism at School'

The aim of the project 'Bilingualism at School' (the BAS-project)[2] is to describe the parallel development of L1 and L2 in bilingual children in Swedish comprehensive school as a contribution to a general theory of language acquisition. The

---

[2] The project 'Bilingualism at School' (The BAS-project) is financially supported by The National Swedish Board of Education (Skolverket, former Skolöverstyrelsen). Project leader: Åke Viberg. Other researchers: Päivi Juvonen, Inger Lindberg and Tua Abrahamsson. In parallel with this project, Maria Borgström is preparing a doctoral thesis on the Spanish/Swedish bilingual development of Latin American children from grade 4 to 6 in Spanish home language classes.

linguistic development is studied in relation to the characteristics of the teaching and of the social background of the children. From a theoretical point of view, the study cuts across the division between first and second language acquisition research, since both age-related and bilingual aspects of development are studied.

In the main study, data on language proficiency were collected from 60 bilingual students with Finnish-speaking parents at two points in time: the school year 87/88 and 89/90. The main criteria for the selection of informants are summarized in Table 1. To obtain a general picture of the development throughout school, two grade levels are compared. At the first point in time, half of the students were in grade 4 (approximately 10 years old) and half in grade 7. At the second point in time, the same students were in grade 6 and 9, respectively.

Table 1. Subjects in the main study.

	Number of students	
Time 1	Grade 4	Grade 7
Time 2	Grade 6	Grade 9
Bilingual students		
Home-language classes	20	20
Regular Swedish classes	10	10
Monolingual controls		
Finnish	10	10
Swedish	10	10

Two teaching models are compared: Home language class and Swedish class. In a home language class, which consists entirely of pupils sharing another home language than Swedish, a considerable amount of instruction is given in the home language, especially in the earliest grades. In a regular Swedish medium class, a student with another language than Swedish used actively at home can participate in a few hours of home language instruction a week. The difference with respect to the amount of instruction in Finnish and Swedish is thus considerable in the two teaching models. In actual practice, this difference is often reinforced by the fact that home language classes tend to be organized in residential areas where the home language has a relatively strong position outside school. According to a study by Liebkind (1989), there is also a difference with respect to the identification pattern and ethnic ideology. Families with adoloscents in regular Swedish classes had a more 'assimilationist' orientation in comparison to families with adolescents in home language classes. The latter were characterized by a stronger Finnish identity.

Since the aim of the project is to give a relatively detailed picture of the linguistic proficiency of each student, the total number of students has had to be limited. At the same time, it is important that several schools in different types of residential areas are represented. For this reason, only a small number of students were selected from each class. In the home language classes, 5 students were selected from each class, which makes it possible to look at 4 classes at each grade level. As for the students in regular Swedish classes, there is some variation for practical reasons, but in most cases only a few or a single student with Finnish background is found.

In order to determine to what degree the bilingual development in Swedish and Finnish parallels monolingual development in both languages, data has been collected from monolingual Swedish and Finnish students of the same age. In general, data from 10 monolingual students have been collected at each grade level. Age-related development can be studied by comparing students at different grade levels, but for this purpose, parallel data have, to a limited extent, also been collected from adult controls in both languages.

As can be seen from Table 2, three types of data were collected. What will primarily be discussed in this paper is one type, i.e. data on oral language proficiency, which was collected individually from each of the students.

Table 2. Types of data.

A. Data on language proficiency

INDIVIDUAL	GROUP
Oral	
- Semi-structured interview	Pair work
- Retelling of videos	Role play
Written	
- Free composition	
- Retelling of videos	

B. Classroom observations (& recordings)

C. Background questionnaire
Social background
Patterns of language use

From the bilingual students, data on Swedish and Finnish were collected on two different occasions by different interviewers, each having the respective language as a first language. The oral recordings have been transcribed and annotated with a computer program, which attaches word class and other grammatical lables to each word and makes it possible to form concordances based on word forms and/or grammatical tags. Primarily, the PC Beta program (Brodda 1991) has been used but most of the CLAN-programs (MacWhinney 1991) can be used as well.

In order to study the characteristics of the teaching, classroom recordings should ideally be made in all classes simultaneously with the collection of data on language proficiency. This, however, was not possible due to a lack of resources. Since we suspected that there would be great variation between schools and between teachers, data on the teaching situation were collected primarily by an ethnographic method through classroom observations. The observations were carried out by Bergman (1992), an experienced bilingual teacher trainer, and covered around 40 lessons in Swedish and Finnish in grade 7-9. The study confirmed the suspicion that there was very great variation within programs and even within individual schools. Particular attention was paid to language distribution. Three different patterns were found. 1) Complete separation of languages. Each language is used by separate teachers. This was the most common pattern. 2) separation by person within individual lessons, i.e. team teaching by a Swedish and a Finnish teacher. 3) bilingual teaching by a bilingual Finnish teacher who switches between Finnish and Swedish during the lesson.

Data on the social background and on the patterns of language use outside school were collected by means of a background questionnaire administered individually to all of the students. The questions on language use are partly based on Boyd (1985), which makes it possible to compare the two studies. The questionnaire is analyzed in Tuomela (1992). According to self-ratings, students in home language classes judge that they are better in Finnish than in Swedish or know both languages quite well, while the majority of Finnish students in regular Swedish classes rate their Swedish as better than their Finnish. Most students irrespective of program speak Finnish to their parents, but students in home language classes use Finnish also with their siblings, while students in regular classes alternate between Swedish and Finnish in this case. Language with friends varies for students in home language classes, while students in regular classes in general use Swedish with friends.

One of the most important findings in Boyd's study was that immigrant students tended to use the home language primarily with the older generation, while Swedish dominated with peers to the extent that it even tended to be used with siblings at home. This was interpreted as a sign of language shift in progress. As Boyd notes, few of the students in her study had been offered more than two hours a week of home language instruction. The results of Tuomela's study indicates that the tendency to use the home language only with the older generation does not apply for Finnish students in home language classes, while it applies to a great extent for Finnish students in regular Swedish classes. (It would be premature to generalize these findings to other minority groups. It hardly applies, for example, to many of the Turkish and Assyrian children, who live in areas with a high concentration of immigrants. Even if they attend 'regular' Swedish classes, many of the students share the same home language and very few of their classmates, if any, have Swedish as their first language.)

Bilingual proficiency

The nature of bilingual proficiency

The data on language proficiency in the computerized corpus are being studied from several perspectives. As a point of departure, a number of general components of linguistic proficiency along the lines of communicative compentence in the sense of Canale & Swain (1980) are distinguished, but the analysis will focus on a number of more narrowly defined functionally integrated subsystems within these wider components. A few structures will thus be singled out for closer examination at each linguistic level

At the level of discourse, a distinction is made between a textual and an interactive subcomponent. Within the textual component, a study has been carried out on the narrative skills of the bilingual students as evidenced in the renarration of one of the video-clips, which was renarrated both in Finnish and Swedish on different occasions (Juvonen, Lindberg & Viberg 1989). The contents of the story were represented by a number of propositions and the various functions of the propositions were described with a variety of story grammar. By observing which propositions were realized in some way in the individual renarrations, it was possible to compare the Finnish and the Swedish versions of the bilingual students with versions from monolingual controls in each language. One finding was that the bilingual students expressed more or less the same core popositions in both their languages. They also tended to favour more detailed and concrete propositions, while the monolingual controls gave more condensed versions. An aspect of the interactive component which is studied in a parallel study on Spanish-speaking Latin American children by Borgström (1992) is the realization of speech acts such as Request and Apology. Data for this study are collected in a role-play task.

At the level of the lexicon, one subsystem is that of basic verbs which are studied by frequency ranking and classification into semantic fields according to a method presented in Viberg (in press), where it is applied to six- and seven-year-old learners of Swedish as a second language. In the earlier study, it was found that learners at a relatively early stage had a strong tendency to overuse certain very frequent basic verbs (the nuclear verbs). In the present study, the same method has so far been applied to the Swedish data from grade 4 and 6. No strong tendency to overuse the nuclear verbs was found, which confirms the general impression that the bilingual students are at a relatively advanced level even in their weaker language, Swedish. There were, however, some indications that certain basic but relatively language-specific verbs were underrepresented in comparison with the usage patterns of the monolingual Swedish controls.

At the morpho-syntactic level, particular attention has been devoted to clause-combining and the system of sentential connectors, which will be treated somewhat more in depth in the next section.

From a somewhat different perspective, we also plan to study features which reflect aspects of control (fluency etc). A preliminary analysis of this type is the study of self-repairs by Juvonen (1991).

Sentential connectors

In Swedish, several of the children in home language classes show clear signs that this is a second language. In many cases, however, the divergencies from the native

Swedish norm as represented by the monolingual controls of the same age are relatively subtle. Within various structural subsystems, the difference is primarily reflected in the choice of options and, in particular, by the overrepresentation (in terms of frequency of use) of the least marked alternatives. This section will be devoted to one aspect of the oral linguistic proficiency that illustrates this, namely clause combining and sentential connectors. In this paper, only data on Swedish will be presented. Eventually, the findings from this study will be combined with similar data on Finnish from the same bilingual students. First, a short sketch is given of the structure of Swedish in this area and then data will be presented and analyzed from the younger half of the bilingual students, i.e those students who have been followed from grade 4 to 6.

Clause-combining and sentential connectors is a functionally integrated area, which provides clear examples of both age-related and L2-related developmental patterns, (see Viberg 1991 for more detailed information). In particular, the usage patterns of sentential connectors have turned out to serve as good indicators of developmental trends and can be relatively easily analyzed (semi)automatically in computerized corpora in a scale that makes it possible to carry out quantitatively based comparisons between groups of learners and various other types of speakers. More detailed, qualitatively oriented analyses can then be performed on restricted samples (such as one of the renarrations in our material).

'Sentential connector' is a cover term for a number of grammatical words appearing in clause-initial position and serving to connect clauses. It comprises what traditionally is called (coordinating) conjunctions (*å/och* 'and', *men* 'but' etc), subordinators in circumstantial clauses (*när* 'when', *om* 'if' etc), relative-clause markers (primarily the indeclinable particle *som),* the that-complementizer (*att)* and question-words in indirect questions. In addition, there is a small number of adverbs which serve as sequential markers and correspond to English clause-initial *then*. There are three common equivalents of this marker in Swedish, which form a small subsystem among the sentential connectors: *då* ('simultaneous then') indicates simultaneity with the preceding clause, *sen* ('sequential then') indicates sequence and *så* ('sequential so') in this particular function can often be substituted for *sen*. (*Så* in addition has several other distinct functions as a connector.) Unlike conjunctions, these adverbs trigger inversion, which is obligatory in Swedish main clauses which are introduced by an adverbial or other major constituent which does not function as subject. The most basic facts are illustrated by the simple sentences below:

Bonden   dödade   ankungen   igår.
farmer-the kill-ed   duckling-the yesterday
The farmer killed the duckling yesterday.

If the adverbial is topicalized, inversion is obligatory:

Igår dödade bonden ankungen. Yesterday the farmer killed the duckling.

In this respect, the connective adverbs are similar to ordinary adverbs:

Då dödade bonden ankungen.(Just) then the farmer killed the duckling.
*Sen dödade bonden ankungen.*Then (after that)-"-
Så dödade bonden ankungen.-"-

What motivates the attribution of a special status to these adverbs is primarily the remarkably high frequency with which they appear in spoken language in narrative contexts.

A topicalized adverbial can be followed by a topic place-holder (TP), which also will be analyzed as a connector:

Igår, så (TP) dödade bonden ankungen.
Yesterday, the farmer killed the duckling.

In the example underneath, the use of connectors is illustrated in a renarration of a video-clip produced by one of the monolingual Swedish students in grade 4. Connectors are shown in bold-face and subordinate clauses are marked by indentation.

(1)		de / de va på nån cirkus eller nåt
		it was at a circus or something
(2)	ADVK	**så** va de en tjej
		then there was a girl (Literally: so was it a girl)
(3)	REL	**som** skulle stå mot en vägg sådär
		who should stand agaist a wall like that
(4)	ADVK	**så** va de en man
		then there was a man (Lit.: so was it a man)
(5)	REL	**som** kasta knivar runt om henne
		who threw knives around her
(6)	K ADVK	**ja å sen** skulle han ta nån filt för ögonen
		yes and then he should take some blanket over his eyes
(7)	SUB	**så** han inte s- såg
		so he couldn't s-see (Lit.: so he not saw)
(8)	K ADVK	**å då** gick den här tjejen / .hhh bakom
		and then this girl went erhh behind (the wall)
(9a)	K ADVK	**å sen / sen**
		and then / then
(10)	SUB	**när** han tog av sej filten
		when he took off the blanket
(9b)	TP	**så** ställde hon sej dära
		she went and stood there (Lit.: so stood she herself there)

K = Conjunction   ADVK =   Connective adverb
TP = Topic place-holder   REL = Relative-clause marker
SUB = Subordinator (in circumstantial clauses)

As can be observed, the sequential connective adverbs are used abundantly, which is characteristic of the renarrations by the children in general. Many of the connectors interact in a subtle way with word order (and intonation) to signal several clearly distinct meanings. When *så* functions as a connective adverb and marks sequence as in (2) and (4), word order in the form of inversion serves as a formal cue that this is the intended interpretation. In (7), where *så* functions as a circumstantial subordination marker and signals a result, there are two word order cues, namely non-inversion and preverbal position of the negation particle. (In main clauses, the negation is postverbal.) The mastery of the functional contrasts thus requires a command both of the system of connectors and of the basic word order rules in Swedish, which by themselves represent a learning problem for second language learners.

One area where most of the bilingual Finnish children differ clearly in their Swedish from the monolingual controls is the usage pattern of the connective adverbs *sen - så- då*. The scope of the difference is evident from Table 3, which shows the frequency of use of these markers by the two groups.

Table 3. The use of connective adverbs. The development from grade 4 - 6.

	Swedish control 10			Bilingual children 20			Significant over-/ under-representation	
Grade 4								
Connective adverb	n	f	mean propor.	n	f	mean propor.		p
sen 'then (seq.)'	10	156	0.31	20	601	0.65	OVER	.001
så 'so; then'	10	244	0.45	18	130	0.15	UNDER	.01
då 'then (sim.)'	10	82	0.16	18	156	0.16		ns
först 'at first'	8	30	0.06	10	26	0.03		ns
Other connective adverbs		15	0.02		7	0.01		ns
TOTAL		527	1.00		920	1.00		
Grade 6								
Connective adverb	n	f	mean propor.	n	f	mean propor.		
sen 'then (seq.)'	10	201	0.26	20	845	0.57	OVER	.001
så ' so; then'	10	425	0.55	20	514	0.27	UNDER	.001
då ' then (sim.)'	10	141	0.17	19	177	0.13		ns
först 'at first'	5	7	0.01	9	28	0.02		ns
Other connective adverbs		9	0.01		7	0.01		ns
TOTAL		783	1.00		1571	1.00		

All three markers are used by all the monolingual children. This is shown in the column marked n, which indicates the number of speakers who use the marker at least once. (The other connective adverbs which have been included for the sake of completeness will be disregarded, since the frequency is too low to merit any further comparison.) Even if there are one or two Finnish children who do not use all three markers, it can be safely concluded that even the majority of these children know the markers in principle. The high over-all frequency of the connective adverbs is evident from the column headed by f, which shows the absoulte frequency of occurence at the group level.

To study the individual variation within and between groups, the proportion between the frequency of use of each connective adverb and the total number of connective adverbs was calculated for each individual student. For the purpose of comparison, this gives a more reliable picture of the usage pattern than the absolute frequencies, since variation due to the varying length of the recordings is neutralized. What is striking is the differences between the two groups with respect to the proportions with which the three markers are used. The bilinguals have a very strong tendency to favour *sen,* while the monolingual Swedish children rather favour *så.* This is shown in the column mean propor(tion), which shows the means of the proportions. These proportions were also used to test the significance of the differences between the monolingual and the bilingual group with a two-tailed t-test[3]. The results of this test are indicated as OVER, when the marker is significantly overrepresented by the bilingual group with respect to the monolingual group which is regarded as a norm. UNDER indicates that a marker is significantly underrepresented by the bilingual group. As can be observed, *sen* is over- and *så* is underrepresented in grade 4 and this pattern is repeated in grade 6.

The most striking feature is thus the favouring of *sen* by the bilingual Finnish students. The individual usage patterns with respect to the proportion with which this marker is used are shown in the scatterplot in Figure 2. In this figure, each letter stands for an individual. The vertical line (at 0.26) shows the mean proportion of the monolingual control group in grade 4 and the horizontal line (at 0.31) shows the corresponding mean in grade 6. All Finnish students except 4, are above the monolingual mean at both times. The diagonal line shows the position of values which are identical at the two grade levels. The students below this line have approached the monolingual pattern in grade 6 and those above it have deviated further, while those at (or close to) the line have not changed. As can be observed, the number of students who have approached the monolingual pattern form the majority, even if there are a few who have moved in the opposite direction. Three bilingual students (A, D, F) are close to the monolingual pattern at both times and even a little below it in grade 6, while one student (O) has changed from 0.77 in grade 4 to a position below the monolingual mean in grade 6. In essence, the figure

---

[3] It might be argued that a non-parametric test is preferable. Very similar results were obtained with a Mann-Whitney test (run on MINITAB).

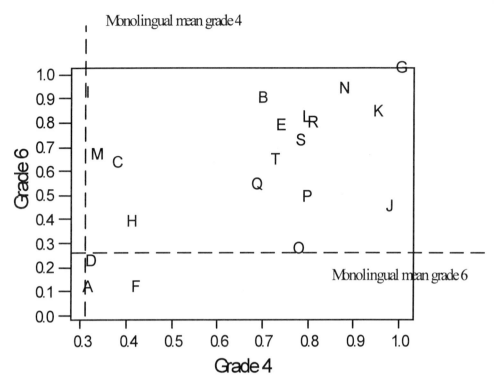

Figure 2. The proportion of Swedish *sen* ('sequential then') in the usage of the individual bilingual Finnish students in grade 4 and grade 6.

shows that there is a rather great variation within the group, at the same time as there is a consistent difference in comparison to the monolingual pattern, since most of the values fall above the monolingual means. There is also a clear indication that a majority of the individual students have moved towards the monolingual pattern in grade 6 without yet having reached it.

The favouring of *sen* has a parallel in an earlier study (Viberg 1991) of the acquisition of Swedish as a second language by six-year-old preschool children, who had a much lower general proficiency in Swedish than the bilingual children in the present study. These children favoured *sen* to an even greater extent (around 78% of the connective adverbs against 37% for a monolingual control group of the same age). In recordings one year later, this pattern was practically unchanged (81% against 31%). A few non-native children who had not used any connective adverb in the first recording had begun using *sen* as the only connective adverb. The tendency to reduce the contrast between *sen-så-då* to a generalized use of *sen* is thus a characteristic feature of Swedish as a second language. It is also a feature that appears early and that changes very slowly in the direction of the native pattern.

I will turn now to possible explanations for the favouring of *sen*. One reason is semantic salience in the input. Out of *sen-så-då*, *sen* has the most consistent and transparent meaning, approximately 'temporal sequence', while in particular *så* has a less transparent meaning and in addition is very polysemous. The three-way constrast found in Swedish also seems to be rather language-specific. In English, all three markers have one primary equivalent: *then*. Some languages, like Spanish, have a two-way sequential/simultaneous contrast (*después* / *entonces*). In German and Dutch, the past/non-past distinction plays a central role for the choice of marker (Ger. *da* / *dann;* Du. *toen* / *dan)*. Even if the number of languages considered is very small, the fact that even relativley closely related languages show so varying possibilities indicates that at least some of the patterns are highly language-specific. (Some of the video-clips used in the present study are being used as stimulus for renarrations in a number of other minority languages in Sweden, which will make it possible to widen the empirical basis for this claim.)

A further reason, in particular for the underrepresentation of *så,* is that the use considered here is rather colloquial and characteristic in particular of idiomatic, spoken Swedish. Such features have a general tendency to be underrepresented in the speech of second-language learners with a limited contact with native Swedes outside the school context. (Some Swedish examples are given i Viberg 1991). Actually, one such example was found even in the Finnish of the bilingual children as compared with a monolingual control group recorded in Finland (see Juvonen & Viberg 1992). In the usage of the bilingual children, Finnish *mikä* 'what' was underrepesented in its function as a relative-clause marker. In the spoken language, this marker can be used after a wider range of antecedents than in the writtten standard language. This tendency to avoid certain colloquial variants can be interpreted as a result of a somewhat restricted input from monolingual peers in informal contexts outside school.

The frequent use of connective adverbs seems to be an age-related characteristic. In Lindberg, Juvonen & Viberg (1990), which is based on a study of the renarration of one of the video-clips in both Finnish and Swedish using both child and adult monolingual control groups, it was shown that both monolingual and bilingual children tended to use a much larger proportion of connective adverbs than adults. The favouring of connective adverbs at the expense of other sentential connectors is thus an age-related characteristic which is shared by children speaking a language as a first or as a second language (after an initial phase), while the favouring of *sen* in relation to the other connective adverbs is a typical characteristic of second language learners. A similar tendency to reduce the system of temporal connective adverbs to one marker at early stages has been reported for Dutch by Extra & Van Helvert (1987) in a longitudinal study of two adult learners.

Conclusion

So far, the major result of the project has been to establish a relatively large computerized database of bilingual oral production data. The last section gave an example of the kind of analyses that can be performed on the data. It would be premature, however, to draw any more far-reaching conclusions at this stage. Only through detailed analyses of a number of structural areas will it be possible to provide an empirical foundation for a general theory of bilingual proficiency. A better understanding of the nature of bilingual proficiency in its turn is a necessary component of a more comprehensive theory of bilingual development comprising the wider socio-cultural context and language use in and out of school as outlined in the beginning of this paper (cf. Figure 1 and the comments to that figure).

References

Bergman, P., 1992. Att undervisa på två språk. Centre for Research on Bilingualism, Stockholm University.

Borgström, M., 1992. Utveckling av tvåspråkig kompetens hos latinamerikanska barn i Sverige, exemplifierad i talhandlingar och rollspel. *Utvecklingspsykologiska seminariets skriftserie nr 40.* Department of Education, Stockholm Univeristy.

Boyd, S., 1985. *Language survival: A study of language contact, language shift and language choice in Sweden.* Department of Linguistics, University of Göteborg.

Brodda, B., 1991. Doing corpus work with PC Beta; or how to be your own computational linguist. In: Johansson, S & Stenström, A-B (eds.), *English computer corpora. Selected papers and research guide.* Mouton de Gruyter, Berlin & New York.

Canale, M., 1983. From communicative competence to communicative language pedagogy. In: Richards, J C & Schmidt, W (eds.), *Language and Communication.* Longman, London.

Canale, M. & Swain, M., 1980. Theoretical bases of communicative approaches to second language teaching and testing. *Applied Linguistics 1:1,* 1-47.

Eldering, L. & Kloprogge, J. (eds), 1989. *Different cultures, same school. Ethnic minority children in Europe.* Swets & Zeitlinger, Amsterdam.

Extra, G. & Van Helvert, K., 1987. Référence temporelle dans l'acquisition d'une seconde langue par des adultes. In: Blanc, M, le Douaron, M & Véronique, D (eds.), *s'Approprier une langue étrangère. Actes du 6ᵉ Colloque International Acquisition d'une langue étrangère'.* Didier, Paris.

Fishman, J., 1971. The sociology of language: an interdisciplinary social science approach to language in society. In: Fishman, J (ed.), *Advances in the sociology of language I.* Mouton, The Hague.

Giles, H, Bourhis, R. Y. & Taylor, D. M., 1977. Towards a theory of language in ethnic group relations. In: Giles, H (ed.), *Language, ethnicity and intergroup relations.* Academic Press, New York.

Harley, B., 1986. *Age in second language acquisition.* Multilingual Matters, Clevedon.

Harley, B., Allen, P., Cummins, J. & Swain, M. (eds.)., 1990. *The development of second language proficiency.* Cambridge University Press, Cambridge.

Heath, S. B., 1986. Sociocultural contexts of language development. In: *Beyond language: Social & cultural factors in schooling language minority students.* California State Department of Education, Sacramento.

Hyltenstam, K. & Viberg, Å. (in press), Linguistic progression and regression. An introduction. In: Hyltenstam & Viberg (eds.), *Progression and regression in language.* Cambridge University Press, Cambridge.

Juvonen, P., 1991. Self-repair in bilingual children: a study of Finnish-Swedish schoolchildren's self-repairs in narrative discourse. In: Herberts, K & Laurén, C (eds.), *Multilingualism in the Nordic countries and beyond. Sixth Nordic Conference on Bilingualism.* Institutet för finlandssvensk samhällsforskning, Va(a)sa/Finland.

Juvonen, P., Lindberg, I. & Viberg, Å., 1989. Narrative skills in two languages. *Scandinavian Working Papers in Bilingualism 8.* Centre for Research on Bilingualism, Stockholm University.

Juvonen, P. & Viberg, Å., 1992. Tvåspråkighet i skolan: Användandet av konnektorer och lexikala val på svenska och finska. To appear in: Wande, E & Almqvist, I (eds.), *Finska varieteter utanför Finland.* Department of Finnish, Stockholm University.

Liebkind, K., 1989. Patterns of ethnic identification amongst Finns in Sweden. In: Liebkind, K (ed.), *New identities in Europe.* Gower, Aldershot/England.

Lindberg, I., Juvonen, P. & Viberg, Å., 1991. Att berätta på två språk. In: Nettelbladt, U & Håkansson, G (eds.), *Samtal och språkundervisning.* Tema Kommunikation, Linköping University.

Long, M. H., 1990. Maturational constraints on language development. *Studies in Second Language Acquisition 12:3,* 251-285.

MacWhinney, B., 1991. *The CHILDES project: Tools for analyzing talk.* Lawrence Erlbaum, Hillsdale/NJ.

O'Malley, J. M. & Chamot, A. U., 1990. *Learning strategies in second language acquisition.* Cambridge University Press, Cambridge.

McLaughlin, B., 1987. *Theories of second-language learning.* Edward Arnold, London.

Municio, I., 1987. *Från lag till bruk. Hemspråksreformens genomförande.* ('From legislation to implementation. The home language reform in Sweden.' In Swedish with a summary in English.) Doctoral thesis. Department of Political Science, Stockholm University.

Nilsson, M., 1992. Rapport från en enkät som belyser situationen och förändringarna av invandrarundervisningen inom grundskolan. Kommunförbundet.

Ogbu, J. U. & Matute-Bianchi, M. E., 1986. Understanding sociocultural factors:

knowledge, identity, and school adjustment. In: *Beyond language: Social & cultural factors in schooling language minority students.* California State Department of Education, Sacramento.

Skehan, P., 1989. *Individual differences in second-language learning.* Edward Arnold, London.

Statistics Sweden, 1992. Home language and home language instruction. Comprehensive school and integrated upper secondary school 1991/92. *U72 SM 92011.* (In Swedish with a short summary in English.)

Tuomela, V., 1992. Självskattad språkfärdighet och språkval hos finska elever i Sverige. Centre for Research on Bilingualism, Stockholm University.

Viberg, Å., 1990. Språkinlärning och språkundervisning. In: Adelswärd, V & Davies, N F (eds.), *På väg mot ett nytt språk.* ASLA, c/o FUMS, University of Uppsala.

Viberg, Å., 1991. The acquisition and development of Swedish as a first and as a second language: the case of clause combining and sentential connectors. To appear in: Kettemann, B & Wieden, W (eds.), *L2 acquisition research in Europe.* Gunter Narr, Tübingen.

Viberg, Å. (in press), Crosslinguistic perspectives on lexical organization and lexical progression. In: Hyltenstam, K & Viberg Å (eds.), *Progression and regression in language.* Cambridge University Press, Cambridge.

Anneli Schaufeli

First language text cohesion in a Turkish-Dutch bilingual setting

Although during the last decade language-acquisition researchers in Western Europe are engaged into the first-language acquisition of immigrant children, they mainly focus on the development of lexical and morphosyntactic skills. Research on Turkish immigrant children showed that from an early age on, their first language proficiency is lagging behind that of their monolingual peers (Boeschoten, 1990; Pfaff, 1991). Moreover, as age increases, the differences on the lexical and morphosyntactic levels become larger (Verhoeven & Boeschoten, 1986; Schaufeli, 1990).

Verhoeven (1988) focused on the development of discourse oriented skills of Turkish children in the Netherlands. His overall conclusion was that universal strategies underlie this development. The cohesion devices which 8-year-old Turkish children in the Netherlands use, turned out to be very similar to those used by 5-year-old monolinguals in Turkey. However, there was a considerable delay in the development of discourse skills among the children in the Netherlands. Verhoeven explained the stagnation in the development of discourse cohesion by the restricted Turkish input these children receive. Assuming that language proficiency is the only dimension on which the mono-and the bilingual groups diverge, this is a remarkable outcome in the light of earlier research findings on similar phenomena. Scinto (1983), Hickmann (1987) and Wigglesworth (1990) all report a relationship between level of cognitive functioning on the one hand and degree of text cohesion or use of linguistic reference devices (i.e., discourse oriented skills) on the other rather than between age and the acquisitional level of these skills.

No matter what causes the stagnation in the development of discourse cohesion, a second question arises, i.e., wether this stagnation is maintained and the differences between the groups will increase, as was the case on both lexical and morpho-syntactic levels. This question may be answered by investigating the language use of older bilingual children. In the present chapter the discourse skills of 12-year-old Turkish children in Turkey and the Netherlands will be compared. Text cohesion will be measured by means of the degree of cohesiveness. More detailed insight will be obtained (a) by analysing the various types of cohesion devices used within both groups of children, (b) by examining the way participant continuity in narratives is realized. Furthermore, a comparison will be made between oral and written language samples. As the bilingual children in the Netherlands had only very little writing experience in Turkish, there may be larger differences between the groups on written narratives than on oral narratives.

Background of the study

Text cohesion and its acquisition

Given the fact that every language has its own linguistic devices for establishing text cohesion, Hickmann (1987) discussed the relation between cognitive and linguistic development of reference in relation to the theories of Piaget and Vygotsky. On the basis of cross-linguistic research results showing the importance of linguistic constraints for cognitive organization, she argued that the differences in the devices of individual languages may influence the acquisition of reference. However, her own research results on native English children (Hickmann, 1982) pointed out that 10-year-olds already use linguistic reference devices appropriately.

Scinto (1983) investigated text cohesion in various types of texts produced by 8 to 15-year-old native speakers of English, and found – rather than an age effect – a strong correlation between developmental level, i.e., level of cognitive functioning in Piagetian terms, and performance in (written) text production. Subjects functioning on the relatively high, low-formal operational level produced texts that were more cohesive and more compact than texts produced by subjects functioning on the lower concrete-operational level. So proficiency in producing texts, measured by means of the text variables cohesion and compactness seems to increase with developmental stage (even in 15-year-olds) rather than with age.

Although Scinto's results show that the various age groups do not differ with respect to the degree of cohesion and compactness in the texts the children produce, Yde and Spoelders (1985) obtained different results. They found on these same variables a difference between Dutch-speaking 8 to 9-year-olds and 10 to 11-year-olds. The latter used significantly more cohesion devices and their texts were more compact. The number of children studied was limited (N=2x14) so per age level they may not have represented different levels of cognitive functioning as was the case in Scinto's investigation. Therefore, in Yde and Spoelders' study the difference in age may have been equal to a difference in cognitive developmental level.

Furthermore, the authors reported a difference in distribution of the various types of cohesion devices. Among the oldest children, compared to the younger ones, a significant decline was found in conjunctive cohesion. The authors argued that a decrease in the use of conjunctions may be caused by an increase in sentence-internal structuring i.e., as more complex sentence structures are acquired, more possibilities for signalling relations within sentences are available.

If we narrow the subject of text cohesion down to participant continuity, the effect of age seems to be less open to question. On the basis of empirical evidence from English speaking children, Karmiloff-Smith (1985) developed a three-phase model for the development in children's use of cohesive markers in narratives. In the first phase (3-5 years of age) children use pronouns and full noun phrases in their deictic function, i.e., to refer directly to the extra-linguistic antecedent. In the second phase (5-8 years of age) children start to use referential expressions in their discourse functions, i.e., for co-reference to another element in the text. They create a thematic subject by which they hold the story together – the subject position is reserved for the thematic subject. This places constraints on the positioning and types of referring expressions used for non-thematic subjects. This urge to distinguish between thematic and non-thematic subjects sometimes even results in slightly ungrammatical structures. In the third phase (8-12 years of age) children occasionally let non-thematic subjects occupy initial positions, although this is generally clearly linguistically marked, for example by using full noun phrases.

Bamberg (1986) obtained similar results for German-speaking children, but where this concerned evidence for a thematic subject, it appeared much earlier in the narratives of these children. Moreover, he found differences between the language use of native speaking German children aged 9-10 and adults, with respect to reference switching.

A taxonomy of text cohesion devices in Turkish

Hallliday and Hasan's taxonomy (Halliday & Hasan, 1976) for cohesion devices was used for the analyses in the current study. As they state,

> 'a text has texture, and this is what distinguishes it from something that is not a text" (1976:2).

According to the authors, this texture is realised by cohesive relations between elements in the text. This means that there should be presuppositions, and these presuppositions must also be fulfilled within the text. One instance of such a relation is called a cohesive tie. Every language has its own linguistic devices for creating texture, i.e., for establishing cohesive ties.

Durmuşoğlu, in her paper on cohesion in Turkish (1987), gave an overview of several cohesion devices. For the coding of the various devices, Halliday and Hasan's classification (1976) was used. The major categories they distinguish, as applied to particular devices in Turkish, resulted in the following categorization:

Co-reference (Cr)
Halliday and Hasan's term is 'reference', but, as Brown and Yule (1983) suggested, this term ought to be substituted by the term co-reference. It is applied to non-lexical elements such as pronouns, which can only be interpreted on the basis of other elements in the text. Besides personal pronouns as 'o' (3SG) the following elements are also involved: possessive pronouns such as 'onun' (3SG), possessive markers as for example in 'evi' 'her house', personal markers on the verb such as in 'geldiler' 'They came' and deictical terms as for instance 'bu' 'this'.

Substitution

Halliday and Hasan's definition of substitution of linguistic terms by others on the lexical level could not be applied unambiguously to Turkish. In the material under investigation, all possible instances of substitution could either be classified as coreferential or as lexical ties. Therefore the category substitution was not distinguished in the material under investigation.

Ellipsis (E)

Ellipsis is defined as *'substitution by zero'* (Halliday & Hasan 1976:142): *'An elliptical item is one which, as it were, leaves specific structural slots to be filled from elsewhere [in the text AS]'* (1976:143). In Turkish, zero anaphora frequently occur, also in cases where English (and Dutch) make use of a pronoun, for example, to refer to a grammatical object. To give an example:

2. *Bisikletle geldim. # Dışarı bıraktım.*
   bicycle-with come-PST-1SG ZERO outside leave-PST-1SG
   'I came by bicycle. I left (it) outside.'

In the second sentence, the object slot is empty and has to be filled with information provided by the first sentence.

Conjunction (C)

Conjunction concerns formal markers which establish relationships in texts. All types of conjunctions are involved, e.g., adversives such as 'ama' 'but', causal conjunctions as 'çünkü' 'because' and temporal conjunctions as for example 'sonra' 'then'.

Lexical cohesion (L)

Lexical cohesion is the last possibility to be discussed. Besides repetition or partial repetition of a form, lexical replacements are also involved. Only replacements based on formal semantic relations between lexical items were taken into account, i.e., semantic relations as defined by Lyons (1977) such as hyponymy ('söğüt-agaç' 'willow-tree') or part-whole ('kapı-ev' 'door-house').

Episodic (causal or associational) relations between certain meanings were not taken into account. These would be too susceptible to individual – and not necessarily objective – judgements.

In the texts under investigation, only intersentential cohesive ties were analysed. In every sentence the number of cohesive items was established and the antecedent was determined for each item. Where a presupposition should have been but was not satisfied, i.e., a cohesive item without a proper antecedent (co-referent), the cohesive item was categorized as an error.

Participant continuity

According to Givon (1983), three types of continuity can be distinguished in discourse: thematic continuity, action continuity and topic/participant continuity. Thematic and action continuity are very much related to text coherence, which was considered to be beyond the scope of this study. Topic or participant continuity is again established by formal linguistic means, therefore this was selected for further analysis.

Participant continuity concerning the major characters in a story may be considered to be a specific requirement of narratives – once a participant is introduced in a story (s)he has to be maintained and sometimes reintroduced. Investigating this type of continuity therefore gives more detailed insight into not only reference strategies, but also the introduction of new information.

Givon (1983) considered the thematic paragraph – in which it is most common for one topic to be the continuity marker – to be the smallest textual entity. This topic is often the participant most crucially involved in the action sequence running through the paragraph. There are several linguistic devices for establishing topic continuity, depending on the degree of availability of a topic or participant. Definite descriptions can be used in the case of participants available for quick retrieval; indefinite ones can be used for introducing a new participant. The various ways in which the major characters in a narrative can be presented are a full noun phrase, a reduced noun phrase or a deleted noun phrase. These devices are considered to represent an increasing level of topic continuity, in the order mentioned (Givon, 1983).

Turkish has several linguistic devices for reference, some of which were already mentioned in the preceding section. The most important characteristics of the Turkish pronominal reference system are the following. In Turkish the grammatical subject is realized by means of a personal suffix attached to the verb and only for reasons of contrast or emphasis is a subject realized by means of a pronoun. There is no constant marker of definiteness vs. indefiniteness. Turkish lacks articles for signalling these features. Only direct objects can – by means of the accusative case – be marked for definiteness. Furthermore Turkish has only one third person singular and has no distinction for gender. Consequently, in certain ambiguous cases reference has to be more explicit.

The (re)introduction of a character is usually coded by a full noun phrase. For an easily recoverable (available) participant, a zero representation can be used – in the case of a grammatical subject the verbal marker is the unmarked form. A possessive marker can only be used when the antecedent is immediately available. A more marked form of presenting characters is the use of overt pronouns (including deictical pronouns) for the sake of emphasis or contrast.

Design of the present study

Data collection

The material discussed here was collected within the framework of a broader study on the first language proficiency of Turkish-Dutch bilingual children (Schaufeli, 1991). In order to describe the language behaviour of this group of children on the various linguistic levels, spontaneous speech was collected and additionally some language tests were conducted. Eighteen bilingual children aged 12, living in the Netherlands for at least 8 years, participated in the research. Their language use was compared to the language use of a control group consisting of again 18 children of the same age. Furthermore the two groups were matched on sex, socio-economic and (first language) dialect background.

The children were – amongst others – asked to tell story's from 11 picture series and to write two compositions. For the analyses of text cohesion of each child one oral text and one written text were selected. The oral text was the first story the children had to tell. Almost all stories were about the same two people – a father and his son. In the first story they had to be introduced, whereas in the subsequent stories they could be considered to be known to the listener. The written text was a composition on the subject 'yürüyen ağaç' 'the walking tree'. Accidentally a few days before the data collection in Turkey, a cartoon about a walking tree was broadcast on television. This apparently affected the compositions of some of the monolingual children. As punctuation, especially in the compositions of the bilinguals, was lacking or seemed unreliable, the compositions were divided into sentences (i.e., a main clause with all its subordinate clauses) in the same way as the oral samples were. The individual compositions differed in length, as did the oral narratives. In Table 1 the average number of sentences of the narratives is given.

Table 1. The number of sentences of the language samples.

Number of sentences	N-group	N = 18	T-group	N = 18
Oral sample	227		166	
Written sample	440		274	

The narratives of the bilingual children (N-group), oral as well as written, appeared to be longer than those of the monolingual children (T-group). This holds especially for the written narratives. Thus, it seems that little experience with writing in a particular language does not necessarily influence text length in that same language. However, it must be kept in mind that the sentences the children in Turkey produce, are longer than those produced by the children in the Netherlands. The average MLU, expressed in morphemes was 7.1 for the N-group and 8.6 for the T-group.

Data analysis

On the basis of the number of cohesive items per sentence, a degree of cohesiveness was be calculated for each text.

As already mentioned, errors in cohesion devices were recorded as well. These errors will be discussed separately. As the formula below shows, incorrectly used ties were not incorporated into the calculations of the indices for cohesiveness. The degree for cohesiveness was obtained by applying the following formula:

$$\text{Cohesiveness index} = \frac{\text{total number of correctly realized cohesive ties}}{\text{total number of T-units}}$$

It seemed interesting not only to find out to what degree the texts were cohesive, but also which devices were used for establishing cohesion. Therefore the cohesion devices were not only counted but also categorized according to the taxonomy mentioned before. This allows us to calculate the proportional distribution of the various devices and to discover further differences between the groups.

Both the oral and the written text were analysed for participant continuity. For the oral text – because of the use of pictures – the central figures were fixed. The father and his son play the leading part and, in addition, the teacher is focused on from time to time (cf. Figure 1).

Figure 1. The first picture series used for eliciting spontaneous speech.

Because in all written stories at least two characters were present (sometimes more but never less), the analysis was limited to two principal characters. Generally the 'walking tree' was one of them, the second one varied from composition to composition. Within a sentence, two levels of participant representation were distinguished: agents were labelled as 'primary' participants, the remaining characters (generally only one) as 'secondary participants'. Because the relations between sentences are the focus of this paper, only one representation per character (the one on the highest level) was taken into account in each sentence. These participant representations were categorized into introduction, maintenance or shift. In each narrative, every character is introduced only once, i.e., the first time it is mentioned. After that, it is either maintained, i.e., continues to be referred to on the same or on a lower level, or reintroduced, i.e., referred to after a few sentences of non-use or referred to on a higher level. The latter implies a participant shift on this higher level. On top of this, the references were divided into formal linguistic categories such as full noun phrase, pronoun, etc.

Results

Degree of cohesiveness

Table 2 shows the difference between the two groups on the cohesiveness index.

Table 2. Mean cohesiveness index (M) and its standard deviation (SD) in the two text types.

	N-sample (N = 18)	T-sample (N = 18)	t	p (Df=34)
Cohesiveness oral text				
M	1.8	2.1	1.77	n.s.
SD	0.46	0.56		
Cohesiveness written text				
M	2.4	2.4	0.17	n.s
SD	0.51	0.50		

For the oral texts this is very small whereby the monolingual children score higher – expressed in standard deviations of the T-group: 0.54 SD. However, the difference is not statistically significant (t-test independent samples, Df=34, $p<.05$).

On the written narratives the scores are exactly equal. Considered in the light of the fact that the children in the Netherlands have substantially less writing experience – at least in Turkish – this outcome supports the idea that the establishment of text cohesion is a skill which is relatively mode-independent.

The overall results indicate that the monolingual and bilingual children produce texts with (almost) the same degree of cohesion. According to Scinto (1983), as

First language text cohesion in a Turkish-Dutch bilingual setting already mentioned, this should be interpreted as showing no differences in the level of cognitive functioning.

An example from a written text with a low cohesiveness score is given below. Cafer, a boy living in Ankara, wrote a text in which the main cohesion device was personal marking on the verb. Apart from that, every sentence contains a new situation or event.

3. *Ne yapacağını şaşırdı. Hızla*
    what do-FUTNSP-PS3SG-ACC confuse-PST:3SG fast
    düştü. Bir an bayıldı. Kendisini
    fall-PST:3SG a moment faint-PST:3SG himself-ACC
    nehir kıyısında buldu.
    river side-PS3SG-LOC find-PST:3SG

    'He was confused about what he should do. He fell fast. He fainted for a moment. He found himself at the riverside.'

Dilek, a bilingual child, wrote a quite cohesive text partly due to frequent use of the conjunction 've' 'and' and to the strategy of repeating the verb (lexical cohesion) of the previous sentence by means of the converbial suffix '-IncE' 'when':

4. *Ve hemen kapıları kitlemişler. Kitleyince*
    and immediately door-PL-ACC lock-IPST-3PL lock-WHEN
    hemen karısına söylemiş. Ve çok çok
    immediately wife-PS3SG-DAT tell-IPST-0 and very much
    korkmuş. Korkunca da oğlu koşmuş.
    fear-IPST:3SG fear-WHEN and son-PS3SG run-IPST:3SG

    'And they immediately locked the doors. Locking (them) he told (it) immediately to his wife [..] And he was very much afraid. And while being afraid his son ran.'

To get more insight into the relation between the degree of cohesion in the two text types, Spearman rank-order correlation coefficients were calculated (Siegel, 1956) between cohesiveness in the oral and the written texts. They are given in Table 3. The correlation coefficients within the N-group can be found in the left part of the table, within the T-group in the right.

Table 3. Spearman rank-order correlation coefficient between cohesiveness scores.

N-group		N = 18	T-group		N = 18
	oral text			oral text	
written text	.29		written text	−.23	

*p<.05

Within the N-sample the correlation is positive but very weak. This means that children in the Netherlands who produce a relatively cohesive oral narrative do not necessarily produce a relatively cohesive written narrative, and vice versa. Within the T-sample the correlations are – although very weak – even negative.

For both groups, the correlation for cohesion is not significant. However, remarkable is the outcome for the monolinguals. There seems to be a weak tendency to produce a relatively cohesive oral text and at the same time a written text with a relatively low degree of cohesiveness, and vice versa. After a closer look at the narratives of the eight T-children who obtained the highest rank-order differences, two different reasons offering an explanation appeared. Five of these eight children missed the point of the picture story, they just described the pictures one by one without stating relations between them. In their written work, however, they appeared to be able to produce a moderate or even very solid story – in terms of cohesiveness. For three of these five, the cartoon on television provided the framework for their narrative (cf. § 4). The remaining three children (of the initial eight) produced cohesive oral narratives, but were not able to invent an attractive story for the composition task. So in both cases the lack of a story framework in general resulted in a rambling story, either because the pictures were not understood or because of a lack of imagination.

To summarize, bilingual children produce texts which are as cohesive as those produced by monolinguals. Furthermore, a framework seems to be necessary for producing a cohesive story. Within the T-sample, such a framework seemed to be absent relatively often, either in the written or in the oral text, resulting in a negative correlation between the narrative skills in these two kinds of texts.

The use of cohesiveness devices

In Table 4, the frequencies of the various cohesive ties in the oral sample are given. Besides the categories already listed (cf. § 4), a category P (Picture) is added. It covers the use of deictical terms which refer directly to the picture. On the basis of audio tapes it is of course difficult to judge wether a child uses a deictical term extra- or intra-linguistically. Therefore only reference devices which were uncomprehensible without the presence of a picture were categorized as 'P'. This implies that only deictical terms used for participant introductions could unambiguously be judged as referring to the picture.

Table 4. The absolute frequencies (f) and percentages (%) of correctly and incorrectly used cohesive ties in the oral text.

	Oral N-sample (227 T-units)				Oral T-sample (166 T-units)			
	incorrect		correct		incorrect		correct	
	f	%	f	%	f	%	f	%
Cr	148	25.2	77	13.1	105	21.3	44	8.9
L	163	27.7	32	5.4	182	37.0	19	3.9
C	95	16.2	16	2.7	58	11.8	4	0.01
E	16	2.7	21	3.8	8	1.6	12	2.4
(P)	17	2.9	3	0.01	48	9.8	12	2.4
Tot. %	74.7		25.3		81.5		18.5	
Total ties			588				492	

This strategy is strictly speaking not a text cohesion device. However, in the presence of pictures, deictic referential devices are (generally) unambiguous and consequently cannot be judged to be unacceptable. Because these items establish some sort of cohesion and should also not be counted as an error, they are considered separately. The children in Turkey score substantially higher in this category.

The differences between the groups in proportional distribution of the correctly used cohesive ties are statistically significant (X^2=33.5. p<.001; Siegel, 1956).

As far as the 'real' text cohesion devices are concerned, the major difference between the groups seems to be found with respect to lexical cohesion (L). The children in Turkey use this device more frequently (37 per cent) than the children in the Netherlands (27.7 per cent), who use the various other devices more frequently instead – they in fact score higher on all other categories.

This implies that the children in Turkey are more redundant when referring in their oral narratives – they use in 37 per cent of the cases a lexical item for establishing a cohesive tie – whereas the children in the Netherlands rely more on devices as co-reference and ellipsis. Conjunctive cohesion also occurs more often in the N-sample, which – according to the results of Yde and Spoelders (1985) – is an indication of a less mature stage of narrative organization. The cause is probably the same as in Yde and Spoelder's study – the children do not have the means to establish sentence-internal relations by means of clause linking devices (Schaufeli, 1991:Ch. 8).

The error percentage in the oral N-sample is higher than in the T-sample, respectively 25.3 per cent and 18.5 per cent. The amount of errors seems to be reasonably high in both groups. Because (P) is not considered to be a text cohesion device, it was not incorporated into a Chi-squared test conducted on the proportional distribution of error types. The differences between the groups were not statistically significant (X^2=2.2, Df=3; Siegel, 1956).

If the percentages of correct and incorrect usage of the various devices are considered, it appears that ellipsis occurs relatively infrequently. However, the frequency of incorrect usage is higher than the frequency of correct usage – both in the N-sample and in the T-sample. This means that the majority of the ellipsis ties are incorrectly used. An incorrectly used ellipsis is a *'substitution by zero'* in which case it is not clear from where the empty slot in the sentence should be filled:

5. *Ordan öğretmen geldi. # Çocuğuna*
   there-ABL teacher come-PST:3SG ZERO child-PS3SG-DAT
   verdi galiba.
   give-PST:3SG probably

   'The teacher came from there. He probably gave (it) to the child'

The direct object slot in the second sentence was not filled. Although the sentence in itself is not ungrammatical, it is not clear what the zero element refers to.

In Table 4, errors in deictical reference to the picture are also listed. The children in Turkey make relatively frequent use of this device incorrectly. Because it might not be clear what is meant by 'incorrectly' in this context, an example will be given. Sometimes the children refer to something in the pictures which is not present or not clear. In the next example, the child mentions a heavy thing, although nothing of that nature can be found in the pictures.

6. *Veya bu ağır şey üstüne düşmüş.*
   or this heavy thing top-PS3SG-DAT fall-IPST:3SG
   'Or this heavy thing fell on him.'

Cases like these may be judged as perception errors. However, the pictures were quite clear and unambiguous, therefore all instances of unfulfilled presuppositions were regarded as incorrect cohesive ties.

With respect to the written texts, the category *deictical reference to pictures* was of course dropped. The frequencies of the cohesive ties for these texts are shown in Table 5.

The differences in proportions between the groups are statistically significant (X^2=16.1, p<.005; Siegel, 1956). The major difference was found in conjunctive cohesion. This tendency, which could already be observed in the oral narratives, seems to be slightly stronger in the written texts.

In the T-sample, a slightly higher percentage of lexical and referential cohesion is found compared to the N-sample. The error percentage in the written samples seems almost equal for both groups. The difference in proportions between both groups is again not statistically significant (X^2=4.2, Df=3; Siegel, 1956).

Table 5. The absolute frequencies (f) and percentages (%) of correctly and incorrectly used cohesive ties in the written text.

	Written N-sample (440 T-units)				Written T-sample (273 T-units)			
	correct		incorrect		correct		incorrect	
	f	%	f	%	f	%	f	%
Cr	368	32.5	27	2.4	256	36.8	17	2.4
L	444	27.7	18	1.6	290	42.7	16	2.3
C	232	20.5	12	1.1	94	13.5	5	0.01
E	16	1.4	14	1.2	7	1.0	4	0.01
Tot. %	93.7		6.3		94.0		6.0	
Total ties	1131				696			

The children in Turkey more frequently use co-reference as a cohesion device in their written narratives compared to their oral narratives. Because the possibility of referring to a picture is absent, they seem to use co-reference instead.

Frequent use of lexical ties gives a rather formal impression. There are some indications that indeed the children in Turkey may have used a slightly more formal register (Schaufeli, 1991:52). The majority of these lexical cohesion devices consist of repetition, i.e., the same noun is used for referring to a certain entity. So a higher percentage of lexical cohesion must not immediately be interpreted as a more detailed and lexically richer reference strategy, as the example below will show.

7. *Bir baba var. Bu baba çocuğunun*
   a father exist this father child-PS3SG-GEN
   ders çalışmasına yardım etmiyor.
   lesson work-INF-PS3SG-DAT help do-NEG-PRGR-0
   Sonra çocuğu ağlıyor, yapamadığı
   later child-PS3SG cry-PRGR:SG make-POT-NEG-NsP-ACC
   için. Babası yanına geliyor.....
   because father-PS3SG side-PS3SG come-PRGR:SG

   'There is a father. This father is not helping his child with his lessons. Then the child is crying, because he's not able to do it. His father is coming next to him...'

This child goes on referring to the two main characters as 'baba' 'father' and 'çocuk' 'child'. The use of for example 'adam' 'man' and 'oğul' 'son' would have been possible and would have caused some lexical diversity, which is now completely absent. The strategy this child uses makes a rather rigid impression. In the second sentence, for example, 'bu baba' 'this father', may be judged as redundant. Personal marking on the verb, a co-referential cohesion device, would have been sufficient and more 'natural'.

Establishing participant continuity

In Table 6 the results of a frequency count of the various devices for establishing participant continuity occurring in both text types are given. The proportional distribution of introduction, maintenance and shift of participant are almost equal in the N and the T samples, in both the oral and the written texts. The lower percentage of participant introductions in the written texts in Table 6 is due to the number of characters taken into account for this analysis (two per story).

Table 6. Frequency (f) and percentages (%) of topic introduction, maintenance and shift.

	N-sample		T-sample	
	f	%	f	%
oral text				
intro	63	19	57	21
maint	191	57	167	62
shift	83	25	47	17
written text				
intro	34	8	33	9
maint	272	67	269	73
shift	98	24	65	18

The children in the Netherlands have a slightly higher percentage of shift than the children in Turkey, who consequently have a higher percentage of maintenance. So the children in the Netherlands switch more frequently between levels of participant representation in their stories. This is in line with the findings of Verhoeven (1988) who found that proportionally 7 and 8-year-old children in the Netherlands tend to shift reference to a greater extent in oral narratives. In the following example, taken from the oral N-sample, a continuing shift of participants takes place. The father and the child have been introduced. In the first sentence the father is the primary participant. In the second, the child is again put forward (participant shift). Then the teacher is introduced in a primary role and after that the primary participant role switches to the child again.

8. *Anlatıyor. Sonra çocuk okula gidiyor.*
   explain-PRGR:3SG then child school-DAT go-PRGR:3SG
   Öğretmen anlatıyor. Ama çocuk yine anlamıyor.
   teacher explain-PRGR:3SG but child again understand-NEG-PRGR:3SG

   'He [=the father] explains it. Then the child is going to school. The teacher explains it. But, again the child does not understand.'

In example (9), of a monolingual child telling the same story, the father is the primary character in the first three sentences, then the teacher is introduced and remains the primary character in the following sentences (which are not shown).

9. *Burda babası çocuğun dersinde*
   here father-PS3SG child-GEN lesson-PS3SG-LOC
   yardım ediyor. Onu okuluna götürüyor.
   help do-PRGR:3SG he-ACC school-DAT take-PRGR:3SG
   Çocuğu dersini yapmadığı
   child-ACC lesson-PS3SG-ACC do-NEG-NSR-PS3SG
   için dövüyor. Öğretmeni çocuklara
   because hit-PRGR:3SG teacher-PS3SG child-PL-DAT
   bir kitap gösteriyor....
   a book show-PRGR:3SG

   'Here the father helps the child with his lessons. He takes him to school. He hits the child because he (=the child) didn't do his lessons. His teacher shows the children a book...'

The various linguistic devices for realizing participant continuity are listed in Table 7, together with the absolute frequencies of occurrence. (Chi-squared tests were not carried out because of the low frequency in the majority of the cells). Next to full noun phrases (NP), deictical (Deic) and personal pronouns (Ppron), possessive markers (Poss), personal marking on the verb, i.e., verb agreement (Agr) and zero representation (Zero), were distinguished. 'Other' refers to a residual category mainly consisting of reflexive pronouns.

It can be inferred that both in the written and in the oral text, participants are generally introduced by means of a full noun phrase. For the reintroduction (or shift) of a participant, a full noun phrase is also the most frequently used device. In the two fragments above (8) and (9) these strategies were demonstrated.

Table 7. Frequencies (f) of the various ways in which main characters are represented.

	N-sample			T-sample		
	intro f	maint f	shift f	intro f	maint f	shift f
oral text						
NP	60	33	45	54	63	39
Deic	–	1	–	2	3	1
Ppron	1	11	15	1	15	–
Poss	1	51	2	–	16	–
Agr	–	76	17	–	62	6
Zero	–	18	–	–	6	–
Other	1	1	4	–	2	1
written text						
NP	32	50	92	31	45	48
Deic	–	2	–	–	4	–
Ppron	2	27	1	–	21	8
Poss	–	30	–	–	21	1
Agr	–	140	5	2	172	7
Zero	–	21	–	–	5	1
Other	–	2	–	–	1	1

Although this is generally the most appropriate strategy – as the scores in the T-sample may show – the children in the Netherlands also use personal pronouns and verb agreement for this purpose. So participant shift in the N-sample may not always be adequate. Verhoeven (1988) signalled a similar tendency in the language use of 7 and 8-year-old bilinguals. Contrary to their monolingual peers, in quite a lot of cases they do use personal marking on the verb (verb agreement) for shifting to another participant.

For participant maintenance, various strategies are used. The children in Turkey prefer to maintain a character either by means of a full noun phrase or by verb agreement, whereas – at least in their oral narratives – the children in the Netherlands also make use of possessive marking. In example (10) of a bilingual child, the primary participant in the first sentence (i.e., 'çocuk' 'the child') is maintained in the second by means of a possessive in 'babası' 'his father'. This strategy is used quite infrequently in the T-sample.

10. *Çocuk bilmiyor, bir dersini.*
    child know-NEG-PRGR a lesson-PS3SG-ACC
    Sonra babası yardım ediyor.
    then father-PS3SG help do-PRGR

'The child does not know his lesson. Then his father helps.'

From the findings concerning participant continuity, it again appears that the children in Turkey use lexical devices more frequently in their oral language use. An example of this strategy worth noting is given below.

11. *Okulda yaptığı iş yanlış olduğu*
    school-LOC do-NsP-PS3SG work wrong be-NsP-PS3SG
    için öğretmeni çocukla birlikte evlerine
    because teacher-PS3SG child-WITH together house-PS3PL-DAT
    gidiyor. Ve öğretmen çocukla birlikte
    go-PRGR:3SG and teacher child-WITH together
    evlerine gittikten sonra kapıyı çalıyorlar.
    house-PS3PL-DAT go-NsP-ABL after door-ACC ring-PRGR-3PL

    'Because the work he did at school was wrong, the child together with his teacher goes to their home. And, after the teacher went to their home together with the child, they ring the bell.'

In addition to the rather redundant use of full nouns in the second sentence of this example – within the sentence – other reference devices, particularly possessive markers, are also frequently used. Such a degree of reference is seldom found in the N-sample. As already suggested, this may be a characteristic of more formal language use.

The findings presented in the former section (concerning the category P), amongst others, showed that deictical terms occur relatively frequently in the T-sample. From Table 7, it will be clear that they are not used for presenting the major characters in a story.

For the written texts (cf. Table 7), the language use of both groups is very similar. Considerable differences between the two samples in the use of the possessive marker for participant maintenance was not found as was the case in the oral texts.

The amount of shift in the N-sample is probably influenced by text length. The children in the Netherlands produce longer texts and consequently have more opportunity for shifting between characters. This of course influences the absolute number of participant shifts.

The proportions of use of the various devices for participant maintenance seem to differ only marginally between the two written samples. The frequency of agreement on the verb as a maintenance device is a little higher in the T-sample, whereas the children in the Netherlands use the other devices somewhat more frequently than their peers in Turkey. They make slightly more use of personal pronouns and possessive markers and they also use ellipsis from time to time, while the children in Turkey almost never do.

Anneli Schaufeli

215

Conclusions

From the results presented in this chapter, it will be clear that as far as text cohesion is concerned the texts the children in Turkey and the children in the Netherlands produce are comparable to a large extent. The degree of cohesion is (almost) the same. Roughly speaking, the same cohesion devices are used and similar errors are made in the same areas. Only with respect to the proportional distribution of the various cohesion devices in both the oral and in the written text, are significant differences found. The bilingual children in the Netherlands use relatively more conjunctive cohesion, and the children in Turkey are inclined to use more deictical terms directly referring to the picture while telling a story from pictures. The latter also use more full noun phrases.

The section on participant continuity confirmed the impression that the narratives of bilingual and monolingual Turkish children, both oral and written, are quite similar. Participant continuity generally seems to be established as it should be, i.e., introduction and shift by means of noun phrases and maintenance by means of the other devices. The only (slight) exception was found with respect to participant shift in the oral narratives. Whereas shift towards another participant is most likely to be realized through the use of a noun phrase (compare the language use of the T-group), the N-children also make use of less appropriate devices as pronominal reference or verb agreement. This same tendency was found by Verhoeven (1988) in the language use of 8-year-old bilingual children.

The fact that only marginal differences were found between bilinguals and monolinguals is remarkable in the light of Verhoeven's research. He found that, amongst other things, the devices which 8-year-old Turkish children in the Netherlands use are very similar to those used by 5-year-old monolinguals in Turkey. This suggests that, between age 8 and age 11, the narrative skills of the children in the Netherlands develop so fast that within three years they reach the same proficiency level that the children in Turkey reach in six years time.

When the results presented here are related to earlier research findings, it can be concluded that certain first language discourse oriented skills in a bilingual setting develop differently from lexical and morphosyntactic skills, as compared to the language development in a monolingual context. Whereas bilingual children lag more and more behind their monolingual peers where lexical and morphosyntactic proficiency are concerned, on the discourse level they seem to catch up with their peers between ages 8 and 11.

Despite the limited Turkish input the bilingual children receive, they use text cohesion devices to the same extent and almost in the same way as their monolingual peers do in both written and oral narratives. The developmental catching-up manoeuvre of the bilingual children may indicate that once the formal linguistic means have been acquired, their appropriate application does not pose any problem. Training narrative skills at Dutch schools may offer an explanation for the fast development of the bilingual children. This experience of practising narrative skills, although it takes place in Dutch, may have a positive influence on the narrative proficiency in Turkish as well.

The comparison of the oral and the written texts leads to the conclusion that, as far as the nature of the cohesion is concerned, oral and written language use is more similar in the case of the monolinguals in Turkey than of the bilinguals in the Netherlands. This confirms the general impression that the oral language of the monolingual children in this particular situation is more formal than the language use of the bilingual children. Consequently the assumption that the differences between monolingual and bilingual children might be larger concerning written narratives as compared to oral narratives as formulated in the introduction, was not at all confirmed.

Abbreviations used in the glosses

0	zero marker indicating third person singular
1SG	first person singular marker
3PL	third person plural marker
ABL	ablative case marker
ACC	accusative case marker
DAT	dative case marker
FUTNSP	future non-subject participle marker
GEN	genitive case marker
INF	infinitival marker
IPST	inferential past tense marker
LOC	locative case marker
NEG	negation marker
NsP	non-subject participle marker
PL	plural marker
POT	potential stem extension marker
PRGR	progressive tense marker
PS3SG	possessive marker, third person singular
PST	past tense marker

References

Bamberg, M., 1986. A functional approach to the acquisition of anaphoric relationships. *Linguistics,* 24, 227-284.

Boeschoten, H., 1990. *Acquisition of Turkish by immigrant children, a multiple case study of Turkish children in the Netherlands aged 4 to 6.* Ph.D. Thesis, Katholieke Universiteit Brabant.

Brown, G. & G. Yule, 1983. *Discourse Analysis.* Cambridge: Cambridge University Press.

Durmusoglu, G., 1987. Cohesion in Turkish. In: H. Boeschoten & L. Verhoeven (eds), *Studies on Modern Turkish, Proceedings of the third Conference on Turkish Linguistics,* 189-202. Tilburg: Tilburg University Press.

Givon, T., 1983. Topic Continuity in Discourse: an Introduction. In: T.Givon (ed.), *Topic Continuity in Discourse: A Quantitative Cross-language Study,* 1-41. Amsterdam: Benjamins.

Halliday, M. & R. Hasan, 1976. *Cohesion in English.* London etc.: Longman.

Hickmann, M., 1982. *The Development of Narrative Skills.* Ph.D. Thesis, University of Chicago

Hickmann, M., 1987. *Clause Structure Variation in Narrative Discourse.* Nijmegen: Max Planck Institute.

Karmiloff-Smith, A., 1985. Language and Cognitive Processes from a developmental perspective. *Language and Cognitive Processes* Vol. 1 no. 1, 61-85.

Lyons, J., 1977. *Semantics.* Cambridge: Cambridge University Press.

Pfaff, C., 1991. Turkish in contact with German: Language maintenance and loss among immigrant children in Berlin (West). *International Journal of the Sociology of Language* 90, 97-130.

Schaufeli, A., 1990. L1 Morphosyntactic Proficiency of Turkish Children in the Netherlands. Paper presented at the *Fifth Int. Conference on Turkish Linguistics,* London August 15-17.

Schaufeli, A., 1991. *Turkish in an Immigrant Setting: a comparative study of the first language of monolingual and bilingual Turkish children.* Ph.D. Thesis, Universiteit van Amsterdam.

Scinto, L., 1983. The Development of Text Production. In: J. Fine & R. Freedle (eds), *Developmental Issues in Discourse,* 225-268. Norwood N.J.: Ablex.

Siegel, S., 1956. *Non-Parametric Statistics for the Behavioral Sciences.* New York etc.: McGraw-Hill.

Verhoeven, L., 1988. Acquisition of Discourse Cohesion in Turkish. In: S. Koç (ed.), *Studies on Turkish Linguistics, Proceedings of the fourth International Conference on Turkish Linguistics,* Middle East Technical University, Ankara, 437-452.

Verhoeven, L. & H. Boeschoten, 1986. First Language acquisition in a second language submersion environment. *Applied Psycholinguistics* 7, 241-256.

Wigglesworth, G., 1990. Children's Narrative Acquisition: a Study of Some Aspects of Reference and Anaphora. *First Language,* Vol.10, 105-125.

Yde, P. & M. Spoelders, 1985. Text Cohesion: An exploratory study with beginning writers. *Applied Psycholinguistics,* No.6, 407-416.

Temporal reference and narrative structures in Italian and German by Italian migrant children in Germany

In recent linguistic and sociolinguistic research a renewed interest can be observed in questions concerning the relationship between language (also language acquisition and development), culture and cognition (cf. Slobin, 1991; Agar, 1991; Gumperz & Levinson, 1991). Emphasizing the conceptual side and the psycholinguistic aspects of grammar and discourse and assuming a conceptual framework of language systems, some linguists and psychologists stress the universal cognitive constraints on language structure more than the socially, pragmatically, and culturally related constraints on the norms of actualization. In a less universalistic way, dealing with narratives in a cross-cultural overview, Slobin (1991) claims that the expression of experience in linguistic terms constitutes 'thinking for speaking' (p.11); this 'involves picking those characters of objects and events that a) fit some conceptualization of the event, and b) are readily encodable in the language' (p.12). However, assuming a more direct association of the production and interpretation of speech activities with social constraints (cf. Vygotsky, 1962), and looking at language as a social construction (cf. Berger & Luckmann, 1966; Schütz & Luckmann, 1979; Luckmann, 1989; Gumperz, 1982), we can see how the production and interpretation of speech activities in particular social situations are not only related to 'cognition' but also to 'knowledge' and are consequently socially and culturally constrained, and thus both display and typify particular experiences.

In the light of these considerations the language development in a bilingual situation such as that of migrant children, appears to be of great interest. In fact these children internalize two different languages and cultures in a contact situation which displays asymmetrical social and cultural distribution and where the mother language is disadvantaged. How, then, should we consider the conception of Slobin, who proposes that 'in acquiring a native language the child learns particular ways of thinking for speaking' (p.12) or that 'the categories that are not grammaticalized in the native language are generally ignored'? In this respect it is problematic to state which of the two languages is the native one for bilingual migrants' children. And it also appears problematic to find out how the grammaticalization of particular categories in one language influences that in the other language.

The question is how do the cultural backgrounds associated with the two languages or speech styles in contact connotatively interfere with each other.

Within the frame of a research project on *The mother tongue of Italian migrants' children in contact with German* (1985, DFG) we have been able to describe and interpret in particular the use and the meaning of some forms of bilingual speech activities in informal situations in everyday interaction (cf. Auer, 1982; Auer & di Luzio, 1983, 1984, 1988; Bierbach, 1985; di Luzio, 1982, 1991).

But some aspects of language use in specific genres of speech activities of these children in more formal situations and in an institutional setting in which the normative constraints of school teaching are displayed are also useful for understanding relevant features of their grammatical and communicative competence in their migrant situation.

As the comparison of the realization of the same items in both contact languages by the same children is not possible at present as such data are unavailable, useful insights into the characteristics of the grammatical and discursive features of their 'native' speech may also be gained from a comparison with monolingual native speakers in their 'native' social and cultural environment in Italy.

Aims of the present investigation

The aim of this paper is to show some aspects of the construction of temporal reference and narrative structure in narratives of 'vicarious' experience (retellings of films, picture stories and tales) told in Italian by a group of children (aged 8-12) of Southern Italian immigrant workers living in Konstanz, Germany. The linguistic socialization and interaction of these children is predominantly 'German', as they speak a southern Italian dialect or Italian variety only with their parents and relatives and a more standard variety of Italian in the classes in *Italian culture and language* they choose to attend during two hours a week outside the curriculum of German schools. For a sketchy characterization of this group and its environment cf. di Luzio (1982, 1991: 132-33).

Their narrative performance in the mother tongue will be compared with that of a group of monolingual children of Southern Italian immigrant workers in Northern Italy (Varese). The native performance of the monolingual group in Varese will be taken as a basis for comparison, and, as a further point of reference, the standard or near-standard Italian norm as learned and used in Italy will also be used.

Narrative accounts are an important discourse activity in children's everyday interaction. For the normative performance of narratives a good command of complex temporal morphosyntactic and discursive forms and structures is needed in order to produce 'accountable' temporal reference and meaningfully interpretable narrative structure. Further necessary linguistic devices are connected with the foregrounding of narratively 'relevant' points or events as well as the giving or contextualizing of the background information necessary for accounting for the 'motives by reason or in consequence of which' and 'the motives in order to which' actions are carried out and events happen and are fully understandable (cf. Schütz & Luckmann, 1979) .

Both the morphosyntactic forms and textual patterns the speakers have at their disposal and the form of the input constrain the temporal, motivational and relevance patterning in narrative retellings. Thus, in retelling stories, a) reference to agents-patients, acts, means and goals of acting, to the scene of the events and b) the collocation of these elements within a frame of temporal, motivational and relevance relationships in other peoples' narrations, is transformed and projected onto the speaker's own text, who contextualizes it according to his own social and cognitive constraints.

In showing how temporal, motivational, and relevance structure at both the morphosyntactic and textual level are realized in the Italian narrative accounts of bilingual migrants' children in Germany, I also want to indicate some significant differences displayed in comparison with the corresponding group of monolingual children in Varese, Italy.

The investigation will be restricted to the more formal renarrating accounts of 'vicarious experience' of fictional events, in which the children either retell the latest film or episode of a TV series they have seen, formulate a text of a short picture story, or retell a story they have just heard or already know. Only a brief comparison will be made with narratives of personal experience in everyday interaction (cf. Auer & di Luzio, 1988) since, unlike fictional narratives, these do not display significant peculiarities in construction of temporality.

Renarrations of fictional stories are chosen for several reasons. In renarrating, the children have both a communicative and a learning task to solve, and these tasks occur frequently in institutional settings in which the communicative codes are normatively regulated. Renarrations are more decontextualized than personal narratives; their construction requires more lexical, grammatical and textual work because of the different rhetorical or contextualization conventions of the narrative models. The encoding norms of renarrations are a constitutive part of school and mass-media socialization. They display literacy and literary patterns with a higher level of stylistic register and also imply other types of audience expectation. Hence it can be expected that this kind of competence is more restricted in the mother tongue of migrants' children. In fact, unlike that of the monolingual children in Italy, their socialization in regard to normative fictional narrating is very slight. Their parents have no time for telling fairy tales and their grandparents are in Italy. Thus they learn and develop narrative competence in a more spontaneous and less guided way, receiving their models, apart from the one-hour weekly Italian classes, overwhelmingly from the German school. The films and series-episodes they prefer to watch on TV are in German. Consequently it is plausible to assume an influence from German, (the language they prefer and know better) on the morphosyntactic and textual construction of temporality, motivation and relevance in narratives in Italian.

Some preliminary questions to which only partial answers can be sought concern 1) the kind and degree of markedness of temporal forms, 'motivational' forms (causal, final or consecutive) and 'relevance' forms (fore- and backgrounding devices) with reference to Standard Italian; 2) how and to what extent simplification strategies and pragmatic devices are employed in achieving a suitable temporal, motivational, and 'relevance' structure; 3) the way in which the realization of temporal, motivational and relevance categories or functions differs from that of the monolingual children of the Varese group and 4) how these differences can be meaningfully interpreted.

These general questions are interlinked with the following more particular ones at the morphosyntactic and textual levels: 5) the use of 'imperfetto' forms with non-stative verbs, as well as the corresponding neutralization of these forms in their aspectual function and their consequences for backgrounding/foregrounding; 6) the frequency of occurrence of 'passato remoto' forms in alternation with present perfect (passato prossimo) forms, as well as the variation between perfect and plusquamperfect forms; 7) the means and devices for backgrounding/foregrounding; 8) the kind of temporal or motivational binding of clauses (coordination and juxtaposition versus subordination and integration); 9) the use and function of indexical versus lexical or morphosyntactic expressions.

I hope that the treatment of these questions will contribute to a better understanding of the influence which both a) the contact between Italian and German varieties and b) the universal principles of language development and strategies of language learning have on the development of the Konstanz children's Italian competence. In particular this can help to understand better the use of temporal, motivational, and 'relevance' forms in narrative constructions by the Konstanz children in comparison with those in Italy, and cast some light on the relationship between the speech behaviour and the sociocultural situation in emigration.

Methodological remarks

Lexical, morphosyntactic and textual units and their reciprocal relationships and functions, which constitute the internal structure of narrative texts, are patterned according to general and particular activity schemata. These activate and constrain the narrative structure as a whole (grammatical and textual).

With regard to general schemata which are activated by the production and interpretation of narratives and which have to be taken into account by the interpretative analysis, we refer to the 'rhetorical' approach of Burke (1966, 1969) combined with the sociolinguistic textual approach of Labov (Labov et al., 1967), cf. K.A. Watson (1973). The key categories or 'dimensions' which (reinterpreting Burke, 1969a XV, 7) constitute and define the structure and functions of dramatic-narrative activities and their context of occurrence within the narrated story as well as in its narration are: (1) act ('what took place'), (2) scene (the background and the situation of occurrence of the act), (3) agent ('what person or kind of person performed the act'), (4) agency (i.e., means or instruments used by the agent), (5) purpose (the 'why', ie. the motive for which the agent performed the act).

We add to them the essential categories of narrative 'as one method of recapitulating past experience by matching a verbal sequence of clauses to the sequence of events which (it is inferred) actually occurred' (Labov, 1972: 359). The most essential categories are: 'complicating action' the central part of the narrative, optionally followed by its 'resolution' or result, optionally preceded by an 'abstract', associated with an 'evaluation' (internal or external to the narrative clauses), and followed by a final 'coda'. The evaluation, 'the most important element in addition to the basic narrative clause' is 'that part of the narrative which reveals the attitude of the narrator towards the narrative by emphasizing the relative importance of some narrative units as compared to the others' (Labov, 1967). It is interesting to note here that no evaluative devices were found by Labov in narratives of 'vicarious experience' such as television plots.

Constitutive of narrative structures is also foregrounding of what the narrator sees as 'figure' vis-à-vis the 'ground' (cf. Reinhart, 1984), the backgrounding or production of relevant context ('ground') for the foreground (cf. also Hopper, 1982; Klein, 1982; Tomlin, 1987; Von Stutterheim, 1991). Backgrounding work consists, among other things, in both the display of orientation and evaluation devices as well as the account of motivational relationships between the elements of the narration.

With regard to particular schemata for descriptive and interpretive tasks we can integrate within the methods mentioned above those represented by the membership categorization devices (Sacks, 1972) for establishing relevance and motivational structures. These are sociosemantic inventories of categories which collect various reciprocally related social categories and roles (e.g teacher, director, pupil, schoolmate) and connect them with activities (more generally predicates) which are typically bound to these categories ('category-bound activities').

In dealing with the temporal, motivational and relevance structures in narratives I will adopt the reconstructive and interpretative methods employed in interpretative sociolinguistics (cf. Gumperz, 1982; di Luzio, 1991). I further assume that (1) narratives do function – analogously to other communicative genres – as solutions of communicative problems, and (2) that internal narrative structures and functions are constrained by their external structures, i.e., by the relationship of these genres (and their realizations) to social structure and to the type of settings (situations) in which they occur (Luckmann, 1989; see also Blom & Gumperz, 1972). The situation is determined by the type of message (i.e., type of narrative), by the scene or setting, by the agents and recipients, as well as by their social and biographical background, by their reciprocal attitudes, expectations and shared norms, by the communicative purposes and by the means employed.

Apart from the content of the message recognized through 'envisionment of the world of the text' (cf. Fillmore, 1982: 329; Auer & di Luzio, 1988: 160 f.), more is needed, namely representation, production and interpretation of the 'world of the text' with the help of schemata and contextualization devices on the basis of several presuppositions (cf. Gumperz, 1982, 1991; Auer & di Luzio, 1992; Duranti & Goodwin, 1992). The latter is necessary to (re)constitute the background and context necessary for the interpretation of the narration.

Paradoxically on the one hand, the interim language and speech of the children must be interpreted with their own categories and not with those of standard language adult speakers. On the other hand, as adults in everyday life, we must reinterpret the children's utterances and translate them into our own language; and we do this with the categories based on adult linguistic knowledge, which, after all, is also the knowledge we also want to teach them in the process of linguistic socialization.

The construction of temporality in narratives

A story teller or reteller has, as already mentioned above, many tasks to solve. He must activate for himself and the interactants a suitable representation of the narrated events and an accountable presentation of them. The conditions of text cohesion and coherence must be satisfied, and the relevance and motivation structures of actions and events must be pointed out. Important work must be done for the (re) construction of the temporal structure of the events and their functions. From the standpoint of the story (re)teller, a necessary procedure for doing this is temporal reference. The normal device for expressing temporal reference in Italian as well as in German is the use of (1) temporal verb-bound morphemes or other markers for a) tense, b) aspect and c) 'Aktionsart' according to the constraints on the (in)compatibility of the forms of a), b) and c) with each other; (2) of the deictic 'origin'('ego, hic et nunc') and other deictic temporal reference points which are established with reference to the 'origin' (cf. Reichenbach, 1947), if not to the calendar; (3) of temporal adverbs (e. g. *prima, dopo, allora, subito),* conjunctions (e. g. *prima che, dopo che, allorché, appena)* and prepositions (e.g., *durante, dopo di)* expressing time intervals and time relations (relations of anteriority, simultaneity and posteriority, which also are expressed by tense-morphemes of verbs); (4) several presupposed pragmatic principles and parts of knowledge regarding the structure of events and general or particular schemata as well as the application of the well known conversational maxims.

The reference to the type of course of the temporal events expressed by the verb is obtained by choosing the verbs or verb prefixes that semantically express the suitable 'Aktionsart' and also constrain the choice of the verb morphemes for tense and aspect. One device among others for expressing reference to relevance and motivation relationships of the events and actions related to each other and to the speaker is the use of aspectual and modal verb morphemes and of corresponding adverbs and conjunctions .

As pointed out by Bühler (1934), a primary type of deixis, the so-called 'demonstratio ad oculos' is used, when the indexical field is situated in the perceptual space of the interactants at the temporal 'space' of the speech act ; another type of deixis, the 'anaphora' is used, when the indexical field is constituted by the discourse in its course. Finally, a third type of deixis, the so-called 'deixis ad phantasma', which is relevant of the expression and interpretation of the temporal structure of narratives, is used when the indexical field is constituted by the scene which is evoked by means of fantasy or memory. A first variant (3A) of this secondary and displaced deixis is displayed when the speaker carries elements of past events immediately in front of interactants and indicates them as if they were vividly present (idiomatically: 'The mountain comes to Mohammed'). A second variant (3B) is shown when the speaker carries both himself and the interactants into the indexical space of the past, and they move together within it, as if it were the space of the actual speech act situation (idiomatically: 'Mohammed goes to the mountain'). Finally, in a third variant (3C) the speaker and his interactants look at the event situated in the temporal frame of the past from the perspective of the point of view located in the actual speech act situation ('Mohammed and the mountain remain each at their own place, and M. sees the mountain from his own perception point'). The latter is the subtype most frequently employed in narratives, especially in standard, literary and normative performances.

In other words, in the temporal deixis, the speaker-hearer conceives the location of the events in the past (secondary or displaced reference) only with reference to the time of speech act (primary reference). If he disregards the primary reference (and this is the case of most fictional stories), the reference points in the past may function autonomously as reference-points for events or states happening at the same very point or at other points of the past as related to him. If the reference point is not otherwise marked, the event expressed by the verb in the preceding clause will be taken by default as a reference-point for the following events.

We must observe that temporal reference is expressed by signs which denote as well as signal the referent; cf. Jakobson's (1971) category of 'shifters', that is, of elements which are indexical and symbolic at the same time. Using 'shifters' the speaker- hearer refers to the message and characterizes the process of the event with reference to the process of its utterance in the actual speech act situation. Besides tense and modal markers, both markers for 'aspect' (which Jakobson excludes probably because of a supposed overlapping with the category of 'Aktionsart') and markers for signalling relevance and motivation relationships are, in my opinion, also used in the function of 'shifters'. The function of aspect as well as of mood (relevance and motivation ascription) in the process of the narrated event is interpretable only with reference to the perspective from which the speaker looks at the event. Here it is the subjective insight displayed at the moment of the actual speech act into the accomplishment of the process embedded in the event narrated which is at play. The category of 'Aktionsart' is used differently as an inherent feature of the meaning of the verb stems which characterize the course of the process expressed by the verb stems (e.g., +/-durative, +/- terminative, /+/- inchoative, +/- iterative etc.) selected by the speakers in order to define the kind of action going on in the event narrated.

Narrative tenses in German and Italian

Some sketchy information on the contrastive system and the use of tenses and aspects in the German and Italian verb follows (cf. Wunderlich, 1970; Schmidt, 1977; Bertinetto, 1986). I will limit my observations to the tenses of the past. The system of the German tenses for 'past' narratives can be seen in the following chart:

time relations	anteriority	simultaneity	posteriority
field of primary deixis	perfect (er hat gewonnen)	present (er gewinnt)	future (er wird gewinnen)
field of secondary (displaced) deixis	perfect (er hat gewonnen) Präteritum (er gewann) Plusquamperfect (er hatte gewonnen)		

We can sum up the binary choices which the interactants make with respect to the opposite specifications of aspectual-temporal categories according to their functions in the following chart. The marked term of the binary opposition is specified by plus, and the unmarked one, where the opposition appears neutralized, is specified with minus.

	past/non past	perfect/non perfect
er gewinnt	-	-
er gewann	+	-
er hat gewonnen	- (+)	+(-)
er hatte gewonnen	+	+

The following observations can be made: for some discursive genres and styles Standard German speakers may use *Präteritum* forms in perfective as well as imperfective aspectual functions; unlike in the case for Italian *passato remoto* or *imperfetto*. The interpretation may depend on several factors:

a) the type of 'Aktionsart'; e.g., verbs with 'durative Aktionsart' (*bleiben, dauern, essen, schauen, steigen*) are interpretable as having imperfective functions, verbs with non-durative 'Aktionsart' (*beissen, fassen, finden, ersteigen*) are not;

b) the co-occurrence of specific types of particles, adverbs and prepositions (cf. *er las in das Buch / in dem~~*);

c) elements of the contextual environment and knowledge of pragmatic factors about temporality and temporal aspects.

Some constraints on the use of the *Präteritum* may also depend on a) the syntactic or textual environment (cf. its use in imperfective function in relative clauses, forms for retrieval of backgrounding information, explanations, assessments etc.), b) on other pragmatic and contextual factors, such as regional-dialectal provenance of the speakers, the speech register, the written or spoken modus, the genre of texts, the degree of closeness to the standard.

Overwhelmingly the *Präteritum* is limited to northern Germany and to the standard, literary and school skill register. But it is frequently used also in the colloquial register for genres such as fairy tales, legends, remote history, biographies. Its use appears thus limited to narration events scarcely related to the present time and connotated by features of temporal deictic distance (cf. Schmidt, 1977; Harweg, 1975). In Southern Germany, except for a few specific types of verbs and especially for modal and otherwise imperfective functions, the Präteritum is not used in colloquial language (cf. Rowley, 1983; Dietrich, 1988); its functions are expressed by the perfect (cf. *'wir haben gezittert am ganzen Leib' –fuhr er fort 'wir haben ein Vaterunser beten wollen, aber die Zunge ist wie gelähmt gewesen vor Schreck'* (P. Roregger cit. in Schmidt, 1977: 226).

As we can observe, the *Präteritum* in German may express functions which in Italian may be expressed complementarily by either *passato remoto* or by *imperfetto*. But unlike in Southern Germany, Italian preterite perfect or *passato remoto* can never assume imperfective functions, and viceversa the imperfetto is used unmarkedly for imperfective functions.

The system of tense in Italian may be represented as follows:

time relations	*anteriority*	*simultaneity*	*posteriority*
field of primary deixis	present perfect (*ha vinto*)	present (*vince*)	simple future (*vincerà*)
field of secondary (displaced) deixis	plusquamperfect I (*aveva vinto*) plusquamperfect II (*ebbe vinto*)	present perfect (past) (*ha vinto*) preterite perfect (*vinse*) imperfect (*vinceva*)	

The specification of the binary specified temporal-aspectual categories can be seen from the following chart, in which minus specifies the unmarked form:

	past/ non-past	preterite/ non-pret.	anterior/ non-ant.	perfective/ non-perf.	imperfective/ non-imperf.	progressive non-progr.
vince	-	-	-	-	-	-
ha vinto	-(+)	-	+	+	-	-
vinse	+	+	-	+	-	-
vinceva	+(-)	-	-	+	-(+)	-(+)
aveva vinto	+	+	+(-)	-(+)	+(-)	-
(ebbe vinto)	+	+	+	+	-	-
sta vincendo	-	-	-	-	+	+
stava vincendo	+	+(-)	-	-	+	+
(era stato vincendo)	+	+	+(-)	+	+(-)	+

From a comparison of the tense forms in German and Italian and from their temporal and aspectual specifications, some main functional differences can be derived, especially with regard to the preterite forms and their grammatical aspect, as well as to the progressive which is lacking in German. An Italian speaker has to differentiate with morphological means some aspects of states, actions or events in the past he is referring to. If he considers the event expressed by the verb as accomplished, he will refer to it by means of preterite perfect (*passato remoto*) or present perfect (*passato prossimo*) (or historic present too). While the first two forms have perfective aspect, the latter is neutralized in regard to its function of 'aspect'. With regard to real or metaphoric distance or nearness to the time of speech act, *passato remoto* and present are marked, whereas present perfect is neutralized. If the speaker considers the event as unaccomplished or neutral with regard to this category, he refers to it by means of the imperfect past (imperfective aspect) of the 'transferred' historic present. Some observations on some characteristic aspects of the use of Italian tenses (cf. also Bertinetto, 1986) may be useful at this point.

Imperfect forms expressing non-punctual events or states may also be used in the function of temporal interval relations building the frame for the incidence of another event (e.g., *mangiava quando bussarono)*, cf. Pollack (1970). They are also used for the representation of events framed in dependent hypotactical constructions such as reported speech and thought, motivational constructions (causal, concessive, final clauses), relative clauses, insertions, parentheses etc. They thus fulfil the general function of backgrounding and contextualizing, that is of reconstructing and retrieving relevant information and context. This is needed for the interpretation of the events which appear in the foreground and are expressed by perfective forms. It is within this function of a more pragmatic and textual type that imperfect forms are thus used for descriptions in general, as well as to present comments, assessments, clarifications, explanations, modal predicates or attitudes. These are all activities which in general build evaluation constituent into narratives.

Furthermore, in perfective environments, e.g., with telic or punctual verbs which are normally incompatible with imperfect forms, the latter can be used in marked perfective function after expressions of time relations, whether they are calendar-related, e.g., *alle tre,* or more subjective, e.g., *dopo.* With punctual verbs and in contexts in which the non-uniqueness of the event is inferable, the imperfect is used to refer to the usuality and iterativity of the event (*arrivava alle tre*).

In addition, in particular contexts which must also be textually and pragmatically defined, imperfect forms are used in perfective environments, e.g., with dynamic, telic or punctual verbs, and together with adverbs of the primary deixis (*ora, adesso, qui*), in order to indicate a chain of events seen from near their own setting. In this way they appear more connected with each other within a common horizon, like the elements of a picture (cf. Bühler's 'Mohammed goes to the mountain'). They are used when the narrator a) refers to closing events at the end of an episode or narrative, mostly after adverbs of temporal relations, e.g., *dopo, subito;* b) evokes events or states in interior monologues (so-called free indirect discourse); and c) narrates in a sketchy way dreams, events or actions concerning the agent or patient in films, tales, or parts of them. This latter use is especially frequent in mass media reports of earlier public events (e.g., political, social or sport reports).

Like the imperfect tense, present tense forms may also be used in perfective environments instead of perfective forms (present perfect or preterite past tenses) either a) alternating in the narration of temporal sequences in the past, or b) occurring without alternation in a whole narrative or in episodes of it. In both cases the whole action is transferred with its setting to the immediate presence of the interactants, that is to the original or primary field of deixis (cf. Bühler's type 3A, 'the mountain comes to Mohammed'). With regard to the behaviour of the present perfect, this is specified primarily by a relation of anteriority and vicinity to the time and situation of the speech act. However, these features may be neutralized. In this case the present perfect may be used in the function of a preterite past and occur in all its collocations or environments referring to a remote past.The use of the present perfect in the function of the preterite for most types of reference to the past is the norm not only in the vast majority of dialectal and regional Italian varieties (Sicilian and Tuscan varieties are among the exceptions), but also in colloquial Italian. The preterite perfect, which in contrast to German is obligatorily perfective, is, similarly to German, generally used in Standard Italian varieties in rather high speech registers employed in the language of public institutions, and in written or oral literary style, in specific genres such as fairy tales, legends, remote history, biographies and other types of discourse connoted by features of distance (cf. Weinrich, 1964).

In the next three sections, we present exemplary analyses of three types of retellings, namely, retelling a picture story, a short oral story and a film scene respectively.

Retelling a picture story

The analysis of retellings of picture stories provides interesting insights into some fundamentals of narrative construction. This genre of retelling displays devices for transformation of elements of iconic-spatial representation into the textual one within a framework of temporal, motivational and relevance relationships (cf. Bamberg, 1987). It is important to see how that what is iconically represented in the frames of the picture stories is interpreted as event or state, how the events or states of these frames are related to each other and how not only temporal but also relevance and motivation relationships are made explicit.

Furthermore, it is important to see to what extent narrative features are displayed with respect to descriptive features and to what extent reference is produced by means of symbolic signs and 'shifters', or instead by means of indexical or iconic signs.

Consider now a retelling by Clem from the Konstanz group recorded during a Saturday leisure time encounter. He was given an unordered set of six frames from the picture story *Alberetto,* and requested to order them, and then to narrate the story. As we can see in the following example, his performance is rather a description of the main event and its subevents, and is strictly bound to the frames.

EX (1) Alberetto (Clem, 10, Konstanz)

i (1) allora: a: il papà ë: pianda: un - - un alberetto:. (0.5 sec.) //// ii (2) doppo se ne va a ccasa: dendro. //// iii (3) allorä: - - dopo il- un uomo - ë - con un bambi:no; viene:- dava- eh viene: scappando: - sull'alberetto. - //// iv (4) doppo il pa:ttre jess - allOra: vi- viene fuore della caza, // (5) e se mette: davanto: - e i:l ë - il albero. // (6) e- - quest'uomo l'- lo- lo grida: - - grida. //
(7) e- e il bambino si - - si ammuccia: a diretö - il - 'l papà. //// v (8) - do- dopo questo papà eh: prende l'alberetto; // (9) e se ne- e: lo strapp(h)a. //// vi (10) doppo ëh- quest qua si arrabbia: e se ne scappë.

----

i (1) now uh the father is - plants a -- little tree (0,5) //// ii (2) then he goes into the house in. //// iii (3) so -- then the - a man is -- with a child; - he comes - he went eh - he comes running to the tree //// iv (4) then the father comes out, now co- comes out from the house, // (5) and he puts himself before - eh the - the tree. // (6) this man -- sho- shouts at him. // (7) and and the child -- hides behind the father. //// v (8) the- then this father uh takes the little tree; // (9) and he pulls it up. //// vi (10) then this one here gets angry and runs away.

At first sight, the reconstruction of the event is not very clear. On the surface, the structure of the interactions between agents and patients is weakly marked with regard to their temporal, motivational and especially to their relevance structure. The actions are connected by means of entailment and the background information is weakly contextualized. The relationships between membership categories and the activities bound with them are not clear and the presuppositions of content relations are barely inferable. The question is how context presuppositions are in particular activated and signalled and how temporal and motivational structures are realized in detail. Problematic is the fact that in his oral retelling of the picture story Clem uses several types of form neutralizations and simplifications. The 'primary' or non-prospective type of deixis (3A) is preferred to the displaced and prospective one (3C) and deictic expressions are preferred to the anaphoric. Temporal deixis seems based on the spatial; or the point of reference for the following clause is provided simply by the preceding one, and temporal construction reflects the succession of the events according to the order of the pictures and forms the basis for the motivational construction in a referential mood that appears indexical and iconic rather than symbolic.

We can immediately see how temporal patterns are still apparent through the spatial ones, so that divergencies from the descriptive genre are hardly perceptible. The whole story is narrated, or rather described, in the aspectually and temporally unmarked present tense. The orientation part, which is normally performed by means of imperfect tenses, is marked here by means of local or temporal adverbs of the originary and primary deixis , cf. *allora* (line 1, 3, 4). Also the action events normally expressed by means of perfect tenses appear here indicated, together with the present tense, by similar 'primary' deictical expressions like *questo* (1. 6, 8, 10).

With regard to the episodes i-vi, Clem organizes them according to the distribution of the pictures. Nearly every episode is introduced by the deictic adverbial marker for temporal relation (*dopo*). No relevant syntactic or textual marking for signalling different segmental patterning of the sequences of the 'action', the 'complication' or the 'coda' are employed; there is also no 'evaluation'. Each essential event is presented as a binary chain of subevents expressed by two clauses bound by means of the conjuction *e* within a relation of coordination in a paratactic style. In a bounded overt couple of clauses, the second clause, a non-stative verb generally indicates foregrounding in respect to the ground represented by the first one. Thus, if both the subevents expressed in both clauses have telic or punctual 'Aktionsart', the subevent in the second clause may be interpreted - according to schematic knowledge – as consecutive to that expressed by the first clause, which accounts at the same time for its temporal binding. New agents or patients are presented in the first clause. As, in general, the first clause represents the frame reference or background for the second one, the hearer can then interpret the intent, according to his schematic knowledge, when he implicitly relates and connects the subevent expressed in the following clause to that of the preceding one. Thus, the following clause, which reflects the temporal order of events, and conveys the salient thread of the action, is related to the preceding clause by a relationship of foregrounding event, bounded temporality or coherent 'motivation'.

The limited syntactic and textual structure of the text presented above and the difficulty of interpreting it must be related not only to the informality of its production, but also to Clem's limited Italian competence. Apart from the reduced syntactic and textual structure, his Italian delivery is also marked by slow tempo, a rhythm which is interrupted by frequent hesitations and pauses, corrections, restarts and interferences. He produces a type of *'italiano stentato'* which is shared by other bilingual migrants' children (di Luzio, 1991). When speaking German, the preferred language he uses in everyday situations and of which he has a virtually native command, Clem's stories display a much more elaborated performance. The narrative strategies shown above (strategies which are also employed by some other bilingual children of the same age) are in some way related to the disadvantaged status of Italian in the case of migrant children. Characteristically, they involve simplification in the realization of narrative temporality, relevance and motivational structure as well as in the referring devices. Thus sense text formulation expressed with present tenses, and by means of 'primary' or non-prospective deixis displaced by very frequent indexical and iconic signs deixis, characterizes a style of narration-description with not only weakly marked temporal structure, but also an indexical-iconic mode of contextualization. This seems to represent a first developmental stage of narration[1].

Retelling a short story

Oral retellings of short stories read out immediately before are another type of linguistic activity normally performed in school. Their importance derives from the fact that this genre of retelling reflects the effect of the normative stimuli emanating from the model story heard immediately before; these retellings are strongly influenced by the input model and may be considered as repetitions or imitations of it. Some of our examples were recorded during Italian classes, others were elicited from children aged between 8 and 10 outside school classes in Konstanz and Vare-

[1] In comparison with this unusual example of oral retelling of picture stories in a more unplanned style outside school, written examples of picture story renarrating under the normative constraints of language socialization in the school, where they are regularly produced - both in the German school and in the Italian courses - display a higher degree of grammatical and textual elaboration of the temporal and relevance structure. Consider the following example from Clem:

EX. (10) Ghiaccio
i (1) Fa fredo. // (2) Il lago giaccato. // (3) Antonio voleve provare, se si può andare sul giaccio. // (4) Improvisamento quando Antonio si trovava sul giaccio // (5) il giaccio si rotto. // (6) Antonio cridava "Aiuto! Aiuto!" //// (ii) (7) Vicino all lago c'era Alberto // (8) che sentiva il crido di "Aiuto" di Antonio. // (9) Alberto cridava "Aspetto che sto venendo" // (10) Alberto aveva una corda per tirare Antonio dall'ago //// (iii) (11) Antonio era bagnato fino ai capelli. // (12) Antonio diceva "Io non vado mai più sul lago giacciato".
----
i (1) it is cold. // (2) The lake is frozen // (3) Toni wanted to try if one can walk on the ice // (4) suddenly when Toni was on the ice // (5) the ice has broken // (6) Toni shouted help help //// (ii) (7) Alberto was near the lake // (8) who heard the help cry from Toni // (9) Alberto cried wait, I am coming // (10) Alberto had a rope to pull Toni out of the lake //// (iii) (11) Toni was wet from head to toe // (12) Toni said I won't go on the frozen lake any more.

se. We present here in an abbreviated version the first retelling by Lore, one of the 10 Varese children, of a short fantastic story by Rodari, a writer of children's books. The original version by Rodari (approximately 650 words) is written in Standard Literary Italian. As expected, this fantastic story, which is highly distanced from everyday reality, uses preterite perfect tense *(passato remoto)* for the action. We will compare some aspects of Lore's performance with those displayed by the bilingual children in Konstanz. The reason why we have chosen to begin with the presentation of a Varese retelling instead of a Konstanz one is because it is closer to the original story and more suitable as a point of reference and comparison for the performances of the Konstanz children.

EX. (2) Tonino l'invisibile

(1) c'era una volta un ragazzo che- che:- doveva: essere interrogato dal professore; // (2) ma- ma- Tonino non voleva essere interrogato; - // (3) ma andò lo stesso a scuola. - // (4) Quando entrò in classe, be- non voleva:; // (5) - disse che non voleva-- voleva essere invisibile e- // (6) e dopo un tratto - vide che:- il professore lo chiamò. (.....) // (7) lo chiamò, // (8) e lui risponde; eh- rispose. // (9) ma il professore non lo sentì. - // (10) dunque il ragazzo. un pò un pò: si - vide che era invisibile, // (11) e cominciò a fare dei dispetti ai suoi amici. - - a tirargli i capelli, e: - a tirare i capelli.- // (12) poi andò fuori (......) // (13) andò in centro.

// (23) Poi andò a casa che- che la mamma lo aspettava nel balcone. - // (24) e vide- - (...) // (25) andò in casa e - (.....) // (26) e allora la madre: aspettava. // (27) Tonino gli disse - ehi mamma sono qua. // (28) ma la mamma e - n- non non lo sentiva , (29) perchè era invisibile.

// (34) Sedette a tavola; // (35) e:- e vide che non lo vede. // (36) ed era -piangeva, // (37) perchè nessuno lo sentiva. - // (38) andò fuori e vide un vecchietto che era solo; (....) sto vecchietto.// (39) e chiese - m - no - // (40) poi si mise a piangere, // (41) dicendo che non voleva più essere invisibile; // (42) il vecchietto gli disse perchè era lì solo a piangere. // (43) fa a - ( ) gli disse. - disse ma lei mi vede? // (44) e:- e il vecchio gli disse sí che ti vedo, perchè non ti dovrei vedere? // (45) dopo tutto contento andò a casa; // (46) e-. e- e la madre gli disse eh vedrai che sculacciata ti dà papà.
----
(1) Once upon a time was a boy who - was to be tested by his teacher. //(2) but- but Tonino did not want to be tested // (3) however he went to school all the same. // (4) when he entered the class room, well -he did not want to; // (5) he said he did not want to - he wanted to be invisible//(6) and after a while he saw that his teacher called him, eh- (...) // (7) he called him//(8) and he answers e- answered. // (9) but the teacher did not hear him - // (10) so the boy (just)/- (just)/ (..)/ saw that he was invisible; // (11) and began to play tricks on his friends - - to pull their hair-- and -

pull their hair- // (12) then he went outside; // (13) (...) went to the centre of the town.//..... //(23) Then he went home where his mum was waiting for him on the balcony- // (24) and he saw - (25) went into the house and (...) // (26) and so mother was waiting.-//(27) Tonino said to her hey, mum, I'm here. // (28) but his mother did not hear him; // (29) because he was invisible. //.....//(34) he sat down at the table;//(35) and saw that he does not see him. //.(36) and he wept//(37) because nobody heard him. - //(38) he went outside and saw an old man who was alone .. this old man. // (39) and he asked - m - no - //(40) then he started to weep; // (41) and said he did not want to be invisible anymore. (......) // (42) the old man said to him why he was there alone weeping - //(43) he does- he said to him: do you then see me? // (44) and- and the old man said to him sure I see you, why shouldn't I see you? // (45) then he went home very glad; //(46) and- and his mother told him: you'll see what a nice thrashing your Daddy will give you.

In an appropriate way for this genre, and in conformity with the model, Lore uses the preterite perfect tense (*passato remoto*) quite naturally and fairly consistently. The majority of the Varese children (8 out of 10) who retold the same story do the same, or in particular places of the story and in a functional way they alternate preterite perfects with forms of the present perfect and historic present.

Like the other Varese children Lore uses lexical marked devices to produce connection and cohesion. Consider for example the connectives: *ma* (1. 2, 3, 9, 28), *quando* (4), *dunque* (10), *che* (23), *perché* (29,37), *e dopo un tratto* (6), *dopo* (20,45), *poi* (12, 23) and *allora* (26). Repairs are in general interpretable less as due to hesitations or pauses to search for grammatical and syntactical expressions, than as due to a search for better stilistic or textual solutions (cf. 1. 4, 5, 8, 10, 38, 43), and more precision or further specifications (cf. 14, 15, 18). A suitable rhythm is clearly audible, as can be seen also in the reprises in lines 7, 13, 26.

One interesting phenomenon is the occurrence of *allora* (1. 26) instead of *poi*. This occurs in most of the narratives of the Varese children, whereas the children in Konstanz use almost exclusively *poi, dopo*. Interestingly, *allora* is used with deictic as well as with combined anaphoric and cataphoric function. Moreover, besides the temporal function, *allora* also expresses a motivational function in the sense of *dunque* ('consequently', 'therefore'). When used as a deictic it expresses simultaneity with a reference point. Its anaphorical reference may concern a preceding or a following point with regard to the reference point of the speaker or with regard to a displaced one. It is no wonder then that – as we will see – *allora* in this function is hardly used by the Konstanz children. In fact, both anaphoric devices and relationships of simultaneity both seem to appear rather later in the stages of language development.

The examples of the same story retold by the Konstanz children show a different and more differentiated state of affairs. For a comparison of the two different styles of retelling, consider now three excerpts from retellings by Konstanz children.

EX (3) Tonino (ii, Polo, aged 10)

(1) e poi viene una signora; // (2)si mise sulle ginocchia. (..) // (3) allora va fuori, // (4) e là un vecchietto lo vede; // (5) perchè ha detto voglio essere di nuovo visibile.// (6) e poi quel vecchietto ha/ disse; // (7) io ti ho visto tante volte.// (8) e Tonino poi disse io non ti ho visto mai.

----

(1) and then a woman comes, // (2) she sat on Tonino's knees // (3) so he goes outside // (4) and there an old man sees him; // (5) because he has said I want to be visible again. //(6) and then that old little man has/ said //(7) I have seen you many times // (8) and Tonino then said I never have seen you

EX. (4) (T 19, Nora, aged 8)

(1) Tonino ha fatto un salto nel banco, // (2) e ci trovò nel cestino // ....// (7) venn- vinne una signora, // (8) la signora zi sedò // (9) ha visto quel posto libero // (10) e si sedava sui ginocchi di Tonino. //.....//(15) Tonino è andato nel mercato// (16) si mangiò tutti i dolcini. //.....//(21) dopo lui ha detto, ma voi mi vedete? si?// (22) il vecchietto disse ma certo che ti vedo.// (23) poi ha detto pure...

----

(1) Tonino has sprung on the bench // (2) and he found himself in the paper basket. // (.......) // (7) a woman cam/ came, // (8) the woman sat down // (9) she has seen that free seat // (10) and sat down on Tonino's knees.//.....// (15) Tonino has gone to the market;// (16) he ate all the cookies //.....// (21) then he has said, but do you see me? yes?// (22) the old man said certainly I see you.// (23) then he also has said (..)

EX. (5) (T 19, Inno, aged 10)

(1) Tonino risponde presente, // (2) però nessuno lo sentiva e nessuno lo vedeva.// (3) Come l'ha chiamato, // (4) nessuno lo vedeva, nessuno lo sentiva.// (5) (.....). e/ è andato nel bus// (6) e dopo veniva la signora // (7) ha messo la borsa sui piedi.// (8) Lei dice. (.....)// (9) così Tonino se ne andava. (.....)//.....// (19) Lei chiamava Tonino/- e Tonino ci diceva, sono qui. // (20) Tonino gridava, // (21) la mamma non sentiva (.....) // (22) dopo è andato giù/ rimpiangendo e dicendo (che) vuole essere non più invisibile.//

----

(1) Tonino answers at once, // (2) but nobody heard him and nobody saw him // (3) as he has called him // (4) nobody saw him, nobody heard him // (5) (.....) he has gone on the bus; // (6) and then the woman came; // (7) she has put the bag on Tonino's feet. // (8) she says - (.....) / so Tonino went away (.....) //.....// (19) she called Tonino and Tonino said to her, I am here. // (20) Tonino shouted; his mother didn't hear him // (21) then he has gone downstairs / crying and saying // (22) that he doesn't want to be invisible any more.//

Present perfect forms are generally preferred to preterite perfect (*passato remoto*) by the Konstanz children. However, whereas the use of present perfect by the monolingual children in Italy is discourse-functional and represents a free stilistic choice, this is not necessarily the case for the Konstanz children. Their choice of present perfect may be constrained by their lack of 'competence' of Standard Italian. Their use of present perfect in such retellings may thus display a strategy of simplification resulting from the avoidance of more marked or less well mastered *passato remoto* forms and from its convergence with the Southern German use of perfect (instead of the *Präteritum*). The instances of preterite perfect (*passato remoto*) occur mostly in the retellings of the Tonino story by the Varese children who are better acquainted with Standard Italian and more motivated to learn it; cf., e.g., the tellers of EX. (3), (4) and (5). Apart from the fact that its use converges with a dialectal norm (e.g., Sicilian by Nora in EX. (4)), *passato remoto* is more frequent 1) at the beginning of the story retelling, where the echo of the model is still perceptible, and 2) with some verbs that are also sometimes used in the preterite form in Southern Germany, e.g., *kam, ging, sagte* (cf. Dietrich, 1988), s., e.g., EX. (3), 1. 6, 8; EX. (4), 1. 7, 17. Preterite perfect forms used overwhelmingly at the beginning of the story (*arrivò, rispose, saltò* (he 'arrived', 'answered', 'jumped on')) are also displayed by Inno in the text immediately preceding, but not reported here, EX. (5). But thereafter she alternates with these forms foregrounding imperfects with not stative verbs, s. EX. (5), 1. 2, 4, 6, 9, 19, 20, 21; s. also Nora in EX. (4), 1. 10. These imperfects with non stative verbs are abnormal in Standard Italian and – because of their ambiguity in respect to foregrounding or backgrounding functions – not unequivocally interpretable for an adult recipient who has internalized the norms of a native variety of Italian. In these perfective environments and with the verbs having 'telic' or 'punctional' 'Aktionsart' one would expect either present perfect or preterite perfect. One possible way of accounting for these forms could be by interpreting them as transferring the viewpoint of the interactants (Mohammed) to the realm of the 'mountain' by means of the corresponding type of deixis already mentioned and used for (re)evocation of dreams and film scenes or in interior monologues. However, this interpretation does not appear plausible because the situation is different, and because this type of stilistic use and interpretation of imperfect is not normal in stories (re)told by the children until they are older and have acquired a better command of Italian (but cf. Calleri, 1990 and Bazzanella & Calleri, 1991: 181). Nor can these forms be explained by the hypothesis formulated by Antinucci & Miller (1976) according to whom in the earlier learning stages 'the past tense has more of an aspectual than of a temporal value' (cf. also Bronckart & Sinclair (1973) and the reformulation as the 'defective tense hypothesis' in Weist (1986) and R. Andersen (1991)). According to Andersen (1991: 307) 'In beginning stages of language acquisition, only inherent aspectual distinctions (i.e., 'Aktionsart') are encoded by verbal morphology, not tense or grammatical aspects'. The way Inno and Nora (as many children of the same age in our group in several types of story retellings) use these imperfects in EX. (2) and (3) or the way progressive imperfects are used by the same children in other stories seems rather to contradict this hypothesis. The data of the American children learning Spanish to which Andersen refers show that the *preterite perfect* (*se partió*) for the expression of punctual events appears earlier than for that of activity and telic events, while the imperfect (*se partía*) appears later.

How then can we explain our findings? We can plausibly say that the trigger for the perfective or foregrounding use of the imperfect tense can be found in the model of literary German used in formal style for narratives and retellings in school. The transfer of the German use of the '*Präteritum*' to the Italian use of the imperfect or their convergence is not fortuitous. Insofar as it supports a natural process of simplification at the semantic and morphophonological level, it is plausible, natural and functional.

The imperfect form marks the past in the distanced field of displayed deixis which has a weak or neutralized relation to the axis of the 'origo' deixis. The 'perfective' aspect is obligatorily implied by the 'Aktionsart' of the 'telic' or 'punctual' verb lexemes. Thus, by employing imperfect tenses with such verb lexemes and in perfective contexts, the grammatical form of the imperfect tense becomes neutral or unmarked with regard to the 'imperfective'/'perfective' aspect opposition and marks only 'past'. In this sense it is a natural process of simplification like that underlying the use of similar imperfect forms by monolingual children in Italy between 2:10 and 5:10, and like similar processes and temporal uses of tense and aspect in creole languages. The model of the contact language German becomes functional in its transfer. In fact the German *Präteritum* is precisely the form which indicates displaced past and is neutral in regard to the perfective/imperfective grammatical aspect expressed by the lexical 'Aktionsart'. By transferring this use to the employment of imperfect tenses in the same function, the Konstanz children produce a kind of German-Italian convergence which forms the closest substitute for the difficult Italian preterite perfect form (*passato remoto*), which is morphophonologically and semantically more marked (i.e., with regard to the flection and to the features 'past' and 'perfective aspect') and the command of which they have not yet adequately achieved. The case is thus different from that investigated by Andersen, because the Spanish preterite perfect tense in *-ó*, in contrast to Italian, belongs to colloquial speech and occurs very frequently in the input received by native English speaking children learning Spanish in Puertorico.

Among the many factors which trigger the characteristic use of the imperfect in the non-imperfective function, both the particular social factors (that is, the social context which influences or constraints this use) and the universalistic cognitive factors in the acquisition and development of Italian in contact imply, condition and support each other. This use of the imperfect represents an example of several simplifying strategies in the temporal construction of narratives which go hand in hand with other natural creative strategies of simplification in the production of temporal, relevance and motivation forms in narratives in the case of the Konstanz bilinguals. On the other hand it must be said that for the Standard Italian speaking participant or hearer this use of imperfect represents a process of complication; in fact it presents for him interpretation problems especially because of the resulting ambiguity between foregrounding and backgrounding functions of such imperfect forms.

Let us return now to the texts at EX. (2), (3) and (4). Interpreting foregrounding imperfects with non stative verbs is not the only difficulty faced by a Standard Italian speaker confronted with the Konstanz texts. Some difficulty occurs also in the interpretation of sequencing and alternating of present, present perfect, preterite perfect or forgrounding imperfect in perfective environments. This happens because their distribution in unexpected with regard to standard norms, that is, it seems to violate constraints on Italian tense congruence in regard to the ordering of more or less marked forms in contiguous utterances concerning correlated aspects of the same global event, cf. EX. (3), 1. 1/2; EX. (4), 1. 1/2, 9/10, 10/11, 16/17/18; EX. (5), 1. 3/4. For anteriority markers we can observe in EX. (3), 1. 4/5; EX. (4), 1. 9/10; EX. (5), 1. 23 a shift from the field of secondary deixis to that of primary, also a process of simplification displayed also by monolingual children in Italy aged between 2:10 and 5:10 (cf. Bazzanella & Calleri, 1991).

Comparing how the two groups of children perform narrative structure in their Italian story retellings, we can state that, apart from the lower degree of tense differentiation in expressing foregrounding relations of the events narrated, the Konstanz children also display – in comparison to the Varese group – an extremely low use of (redundant) overt syntactic markers such as adverbs and conjunctions for expressing motivation, relevance and subordination relations between the sequential pairs of the subevents narrated. Furthermore, they display a rhythm which is somewhat broken because of the effort to encode in an unfamiliar, poorly mastered and rarely used language. This effort also appears most evident when comparing the slow tempo and brevity of the Italian texts of our bilingual children with their own performance in German or with that of the Varese children (cf. also Auer & di Luzio, 1988). For example Pol's German version of the Tonino story was in terms of words more than double his Italian performance, and also contained many more evaluations. In contrast to this, his Italian performance took longer than the German one. Like him, most of the children use pauses and come to a standstill if the interactants, especially the teacher, do not help.

To conclude, we can interpret several linguistic features in the story retellings of the Konstanz children presented above as being due to processes of simplification and self-help strategies in their production.; this simplification can, however, make the reception by Standard Italian speaking participants more difficult.

Retelling a film scene

In retelling a picture story or an oral story read out before, the possible and obvious reference to a model helps to disambiguate the non-overtly marked elements of temporal, relevance and motivation structure. With a film retelling this is not poss-ible to such an extent. Hence, its interpretation is more difficult. A different type and a large amount of contextualization work in inferring these elements is required of the recipient for a suitable interpretation of the events reported.

In contrast to the types of retellings examined above, retellings of films or film scenes are also embedded in everyday interaction. Apparently the most striking differentiating aspect is the preference for the present perfect and its high frequency in narrating the film actions. This usage is shared by both groups. However, in some contexts and for some particular stretches of the action, the present perfect may alternate with the preterite perfect in retellings of the Varese group, with non stative imperfects in some of the Konstanz group, and with the present for both groups. Among other things, this depends on the degree of informality of the retelling situation, the speech attitudes and the rhetorical competence of the narrators. We observed that, like other retelling genres, the film retellings of the Konstanz children – in contrast to those of the Varese children – are also perceived by Standard Italian speaking recipients as quite abnormal, unclear and difficult to interpret. The question is 1) if this perception depends only on the abnormal use of non stative imperfects and on the different sequential distribution of the tense forms or 2) if there are other characteristic features which differentiate the retellings of film scenes of the Konstanz group from those of the Varese group.

Let us consider two film stories respectively of two Konstanz children (Nic and Luc, both aged 10) and then contrast them with comparable performances of two Varese children.

EX. (6) Das Imperium schlägt zurück (Nic, 10, Konstanz)

/////(i-iv).....////v (40) all' altra mattina, hanno laesciato uscire di quest' astronave, per cercarle, - // (41) erano cosí, ((0,10 he draws) // (42) e cosí che li andaväno a ccerca:re.// (43) e uno li trove. // (44) poi li portä di nuovo al rifugio dei rebelli, // (45) e: vanno là. // (46) e parlano parlano; //// vi (47) e a=n=tra/ mhm a un tratto vedono dei - una flotta di astonave; dei grandi grandi; // (48) è ccosi ((0.12)) ((he draws)) // (49) - che cc'era anche uno più ggrande che era il piú ggrande; //. (50) e arrivava là, // (51) e poi davano allarme. //// vii (52) e c'era uno che si ghiama/ si chiamava das/ la/ da/ do/ lotwer. // (54) e quello là ha detto per eha detto a uno le/ eh ve/ vi hanno scoperti che attaccate. perchè l'avete lasciato?// (55) allora c'era cosí un pi un commandante, ((hhh)) che commandava quella flotta. // (56) e e e e l'ha fatto morire. // (57) l'ha tolto l'aria (h) mhm non so come; // (58) proprio cosí; // (59) perché lui era il - e non te lo dico perchè se no ti (to/ e-em/) cosí allora (hhhh) (.....) eh dopo senti. //// viii (60) mhm e doppo vanno là, a attacare. // (61) arrivono i et et.// (62) sono degli animali cosí. ((he draws)) - non sono animali. - sono dei picco/ eh dei come - sono di ferro; sembrano come animali; ((0.5)) ((he draws)) // (63) e questo qua si poteva muovere // (64) e li attaccavano. // (65) ((0,3)) erano cosí, ((0,5)) ((he draws)) dopo (che) li attaccavano, //// ix (66). e poi c'eran//// (67) e l'hanno dato l'allarme. che arrivavano. - -// (68) e uno skappava. // (69) Nanzolo scappava con la prin/ prinzessa, princes/, pricipessa, // (70) e scappava

- (hhhh) e scappava via con questa n/ astronave, ch'era la piú svelta della galaxis; // (71) ((0,3)) scappava via, // (72) e: - e a un tratto dice l'altro, questo comandante; un altro comandante. // (73) non lo trovava piú,// (74) e l'ha fatto di nuovo morire. //// x (75) e poi eh; a un tratto hanno visto una flotta. // (76) sono usciti là, // (77) aspettava una flotta di tanti di questi qua. (78) aspettava quelli; // (79) e iniziavano a sparare, // (80) e rompevano tutto. // (81) e poi ((hhh)) e poi si ne sono skappati (in) un coso ^{oo} non so come si chiama perche non l'hanno detto il nome^{oo}.

//// v (40) on the next morning they let (them) out of that spaceship to look for them. // (41) (they) were like that, ((0,8)) ((he draws)) // (42) And it is so that they went to look for them. // (43) one of them finds them. // (44) and then brings them back to the rebels' shelter, // (45) and they go there; // (46) and they talk and talk; //// vi (47) and al/ m/ suddenly (they) see some - - a fleet of spaceship; some very, very big - // (48) it is like that ((he draws)) ((0,9)) // (49) - -that there was one even bigger, that was the biggest one; // (50) and (this) got there, // (51) and then (they) gave alarm. //// vii (52) and there was one that - his name is -// (53) his name was das/ la/ da/ do/ lotwer. // (54) and that one has said for / and has said to one (....) 'they have discovered you, that you are attacking. why have you let him? // (55) well, there was a lit/ a commander ((hhhh)) who commanded that fleet. // (56) and- and- and- and he made him die. // (57) he took away the air, but I don't know how; // (58) just like that, // (59) because he was the --, I won't tell you because if I do. you (..). I'll - so -- you'll hear later. //// viii (60) mhm and then they go there to attack. // (61) the.et et come. // (62) they are animals like this. ((he draws)) - they are not animals. (they) are litt- eh- like-- they are made of iron; they seem to be like animals. ((he draws)) ((0,5))// (63) and that one could move; // (64) and they attacked them. // (65) and (they) were like this ((0,5)) ((he draws)) after (that) they attacked them, ((hhhh) ////ix (66) and then there were-- // (67) they have given the alarm that they were arriving. // (68) and one (of them) escaped. // (69) Nanzolo escaped with the pri/ prize- prices/ princess, // (70) and escaped, ((hhh)) and escaped away with that spaceship which was the fastest in the galaxy; ((0,3)) //// x (71) he escaped away, // (72) and- and suddenly the other says; that commander; another commander. // (73) (he) did not find him any more, // (74) and he made him die again (?) too. -- //// x (75) and the, eh, suddenly they have seen a fleet. // (76) they have got out there, // (77) (?) was waiting a fleet of so many of those; // (78) (he) waited for those; // (79) and they started to shoot; // (80) and broke everything. ((hhh)) // (81) and then / ((hhh)) and then they have flown away (in) something; I don't know what it's called, the did not say the name.

EX (7) Kurier der Kaiserin (Luc, 10, Konstanz)

Luc: ke:nnscht - Kurier der Kaiserin; lo conosci il filmo - Kurier der Kaiserin?//m: ah: no, - //Luc: vene -- ogni Dienstag;// m: mhm; e bello?// Luc: si (.)alle(.) sei lo fanno ess eff eins.//m: hn - e com=e? - che cosa fa?--////Luc: i (1) (ah) un'altra volta; eh - era com'una: - ah Prinzessin di: (.) da (.) Austria; (0,5) // (2) gli'a: a: la: princessina i tocca un: (.) Kaptitän e/ austrian che sciochë falsch; // (3) perché ten/ - // (4) il capitä;n - che nun vencë // (5) e vvencë sempre, // (6) perché tiene due assi.//// ii (7) e dopë l'ha visto u:/una fimmina, // (8) ch ha m/°° ha- ha menato un uomo con un corte:llo;// (9) però no/ non è muorto°° il - quello ch'ha (ucciso)°°.-//// iii (10) e rropë è mmenutë u kurrier. - u kurier. - // (11) e: - l'ha fattë yu:m, // (12) el'ha minat'u hh - u Kapitä:n p'a: fene:str(ë). //// iv (13.) primë e/--s'avia (prima) teni (e) (a) na cartë (e ne cchiù);// (14) - però dopë l'ha vis/l'ha viste n'ata vo:ta, // (15.) e (.) e v/eh/a l'ha vi:-a (jittà) i carti, //(16) roppe l'ha vistë, hh // (17) e roppë e/ e/ e/ vulía - vulía ngappà, //(18.) però roppe a chjamat '(ukuri) - // (19) è menutë, // (20) e roppë-- a- l'ha menat(ë) prima accussí, // (21) e roppë hhh u Kapite:n i vulí(a) menà nu carbo:në, --// (22.) l'ha mmenatë, // (23) però non l'ha colpitë.// (24) e roppe l'ha: hhh m/ m/ mmenatë iggjë, // (25.) e roppë bu:m//// v (26) (allor) e roppë meníe n'at'uomë(ne), // (27) e l'ha menatë u - buo:.hh he // (28) e roppë ha pigliatë chelle vecchjë, // (29) e l'ha minatë pë a hh fenestrë, // (30.) e mo'non (lu) potía camminà(re) chjú.

Luc: do you know the film Courier of the emperess///M: no// Luc: it's on every Tuesday.// M: is it nice? // Luc: yes at six it comes on SFI (station)). // M: and what is it like? what does he do?
Luc: v (1) another time there was like a princess of- of Austria. // (2) the princess gets (/) a captain of Austria who cheats at cards; // (3) because ha/ // (4) the captain who doesn't win // (5) uhn and (he) always wins, // (6) because he has two aces. /// ii (7) and then a woman saw it (?) (him?) who (?) (that?) he struck a man (?) with a knife. // (8) however he didn't die he the one who(m) he had killed. // iii (10) and then came the courier. the courier. // (11) and he made him yum yum. // (12) and he threw the captain out of the window./// iv (13) first he had- first to - he had one card.) and no more.// (14) however then they ha/ (s) he saw him another time, // (15) and (s)he saw him throwing (?) the cards, // (16) (s)he saw him, // (17) and then (s)he wanted to snatch him, // (18) but then (s)he called (the courier), // (19) and he came, // (20) and then he hit him first like that // (21) and then the captain threw (against) him a coal; // (22) he threw it , // (23) but he missed him. // (24) and then he did hit him, this one, II (25) and then bum. h //// v (26) so and then came another man, // 27 and he hit him we/.// (28) and then he took this old one, // (29) and he threw him out of the window, // (30) and now he couldn't walk any more.

EX. (6) represents only a short excerpt of the initial part of the film retold by Nic (a little after the initial episodes (i)-(iv)). In this film retelling Nic uses imperfects not only for backgrounding in presentative, descriptive and explicative utterances with stative verbs (1. 41, 49, 59, 65, 66) often with the help of drawings and deictic iconic gestures, but also in foregrounding contexts with non stative verbs (1. 42, 50, 51, 64, 67, 71, 73, 77, 78, 79, 80). For the Standard speaking participant these imperfects in perfective contexts imply an interpretative complication because of their ambiguity between back- and foregrounding function (especially 1. 42, 73, 77, 78); however, from the speakers' point of view they display a process of simplifications (s. p. 18) This not only because of the partial convergence of such forms with the familiar German Präterita, but also and especially because of the simpler and less displaced deixis (type 3B) they display; a use differing from that of the monolingual children of the same age but similar to that of such children aged between 3 and 5 (cf. Bazzanella & Calleri, 1991). A similar simple and less displaced deixis (type 3A in EX. (6)) is displayed by historical present or present past for actions at turning points at the begin of the episodes (vi), (viii), (x) and (v), (vii), (ix) respectively.

In contrast to Nic in EX. (6), Luc in EX. (7) almost constantly uses present pasts in the foregrounding function within the episodes (ii)-(v) (s. 1. 7, 8, 9, 10, 11, 12, 14, 16, 18, 19, 20, 22, 23, 24, 27, 28, 29). This seems in part due to the fairly informal and near dialect performance of Luc. The present is used in episodes (i) at the beginning of the narration of the events (1. 2, 5) which displays a primary deixis and the nearness to the reference point of the speech act; it is also used in the backgrounding function, in present-congruent dependent clauses (1. 3, 4, 6). Imperfect is used in the backgrounding function at the beginning of the retelling (1.1) for the initial orientation, in episode (iv) after *prima* (1. 13) for an explicative description, in episode (v), after *allora* (1. 26) for reorientation, or with modal verbs for evaluations (1. 17, 21). The backgrounding present past (1. 8, 9) instead of the expected plusquamperfect to express the anteriority of the action, is a device of shifting back to the primary deixis reference point (simplification device), in which the early stage of language learning and Southern German dialect converge.

Similarly to the tendency according to which different parameters of foregrounding and displacement of temporal deixis in EX. (6) and (7) appear unmarked or only weakly marked at the level of tense representation, the dependency and motivation relation between adjacent clauses reporting immediate constitutive parts of an event also remain unmarked or only weakly marked at the lexical and syntactic level. Such relations are in general not realized by Nic and Luc within hypotactical constructions (as, e.g., in EX. (6), 1..59), that is, are not overtly marked by means of subordinating conjunctions or adverbs, but simply expressed by paratactic chaining of the clauses of a couplet; these are mostly bound together in such a way that one represents the satellite (presupposed member or background) and the other the nucleus (or foreground) as we can see in EX. (6), 1. 42/43, 45/46, 47/51, 54/56, 67/68, 73/74, 75/76, 79/80-81 and in EX. (7), 1. 10/11, 16/17, 19/20(21), 24/25, 26/27, 29/30. The utterances reporting different moves or states are mostly juxtaposed by means of the conjunction *e* 'and' (s. EX. (6), 1. 42, 43, 45, 46, 50, 52, 54, 56, 63, 64, 68, 70, 74, 79, 80; EX. (7), 1. 5, 11, 12, 15, 28, 30, 31), *e poi* (*e dopo, e roppe* in EX. (7)) 'and then' (EX. (6), 1. 51, 60, 66, 75, 81; EX. (7), 1. 7, 10, 17, 20, 21, 24, 26, 27, 29), *e (poi) a un tratto* 'and (then) suddenly' (EX. (6), 1. 47, 72, 75) and adverbial connectives such as *poi* (*dopo, roppe* in EX. (7) of Luc) 'then' (EX. (6), 1. 44, 49; EX. (7), 1. 14, 16, 18). The practice of juxtaposing the clauses reporting events by the use of monotonous paratactic *e dopo* 'and then' is a characteristic of the early stages of childrens' language development. In spite of Luc's attempt in EX. (7) to use some cohesive connectives and adverbials such as *prima* 'before' (1. 13, 20) also in the couplets *prima/ dopo* (1. 13/14, 20/21), *però* 'but', 'however' (1. 9, 14, 18, 23) and *perché* 'because' (1. 3, 6), and in spite of other devices for producing cohesion used by both Luc and Nic as, for example, their arranging and chaining of utterances by means of intonational patterns, these arrangements are perceived as strongly serial and formed from the standpoint of the origin without a relevant perspective. The paratactic mode of juxtaposing the clauses which report events, as well as the absence or scarcity of overt syntactical and lexical markers does not display the dependency framework of temporal structures clearly and unambiguously; it also obscures that of relevance and motivation relationships. Other more pragmatic devices and inferential work are activated and must be taken into account in the interpretation; however understanding is made difficult in cases of insufficiently shared knowledge.

The connections of the events not only to each other (temporal, relevance and motivational deixis) but also to the agents and patients (personal deixis) are only weakly indicated on the surface and are contextualized in a more pragmatic and less grammatical or lexically marked way in Nic's and Luc's texts in EX. (6) and (7). Thus, nominal or pronominal forms for anaphoric reference to agents or patients are very often absent also where they would be necessarily expected (cf. EX. (6), 1. 40, 46, 47, 51, 60, 64, 74, 75, 79, 81 and EX. (7), 1. 13, 16-18, 25, 27-29, 30). Furthermore, besides the absence of anaphoric personal pronouns, the anaphoric pronominal reference or other deictic means for identifying agents or patients is also often ambiguous and may cause difficulties in the identification of the person referred to (cf. EX. (6), 1. 54, 59, 63, 67, 72 and 42, 43, 44, 54, 56, 57, 64, 73, 77, 78 respectively; EX. (7), 1. 13, 16-18, 25, 27-29, 30 and 1. 15-17, 20, 21, 22-23, 27 respectively). For the most part the resulting ambiguity of agent reference can be resolved only with recourse to the situational context and on the basis of simplified and more pragmatic principles as for example: 'refer them to the protagonist or deuteragonist last mentioned' or 'wait for the next move to disambiguate the agent-patient reference'.

We can conclusively affirm that the lack of information on specific features of the narrative elements (scene, act, agents and patients, agency, purposes) and their mutual relationships which characterizes Nic's and Luc's retellings of a film scene makes it difficult for a Standard speaker recipient to situate them within a suitable rhetorical narrative schema in order to reconstruct what is really going on and come to a suitable interpretation of the facts.

To resume, the narrative style of the Konstanz children in retelling a film scene, displays a strong extratextual, i.e., indexical and iconic mode of representation and referring. The iconic representation of events narrated and of the persons acting in them is often displayed in the form of a *demonstratio ad oculos* (i.e., the types of less displaced deixis 3A and 3B) with ellipses of important scene elements. Thus the audience has a great deal of referential work to do in order to reconstruct what the narrator has seen and they must infer. In this way, in retelling film scenes, the Konstanz children use a narrative technique which, being strongly based on types of exophoric deixis, deictic and iconic signalling and contextualizing, reflects the film technique. As in the film, the visualisation of setting, actors, actor-bound actions, action-bound agency and goals or motivation is mediated and organized in a series of scene and action-centered episodes. Undoubtedly this technique, insofar as it relates events more on the basis of their internal structure than by means of syntactic and textual marking - reveals processes of simplification; this can inversely imply in an audience used to normative narrative standard a complication in the interpretive process. This is often the case when a Standard using recipient is confronted with the film retellings of the Konstanz children, where a hypocodification at several levels impedes a suitable envisionment of the world of narration.

Our observations and hypotheses on the structural and communicative characteristics of the film retellings of the Konstanz children will gain more support if we contrast them with comparable performances of the Varese group.

Thus consider the following two examples of Elm (aged 9) and Jan (aged 10) from the Varese group, which display a different and quite opposite state of affairs.

EX. (8) Daltanius (Elm, 9, Varese)
i (1) C'era una volta un pianeta che non era come la terra // (2) e un giorno un professore che aveva una mente piu geniale di un essere umano costruí un leone di ferro //// ii (3) e allora: attacc/ dei esseri mhm s-/di un altro pianeta attaccarono il loro pianeta, // (4) e andarono sulla terra per conquistarla. //// iii (5) allora quei/ quello- quel vecchio costruí una base. // (6) e un pricipe di nome Enzo /- Kento pilotò Dalta:nius/ (....) pilotò Antares. //// iv (7) e quando si agganciarono Antares e il leone, // (7b:) X: [ma scemo! ancora non l'avevano trovato il leone!] - - non l'avevano ancora trovato il leone, // (8) - no - il leone era caduto da- dalla base, // (9) e non lo trovarono più. //// v (10) e quando lo trovarono, // (11) eh - si saldarono Daltanius e Antares // (12) e si trasformarono (in) (di) Daitanius. ...//XY: 13: ora basta eh - basta

----

i (1) once upon a time there was a planet that wasn't like the earth // (2) and one day a professor who had a mind more ingenious than a human being built a lion made of iron. //// ii (3) and so they atta/ beings mhm s/ from another planet attacked their planet, // (4) and came to the earth in order to conquer it. //// iii (5) and so that- that old man built a base, // (6) and a prince named Enzo piloted Daltanius -

piloted Antares. //// iv (7) and when Antares and the lion hooked up// [stupid! they hadn't found the lion yet!] // (8) no/ and the lion had fallen from the base, // (9) and they didn't find it anymore. //// v (10) and when they found it, // (11) Daltanius and Antares soldered together // (12) and they transformed themselves from (?) into (?) Daltanius // (13) XY: enough! enough!

EX. (9) Starsky and Hutch (Jan, 10, Varese)
i (1) Ah si che due poliziotti, uno si chiama Starsky ed A/ - allora questi eh questi due poliziotti - due due - // (2) c'erano degli uomini che - c'erano degli uomini che dovevano fare una rapina - (....) - dovevano fare delle rapine ai porti che arrivano delle navi con dei valori. //// ii (3) allora prima loro hanno rubato delle macchine fotografiche giapponesi, // (4) e dopo dovevano fare un altro colpo. // (5) però dovevano rubare dei diamanti da tremila dra tremila mili - da trecento miliardi di - di dollari. [[M: eh tre milioni di dollari!]] - - tre milioni di dollari. //// iii (6) allora eh - sono andati là, // (7) e con dei - con delle prove li hanno arrestati. // (8) - -no? perché c'era un registrató/ c'era un ricettatore che - - aiutava questi due poliziotti, perchè- // (9) (....) - eh era uno che diceva che s'era messo - - non era più disonesto. // (10) però - però - però ha detto - cercherò d'informarmi. //// iv (11) allora però lui voleva ritirarsi indietro da questo colpo. // (12) perché ce/ eh c'en-trava anche lui. // (13) però il colpo da tre milioni e mmezzo voleva anche lui farlo no? voleva; - // (14) lui era il ricettatore che li pagava - i diamanti. // (15) questi era(no) tre milioni di dollari, - tre milioni di dollari. // (16) e invece lui glie ne dava un milione e mezzo - per tutti quei diamanti lí. //// v (17) allora lui dopo se n'è voluto togliere, // (18) però dopo li hanno sorpreso sul fatto.

----

i (1) Oh yes, two policemen, one called Starsky and A./ so those, those two police-men two- two- // (2) there were men there were men who had to make a robbery (....) - they had to make some robberies in the harbours because ships had to arrive with valuable things. // (3) so first they have stole some Japanese cameras; //// ii (4) and then they had to make another coup; // (5) however they had to steal diamonds (....) worth three thousand billion dollars [M: eh eh, three million dollars!] - three million dollars. // (6) so - they went there, // (7) and with - with -/ they arrested them with proofs. // (8) you know, because he was a registe/ - he was a receiver who helped those two policemen, because/ (..) // (9) eh - he was one who said that he had begun/ he was not dishonest any more. // (10) however - however - however he has said, I'll try to get information. // (11) but then he wanted to draw back from this coup; // (12) because he too was involved. // (13) however the robbery worth three and a half million, he wanted to do this, he too, didn't he? he wanted; -// (14) he was the receiver who payed them - the diamonds. // (15) they were (worth) three million dollars, three million dollars. // (16) but he gave them one and a half million for all those diamonds. // (17) so he has wanted to leave, // (18) but afterwards they have caught them stealing.

In contrast to the retellings by the Konstanz children in EX. (6) and (7), Elm's and Jan's performances display a high degree of elaboration in the narrative organization of temporal, relevance and motivation relationships. Both stories are concisely represented in line with the acquired and practised way of narrating according to normative rhetorical schemata of narratives, whereby Elm applies fairy tale schemata, beginning with *c'era una volta* 'one upon a time' (1. 1) and continuing with *e un giorno* 'one day' (1. 2). The episodes in both retellings do not seem to correspond iconically to the film episodes but only give a sketchy conventionalized account. The adverb *allora* 'then', 'so', 'thus' forms the temporal and motivational deixis in the episodes (ii) and (iii) (respectively 1. 3 and 5) of EX. (8) and at the beginning of the episodes (i) - (v) (1. 1, 3, 6, 11 and 17 respectively) of EX. (9), that is, it connects anaphorically the events occurring there with the foregoing ones in a relationship of temporal sequentiality and motivational consequentiality. Backgrounded events are framed in backgrounding hypotactical patterns introduced twice by *quando* 'when' in the first clause, whereas foregrounding is unambiguously marked without any tense variation by *passato remoto* in the independent clauses (with the second position) optionally preceded by *allora* in the episodes of EX. (8). Back- and foregrounding relations are clearly expressed at the surface structure by lexical and syntactical means in EX. (8) by Elm (e.g., 1. 1, 2, 4, 5, 8, 9, 11-16 and 3, 6, 7, 10, 17, 18 respectively) whenever he does not use hypotactical constructions but rather connectives such as *però* 'but' (1. 5, 10, 11, 13, 18), *invece* 'instead' (1. 16), *perché* 'because' (1. 8, 12).

Personal deixis refers in both texts unambiguously to the agents and patients of the actions; it is expressed endophorically by means of proper names, individualizing names and anaphoric expressions and is clearly interpretable.

In both retellings by the Varese children we can state that inferential work by the recipient is greatly reduced; in any case presuppositions of further context information are better feasible because unambiguous contextualization markers help to activate suitable narrative schemata. That is, scene, acts, agents, patients and goals and their reciprocal relationships are clearly outlined and interpretable within a temporal narrative frame according to rhetoric-narrative schemata (orientation, action, complication, solution). The grammatically and lexically marked temporal and narrative functions and the textual constructions mentioned above display a fairly formal and standard style which is highly conventional and does not reflect an indexical or iconic 'pragmatic mode' of narrating. Strong rhythmical and specific intonational contours characterize (contextualize) the different patterns of relevance within the couplets forming the backgrounding and foregrounding parts of the episodes; moreover the contextualization markers are grammaticalized or lexicalized and the context is situated in the text.

On the basis of similar analyses of the different ways of retelling film scenes by the monolingual group immersed in Italian culture and socialization in Varese and the bilingual group in Konstanz with only minor Italian socialization, we can summarize our observations and make some hypothetical claims.

The two ways of retelling films display different attitudes and two styles of referring. The Konstanz children are closely bound to the situation and require a great deal of presuppositions and inference work. In particular, presuppositions without overt backgrounding markers (verbal aspects, syntactical marking, (pro) nominal reference to agents or patients, syntactic framework for expressing dependency relationships of relevance and motivation) are mostly recoverable from the content and ordering of the utterances. It is as if their narrating procedures are transposed from that of the film. It is also very elliptic and closer to the pragmatic way in which they communicate and narrate in every day interaction, when they refer to schemata based on shared knowledge. When confronted by a retelling of films with a fictional realm, they do not seem aware that the narration of this genre requires a specific style of performance with its own rules even at the temporal structure level. They are simply not trained in it. In addition, they seem to suppose attitudes and expectations from the interactants as in every day conversation: if you need more information you can ask for it. This attitude and the way they perform can be associated with the realization of a strategy of simplification at the pragmatic communicative level. These facts may be connected with their feeling of low competence in Italian and with their avoidance of communicative difficulties. In fact, in German they behave quite differently.

In connection with these facts we can express another hypothetical claim with regard to the deictic temporal structure used by the Konstanz children. The related events seem to be reconstructed and displayed in a way that concerns more the inherent semantic relationship of the events with each other than their deictic temporal and motivational relationships from the viewpoint of the interactants. In other words, the events seem to be first represented and (re)organized according to some principle inherent in the nature of the events themselves and only secondarily according to temporal, relevance and motivation relationships and devices to represent them. That is, the second type of organisation seems less developed than the first. Thus, the Konstanz children - more than those of the Varese group - seem to apply principles for temporal construction and backgrounding/foregrounding which are less grammaticalized and reflect more natural processes. For example, temporal continuity or temporal deictic or anaphoric anchoring of events reported as well as their framing within structures of relevance and motivation relationships are often expressed by the sequential order of textual units which reflect the order of events. Units reporting punctual or completed events are more frequently used as foregrounding and 'relevant' than those reporting non-punctual events. With regard to motivation relations we can observe that backgrounding, motivation and relevance relationships are often presented as inferable from knowledge of the content or from the relationships between adjacent units.

If this hypothetical interpretation fits the facts, then in this regard, too, the Konstanz children seem to display a behaviour with traces of an earlier developmental stage of grammatical and communicative competence. At this stage grammaticalization has not yet replaced the pragmatic mode (cf. Givón, 1979) in many places in which this is already done by the monolingual children of the same age in Varese.

Conclusions

In the context of this paper, we were only able to demonstrate our holistic in-depth analysis of different types of retellings (i.e., picture story, short oral story and film scene retellings) on the basis of a few examples. Derived from an extended comparative analysis of such retellings by both the immigrants' children in Konstanz and the monolingual children in Varese, we summarise the following preliminary observations about the Konstanz group.

– The forms and constructions of temporal and motivational relevance reveal a low degree of markedness.
– Several simplification strategies at the morphosyntactic, textual and pragmatic levels are employed in the construction of temporal deixis, aspectual perspective, motivation and relevance relationships in narrating events.
– Differences from the monolingual children in Italy are displayed with regard to the expression of temporality, relevance and motivation at the morphosyntactic, textual and contextualization level. The children in Varese display structures which are closer to the norm of the Standard Italian style.
– In connection with the simplification strategies, deviant foregrounding imperfects with non-stative verbs are used particularly in retelling picture stories and oral stories read immediately before which contain forms of *passato remoto*. In any case this tense is rare in narrations of films and very rare even in norm-conscious subgroups.
– The use of foregrounding imperfects with non-stative verbs seems to be influenced by the practice of the German *Präteritum* and mediated in the school setting and instructional socialization in contact with the literary language.
– Difficulties in forming and using *passato remoto* forms (which are both semantically and morphophonologically more marked than those of the *imperfetto)* are evident. In its place transfers from German *Präteritum* rendered by Italian *imperfetto* are used in convergence with simplification processes and strategies.
– Imperfect forms are mastered and used in modal constructions, in relating utterances, explanations, descriptions, evaluations and retrieval of information. These uses may also be connected with the fact that verbs used for such activities generally display an *'Aktionsart'* which neutralizes other aspectual marks. Some further stylistic uses of the imperfect which occur among the Varese children do not yet occur in the Konstanz children.
– Devices of parataxis, juxtaposition with ellipsis or lack of temporal and motivational connections are preferred. Devices of hypotaxis are rare. Congruence devices and 'consecutio temporum' devices are also rarely applied.
– The expression of temporal relations prevails over those of causal, concessive, consecutive and final relations. Expression of the latter mostly appears neutralized and must be inferred from the context and intonational contours.
– Transposition from displaced deixis to the 'origo' deixis is frequent and suggests strategies and processes of simplification.

- Deixis prevails over anaphora. Expressions for anteriority and posteriority prevail over those for simultaneity. Since these are more marked, they are avoided in accordance with the simplification principle.
- Indexical or iconical expressions are used occasionally instead of more marked shifters.
- Personal deixis appears to be implied and dominated by temporal deixis, which in turn is dominated by spatial deixis. Deictic use of temporal marks prevails over those of grammatical or otherwise non-lexically inherent aspectual marks. Morphologically marked relations (eg. the aspectual ones) appear neutralized if implied by lexical expressions. The use of deictic marking by *plusquamperfect* is dispreferred.
- Sequential juxtaposing order is preferred to that of perspective, and enchaining to encasing (as less marked versus more marked).
- Relating of events on the basis of their internal structure is preferred to relating by means of syntactic and textual marking.
- Background information is often presupposed and more inferring work is required of the recipient.

After summarizing these aspects of behaviour in narrative constructions, we can state that they conform to general principles which rule the course of language acquisition. The linguistic behaviour of these children with regard to their mother tongue in the situation of migration appears governed by universal constraints on language acquisition which converge with other constraints of a social kind.

The non-standardness of some linguistic structures depends in one part on their scarce contact with Standard Italian and in another part on the intensive contact between the languages available in their repertoire. This consists of German and Italian dialects used to form in an almost natural and unguided way their own variety of Italian which is given only little support by the one-hour weekly Italian classes. Thus this anomaly represents normal and regular phenomena in the stage of an interim language in the process of language acquisition.

The differences between the performance of the Konstanz children and that of the Varese children are to a great extent explicable by reference to the different linguistic and cultural socialization of the two groups. The communicative tasks we have illustrated are highly contextualized, i.e., associated with the factors of the context in which they are learned and used. Both production and interpretation of the performance of these tasks are also influenced and conditioned by these contexts. In the present state of research, nothing precise can be said about the relationships between the speech style or linguistic encoding of these children and the correspondent cultural context. The little that can be assumed concerns 1) the social constraints on this stage of linguistic knowledge and the social effects or consequences of it; 2) the convergence of the universal cognitive constraints on the process of language acquisition by these migrant children with the constraints due to their communicative necessities and goals and to their social and linguistic knowledge, and 3) the interdependence between linguistic and instructional development.

In general, if narratives represent a special way of discursive (re)structuring of vicarious experience, we can state that the way in which the bilingual children of the Konstanz group do this in Italian is significantly different from that of the monolingual children of the Varese group. The preliminary results and the claims presented in the course of this study may serve as a basis for forming further hypotheses. However, more data and intensive research are needed to realise these aims.

References

Agar, M., 1991. The biculture in bilingual. *Language in Society,* 20, 167-181.

Andersen, R., 1991. Developmental sequences: the emergence of aspect marking in second language acquisition. In: T. Huebner & A. Ferguson (eds), *Crosscurrents in second language acquisition and linguistic theories,* Amsterdam: Benjamins.

Antinucci, F. & R. Miller, 1976. How children talk about what happened. *Journal of Child Language,* 3, 167-89.

Auer, P., 1982. *Zweisprachige Konversationen.* Papiere des SFB 99, N. 79, Universität Konstanz. (English Translation 1985: *Bilingual Conversation.* Pragmatics and Beyond. Amsterdam: Benjamins).

Auer, P. & A. di Luzio, 1983. Three types of variation and their interpretation. In: L. Dabène, M. Flasaquier & J. Lyons (eds), *Status of Migrants' Mother Tongues.* ESF, Strasbourg, 67-100.

Auer, P. & A. di Luzio (eds), 1984. *Interpretative Sociolinguistics: Migrants - Children - Migrant Children.* Tübingen: Narr.

Auer, P. & A. di Luzio, 1988. Diskurssemantische Eigenschaften der Sprache italienischer Migrantenkinder. In: A. von Stechow & M.-T. Schepping (eds), *Fortschritte in der Semantik,* 159-199, Weinheim: VCH, Acta Humaniora.

Auer, P. & A. di Luzio (eds), 1992. *The contextualization of Language.* Amsterdam: Benjamins.

Bamberg, M., 1987. *The acquisition of narratives.* Berlin: Mouton, de Gruyter.

Bazzanella, C. & D. Calleri, 1991. Tense coherence and grounding in children's narrative. *Text,* 11, 175-187.

Berger, P. & T. Luckmann, 1966. *The social construction of reality.* New York: Academic Press.

Bertinetto, P., 1986. *Tempo, aspetto e azione verbale nel verbo italiano; il sistema dell'indicativo.* Firenze: Accademia della Crusca.

Bierbach, C., 1985. Nun erzähl doch mal! Textstruktur und referentielle Organisation in elizitierten Erzählungen italienischer Kinder. In: E. Gülich, & Th. Kotschi (eds), *Grammatik, Konversation, Interaktion.* Tübingen: Narr.

Blom, J. & J. Gumperz, 1972. Social meaning in linguistic structures: code-switching in Norway. In: J.Gumperz & D. Hymes (eds), *Directions in Sociolinguistics,* 407-434. New York: Holt, Rinehart & Winston.

Bronckart, J. & H. Sinclair, 1973. Time, tense and aspect. *Cognition,* 2, 107-30.

Bühler, K., 1934. *Sprachtheorie.* Jena: Fischer.

Burke, K., 1966. *Language as Symbolic Action. Essays on Life, Literature, and Method.* Berkeley: University of California Press.

Burke, K., 1969. *A Grammar of Motives.* Berkeley: University of California Press.

Calleri, D., 1990. L'acquisizione dell'imperfetto in bambini di madre lingua italiana. In: G. Bernini & A. Giacalone Ramat (eds), *La temporalitá nell'acquisizione di lingue seconde,* 117-127. Milano: Angeli.

Di Luzio, A., 1982. Problemi linguistici dei figli dei lavoratori migranti. In: G. Braga (ed.) *Problemi linguistici e unità europea,* 112-119. Milano: Angeli.

Di Luzio, A., 1991. On some (socio)linguistic properties of Italian foreign workers' children in contact with German. *International Journal of the Sociology of Language,* 90, 131-157.

Dietrich, M., 1988. *Die Verwendung des Präteritums im Konstanzer Dialekt; Eine Untersuchung gesprochener Sprache.* Staatsexamensarbeit, Universität Konstanz.

Duranti, A. & Ch. Goodwin (eds), 1992. *Rethinking Context.* Cambridge: Cambridge University Press.

Fillmore, C., 1982. Ideal readers and real readers. In: D. Tannen (ed.), *Analyzing Discourse: Text and Talk,* 248-270. Washington DC: Georgetown University Press.

Givon, T., 1979. *On Understanding Grammar.* New York: Academic Press.

Gumperz, J., 1982. *Discourse Strategies.* Cambridge: Cambridge University Press.

Gumperz, J. (ed.), 1991. *Language and social identity.* Cambridge: Cambridge University Press.

Gumperz, J. & S. Levinson, 1991. *Rethinking linguistic relativity;* Report on the International Symposium 112; Ocho Rios, Jamaica, Mai 3-11 1991.

Harweg, R., 1975. Perfekt und Präteritum im gesprochenen Neuhochdeutsch; zugleich ein Beitrag zur Theorie des nichtliterarischen Erzählens. *Orbis,* 24, 130-183.

Hopper, P. (ed.), 1982. *Tense-Aspect: Between Semantics and Pragmatics.* Amsterdam: Benjamins.

Jakobson, R., 1971. Shifters, Verbal Categories and the Russian Verb. In: *Selected Writings II, Word and Language.* The Hague: Mouton.

Klein, W., 1982. Der Ausdruck der Temporalität im ungesteuerten Spracherwerb. In: G. Rauh (ed.), *Essays on Deixis,* 149-168. Tübingen: Narr.

Labov, W., 1972. The transformation of experience in Narrative Syntax. In: W. Labov, *Language in the Inner City,* 354-398. Philadelphia: University of Pennsylvania.

Labov, W. & J. Waletzky, 1967. Narrative Analysis. In: J. Helm (ed.), *Essays on the Verbal and Visual Arts.* Seattle.

Luckmann, T., 1989. Kultur und Kommunikation. In: M. Haller et al. (eds), *Kultur und Gesellschaft,* 33-45. Frankfurt/M.:Campus.

Pollack, W., 1970. Aspekt und Aktionsart. *Linguistik und Didaktik,* 1:40-7, 155-63.

Reichenbach, H., 1947. *Elements of Symbolic Logic.* London.

Reinhart, T., 1984. Principles of gestalt perception in the temporal organization of narrative texts. *Linguistics,* 22, 779-809.

Rowley, A., 1983. Das Präteritum in den heutigen deutschen Dialekten. *Zeitschrift für Dialektologie und Linguistik,* 160-182.

Sacks, H., 1972. On the analyzability of stories by children. In: J. Gumperz & D. Hymes (eds), *Directions in Sociolinguistics,* 329-345. New York: Holt, Rinehart and Winston.

Schmidt, W., 1977. *Grundfragen der deutschen Grammatik.* Berlin: Volk und Wissen.

Schütz, A. & T. Luckmann, 1979. *Strukturen der Lebenswelt* (Bd 1). Frankfurt/M: Suhrkamp.

Slobin, D., 1991. Learning to think for speaking: native language, cognition, and rhetorical style. *Papers in Pragmatics,* 1; 1, 7-25.

Von Stutterheim, C., 1991. Narrative and description: temporal reference in second language acquisition. In: T. Huebner & A. Ferguson (eds), *Crosscurrents in Second Language Acquisition and Linguistic Theories,* 385-403. Amsterdam: Benjamins.

Tomlin, R. (ed.), 1987. *Coherence and grounding in discourse.* Amsterdam: Benjamin.

Vygotsky, L., 1962. *Thought and Language.* Cambridge, Mass. (1st russ. ed. 1934).

Watson, K., 1973. A theoretical and sociolinguistic model for the analysis of narrative. *American Anthropologist,* 75, 243-263.

Weinrich, H., 1964. *Tempus. Besprochene und erzählte Welt.* Stuttgart: Kohlhammer.

Weist, R., 1986. Tense and aspect. In: P. Fletcher & M. Garman (eds), *Language Acquisition,* 356-374. Cambridge: Cambridge University Press.

Wunderlich, D., 1970. *Tempus und Zeitreferenz im deutschen.* München: Max Hueber Verlag.

Second language influence on first language acquisition:
Turkish children in Germany

One central problem in the study of the early bilingualism of second and third generation children from immigrant families ensues from the fact that the properties of the first language which is acquired are not exactly known, i.e., result to a large extent from the acquisition process itself. In principle, of course, this can be said of the monolingual acquisition process as well. However, in that case the change of language resulting from the acquisition process is mostly thought to be negligible and the issue is commonly disregarded in developmental research. We cannot do the same in the case of bilingual acquisition in unstable settings. In this connection an assessment of interference phenomena in the speech of older children must be helpful to gain some insight, both into the measure in which the acquisition of their first language is influenced by their second language, and into the new properties that input varieties offered to younger children may have.

The notion of *error analysis* is vital for the topic addressed here, as it is for bilingual developmental research at large. It is best discussed on the basis of Bowerman's definition:

> The term *error* will be used (...) to refer to deviations from norms of adult usage and presumably from what the child has heard modeled; most of these will not be errors within the rules of the child's own system (Bowerman, 1982: 101).

To my mind this definition shows that the term norm is used in two ways in acquisition research. Firstly, of course, some societal norm is impressed on the child in various ways and with varying persistency during the acquisition process. At the same time, a so-called 'adult norm' is assumed to exist which may serve as a point of reference for error analysis. In this usage the term *norm* is actually more or less equivalent to 'the final result of the acquisition process'. At the same time the concept *norm* as applied in error analysis is stipulated in terms of input-output mapping, whereas possible discrepancies between the language input and the eventual result of the acquisition process are disregarded in the case of monolingual acquisition.

The scheme is inappropriate for bilingual acquisition in an immigrant setting. In second language acquisition research it might be legitimate to term some standard-like variety 'target-language' and label systems of off-target structures 'imperfective learning'. But what about the acquisition of Turkish as a first language in Germany and other parts of Europe? In the light of what we expect as the 'final result of the acquisition process' it makes little sense to select standard Turkish as the norm to be referred to in error analysis. For the analysis of the speech of children from parents with a rural background in Turkey it is, of course, an improvement if we broaden the scope of the 'adult norm' to include characteristics of Anatolian dialects. But that is not enough. In the bilingual situation that the Turkish immigrant children find themselves in the norm of their first language must be conceived of as a very dynamic concept. New norms can be expected to emerge as a result of the first language acquisition process itself, and of sociolinguistic processes. School-going children must be considered a crucial age-group in this respect (see Verhoeven, 1991 for a review of the research to date into the acquisition of Turkish in the immigrant setting).

On an earlier occasion (Boeschoten, 1990) I concentrated on analysing innovative patterns generally to be found in the speech production of Turkish children aged 4-6 in the Netherlands. Those patterns were apparently intralinguistically motivated, but were also different from anything known from the monolingual setting in Turkey. None of the patterns found seemed to be related to interference from the children's second language, i.e., Dutch. This result is not particulary surprising, because the immigrant children are not normally brought up bilingually before they enter kindergarten classes at the age of 4.

At a later stage, as the children become more balanced bilinguals, this changes. I want to illustrate what might happen around the age of 10 on the basis of the data from the contact situation in Germany.

In this chapter I will discuss some patterns to be found in the speech of Turkish children growing up in Germany. The home language situation of these children can be characterised as mixed: with their parents they speak mostly Turkish, but they use at least as much German as Turkish with their siblings. In their Turkish there is ample evidence of interference, as will be shown below.

I will not discuss the concept of *interference* here; the problems concerning its definition, and its application in the present contact situation are dwelled upon in Boeschoten & Broeder (forthcoming). Rather, I will approach the matter from a descriptive perspective on the basis of a relatively small corpus, which consists of speech samples collected in interview sessions of 10-20 minutes each with Turkish children aged 8-12 in Frankfurt and other towns in Hessen[1]. Data were collected from 24 children of different socio-economic background. Most of them were born in Germany and grew up there. The interviews were essentially conducted as free conversation, but were structured in the sense that certain topics of conversations

---

[1] The data were collected and presented during a seminar at the University of Frankfurt during the 'Wintersemester' 1990/91 by the following students: Özgüler Altunay, Birgen Ülker, Gülten Yazıcı, Siret Çelebi, Semra Baykal and Semra Wystrach.

L2 influence on L1 acquisition

were introduced in all cases, e.g., certain aspects of the home situation of the children, experiences the children had during holidays in Turkey and their hobbies and interests.

The interlinguistic level and calques

In [1] we see the general situation exemplified by three variants of denotations for 'writing desk' occurring in the present corpus; the interlingual level is here represented by a loan translation:

1. Schreibtisch   GERMAN
    yazı masası/yazma masası   INTERLANGUAGE
    çalışma masası   TURKISH ('working-table')

Similar cases are the extensions of meaning of Turkish lexemes as a result of interlingual polysemy (i.e., the existence of a German lexeme which could serve as the translational equivalent of the Turkish lexeme, but only if the latter occurs with another meaning); two examples are given in [2] and [3]:

2. I_{14}: Almanca konuşuyorsak, hmm/ ondan sonra Türkçe'ye *varıyoruz*
    'if we speak German/ then we change to Turkish'
    [germ. *über-gehen* > *var*= 'to go (somewh.)', instead of *geç*='to pass']

3. I_{12}: Mesela *Judo* için bir *saat* var.
    'For example, there is one lesson (for) judo'
    [this use of *saat* 'hour' < germ. *Stunde*]

An important type of calque, which is typical of Turkish/German (and Turkish/Dutch; maybe also Turkish/Germanic) contact is exemplified by the compounds in [4]:

4a. I_7: Ben *Georg Büchner*-okula gidiyorum.
    'I visit the Georg Büchnerschule'
    [and not ... *Georg Büchner okul-un-a*]

4b.   MOST INFORMANTS: pop müzik [and not *pop müziği*]

The point in this case is that both Turkish and German have [modifier-head] order in nominal compounds, but in Turkish compounds agreement marking with a 3rd person possessive suffix on the head is obligatory. The agreement marker is lacking in cases like those in [4].

Finally, [5] looks like just another calque, similar to [1]. However, here there might be consequences of a paradigmatic nature, in the sense that *devam*, which is a noun meaning 'continuation' in standard Turkish, might be on its way to becoming a marker of aktionsart in Germanic fashion, cf. [6].

5. I$_{18}$: Devam okuyorum.
'I read on'
[germ. *weiter-lesen* > *devam oku=*]

6. I$_{12}$: Ondan sonra ödevim bitmediyse, onu *devam yapıyorum.*
'Then, if my homework hasn't been finished, I go on with it'
[*devam yap=* < germ. *weiter-machen*]

7. I$_9$: Yemek şey yapıyorduk, ondan azıcık şimdi... azıcık ta *Grammatik yapı-yoduk.*
'We cooked a meal, and then a little now... we also worked a bit at grammar.'

8. I$_{14}$: Bazan Atatürk'ten, bazen de sosyal bilgiler *edi*yoruz.
'Sometimes (the lesson) is about Atatürk, and sometimes we *do* social science'

The dummy verb ('pro-verb') *yap=*, by the way, occurs quite frequently in calques which derive from idiomatic uses of German *machen* (esp. 'to work at a school subject'), as exemplified in [6] and [7], and so occasionally does the verb *et=*, the (apparently essentially intralinguistically motivated) ousting of which by *yap=* from its semantically empty functions is characteristic of immigrant Turkish (Boeschoten & Backus, forthcoming; Boeschoten & Broeder, forthcoming)

Global distribution of language elements

So far, what we know about the acquisition of Turkish in an immigrant setting is mostly based on the analysis of (pseudo-)longitudinal data sets of speech samples, but on nothing resembling diaries. Naturally, we are therefore somewhat bedevilled by the problem that we can't assess global distributions of variable features of the language. Let me exemplify what this means for an assessment of interference phenomena on the basis of the following example:

Consider the word order in Dutch and German relative clauses:

9a. DUTCH: Ik weet dat je gekomen bent.
    GERMAN: Ich weiß, daß du gekommen bist.
9b. DUTCH: Ik weet dat je bent gekomen.
    GERMAN: *Ich weiß, daß du bist gekommen.
             'I know that you have come.'

Whereas in standard Dutch the position of the auxiliary verb is variable, [9b] is ungrammatical in German. As I know from personal experience, a Dutch-German bilingual might well tend to produce only the type [9a] in their Dutch, which would amount to an undergeneralisation of [9b]; a case of interference on the level of performance which can't be detected by means of error analysis and therefore must be assessed on the basis of rather large corpuses.

There is another point to be made about this introductory example. Although the pattern looks neat and clear-cut, it actually is not. In the idiolects of many speakers of Dutch (mostly from the southern part of the language area) [9b] is out, as it is in German. Complications like these of a sociolinguistic nature have to be expected, of course, especially because a variable rule is involved.

In the Turkish-German contact situation we can already discern a number of distributional features. It has, probably rightly, been suggested that in immigrant Turkish an increased frequency may be observed of the overt expression of pronouns, which is not obligatory in Turkish, a 'pro-drop' language (Pfaff, 1991). However, the issue is a purely pragmatic one (i.e., the level of syntactic competence is not affected as far as intersentential anaphora is concerned), and cannot be really clarified on the basis of the data analysed so far in the literature. The data presented here are certainly too limited to contribute to the discussion.

There are, however, other patterns to be considered. A transfer, which generally occurs with all informants, concerns the distribution of a lexical item (cf. [9a]). The meaning 'to go outside' is commonly expressed with *git=* 'to go', and not with *çık=* 'to come out' (as in [10b]), which in standard Turkish is more common.

10a. INFORMANTS: Dışarı(ya) gidiyorum. 'I go outside'
10b. STAND. TURKISH: Dışarı(ya) çıkıyorum.

11. I₁₅: Eşşeğim kuyruğundaki ne kadar saçı varsa...
'whatever hair there was on my donkey's tail...'
[coalescence of *saç* 'hair on the head' and *kıl* 'hair' to *saç*]

12a. I₈: Daha onu *feststellen* yapmadık.
'We have not yet convinced ourselves of that.'
12b. I₁₈: Kalem aldı annem. O zaman ben onu daha kullanmak istemiyorum.
'My mother bought a pencil. At that time I don't want to use it yet.'
[overgeneralising *daha* (for *henüz*) < germ. *noch*(?)]

Examples [10-12] are illustrative of a serious methodological problem: although it is unquestionably true that in these case we witness the phenomenon of redistributions in the lexicon, and, quite probably, at least in some cases the telescoping of two or more lexical items into one. However, it is impossible to ascertain on the basis of the description of a corpus like the present one the role played by interference mechanisms in these changes, as they could as well be motivated by intralinguistical processes taking effect during the acquisition process. Besides, the features we have selected here were fairly generally produced by the group of informants, and should therefore also be judged from the perspective of linguistic change in progress.

One interesting distributional feature to be found in the present data set is the regression of the Turkish imperfective past tense forms *-yordu* and *-rdI* which is in evidence in the narrations of the informants. There are two possibilities here: in the first place, of course, narrations may well be (and those of the informants mostly are) based solely on the perfective (and at the same time, neutral, cf. Johanson, 1971) element of the aspectual opposition *-DI*[2] (the 'preterite').

More interesting are the cases in which the aspectual opposition has been preserved, but present tense forms (*-yor/-r*) are used for information which is intraterminally presented ('backgrounded'), where one would expect the imperfective forms (*-yordu/-DI*) in standard Turkish:

13a. I$_{19}$: Bazen iki tane bisiklet vardı orada; sonra her gün çık*ıyorum*, yani sür*üy-orum*.
'Sometimes there were two bicycles there, too; then I go out (PROGR) each day, that is I ride (PROGR).'

13b. I$_8$: Orda birşey, tahta ev bauen yap*tık*, ondan sonra arkadaşlarımızı falan çağır*dık* (...) ondan sonra halt onu yap*tık*, denize git*tik*, başka hatırlıya-mıyorum, öyle şeyler yap*ıyoruz* fast hergün. Bi de dükkanımız var orda, bazanları oraya gid*iyorum*, babaanneme yardım etmeye.
'We built (PRET) something there, a wooden house, then we invited (PRET) our friends there (...) then, we did (PRET) just that, we went to the sea; for the rest I can't remember; we do (PROGR) things like that almost every day. We have a shop there, too, sometimes I go there in order to help my granny.'

13c. I$_{14}$: Yani önceleri hep düşün*ürüm* küçükken bir diş doktoru olacaktım diye.
'That is, I always used to think (AOR), when I (was) small, that I would become a dentist.'
[Here, the converb *-ken* clearly sets a frame for the (habitual) imperfective form 'düşün*ürdüm*']

We can conclude from examples like those in [13] that the Turkish aspectual opposition, which is so alien to German, is acquired at least by some of the immigrant children, even if the imperfective past tense forms often are not produced. This can hardly be attributed to any 'influence of German'. On the other hand, a reduction of the formal inventory to the preterite *-DI* (and other forms outside the scope of the main aspectual opposition), without any indication that narratives are organised

---

[2] Capitals in suffix forms conventionally indicate 'archephonemes'.

along the lines of verbal aspect, again could, to a certain extent well be attributed to interference. As we have seen, a reduction of the formal inventory does not necessarily impeach the expression of the semantic category of verbal aspect on the level of discourse.

Word order

In spoken Turkish the order of constituents is quite free, at least in simplex sentences. 'Free', of course, means that word order in general is regulated not so much by syntactic rules as by pragmatic principles. An obvious global prediction would be that contact with German will result in a tendency to favour patterns of constituent order conforming to patterns of German, the word order of which is much more rigidly fixed.

Obviously the operationalisation of this idea in first language acquisition research is a tall order to fill, considering the fact that we are again dealing with a very general distributional feature of the language. Here I will not attempt anything like it on the basis of the present data. However, in mixed discourse certain structures persistently crop up which invariably have VO-order:

14. I_{12}: Ondan sonra öğreniyorsun nasıl *umgehen* yap-acağını *Computer*'len
      then learn-PROG-2SG how do-VERB.NOUN-POSS2SG-ACC computer-with
      'Then you learn how to handle a computer.'
      [germ. *Dann lernst du, wie du mit dem Computer umgehen mußt.*]

15a. I_{17}: *Lust*'um yok kitap oku*mağa.*
       'I don't feel like reading (a) book(s).'
       [germ. *Ich habe keine Lust zum Bücherlesen.*]

15b. I_{17}: Sonra Kırmızı Yanaklı Kız bitmiş çiçekler topla*mağa.*
       'Then Red Riding Hood finished collecting flowers.'
       [transfer of meaning: germ. *fertig sein/werden mit* > turk. *bit=*]

15c. I_{17}: Sonra gitmiş dışarı su iç*meğe.*
       'Then he went outside to drink water.'

16. I_9: Daha iyi benim için (diye).
      V   O
      '[Because] it is better for me.'
      [germ. *[weil] (es ist) besser für mich*]

In [14], the calquing of the German idiom, which centres around the lexical combination *umgehen mit...* 'to handle', by no means leads to an exact word-for-word reproduction of the order in the German equivalent in Turkish. But the surface order [main verb – object clause] is highly characteristic of this type: the calquing of [(German) verb-INF *yap=*] + *ile* (calqued on German mit 'with'); in fact, in this case the inverse order, which would conform to the 'normal' Turkish word order pattern, never occurs and sounds decidedly odd. Similar cases are mentioned for Dutch/Turkish 'code-switching' by Backus (1992).

Another relatively frequent pattern is based on subordination marked with *-mAG-A* (INF-DAT) on the subordinate verb. In [15a] the German idiom is reproduced in a straightforward way. Example [15b] also involves a curious transitivisation of the (intransitive) verb *bit=* 'to finish', the use of which seems to be triggered by the intransitivity of the German equivalent. Anyway, a sentence-final position of the subordinate clause again is characteristic of this type. The same ordering is, of course, quite possible for subordinations with *-mAG-A* in the colloquial Turkish of monolinguals (*-mAGA git=* 'to go ...ing', *-mAGA çalış=* 'to try to...', etc.; cf. [15c]), but in these cases the order is variable, as it is in the speech of the bilingual informants.

Finally, in [16] another possibility is exemplified: here, the [head-modifier] order of the german AdjP [*besser für mich*] is reproduced as VO-ordering in a syntactically different constellation.

In instances like the patterns in [14]-[16], interaction of the grammars of two languages has led to conventionalised patterns in one of them (here, the phenomenon is essentially located in the Turkish repertoire of the speakers; cf. Boeschoten & Broeder, forthcoming). As we can account for them neither as purely lexical phenomena, nor solely in terms of the combinability of two independent grammars, they cannot be accommodated by a theory according to which language mixing phenomena are described and interpreted along the lines of a dichotomy borrowing-'code-switching'. This point has been made by Johanson (1992).

In this connection, however, my main objective is to point out the consequences these calques have for the overall distributional features of surface word order patterns, i.e., a shift in the direction of VO-order. How this change in distribution might spread to structures which have not evolved in the linguistic interface is not clear. The investigation of this question is an important topic for bilingual acquisition research.

An odd example is for instance the following:

17 I_9: Daha kolay kullanıyorum, çünkü$_{CONJ}$ öğgrendim$_V$ onu daha küçükken.
       'I handle [German] more easily, for I already learned it when I was small'
       [germ. ..., *denn ich habe es schon gelernt...*]

I get the feeling that instances like these may well be connected with a tendency to apply the odd rule of 'verb-second' in Turkish (see Boeschoten, 1990), although naturally the rule does not apply to the German equivalent of the utterance. However, the present corpus is much too small to yield sufficient evidence for further discussion of this point.

Turkish ablatives induced by German 'von'

A prominent feature of the acquisition of German (and Dutch) as a second language by immigrants is the frequent, often overgeneralised, use made by speakers of the preposition *von* (Dutch: *van;* cf. Boeschoten & Broeder, forthcoming). When the data discussed presently are analysed, it is interesting to notice that the way in which the informants use the ablative case in their Turkish yields certain patterns which seem to be connected with the functions of this German element. In the following examples, the scope of the ablative is definitely widened in comparison with any variety of Turkish known from Turkey itself.

In the first place, partitive meaning of the ablative is in evidence in [18]; here the ablative of the pronoun *o*, i.e., *ondan*, seems to be directly related to anaphoric *davon*.

18a. I_4: Babam... arabaların böyle *Dach'*ında, yani tepesinde, böyle açma şeyi var ya, hava girmesi için, on*dan* yapıyor.
'My father... cars have such on their roof, that is on top of them, such an opening thing, for air to come in. He makes *from* that.'
[on*dan* < germ. da*von*]

18b. I_{14}: Gerisi de böle komik Heft'ler var, on*dan* çoğu saman oluyor.
'For the rest there are those comic strips; most of them are lousy.' (****)
[standard Turkish *on-lar-ın* (-PL-GEN) *çoğu*]
[*saman* (lit.: 'straw') is shortened for *saman gibi* 'like straw']

19a. I_{12}: Mesela Atatürk'*ten*, Fatih Sultan Mehmet'*ten* ödev vermişti bir kere.
'(The teacher), for instance, once gave (us) homework *about* Atatürk and Sultan Mehmed II.'

19b. I_{13}: Savaş*tan* rüya gördüm.
'I dreamt *about* the war.'

20. I_8: Urkunde var, ondan sonra Puzzle'ler*den* resimler.
'(On the wall of my room) there is a diploma, and then pictures (made) from puzzles.'

21. I_{13}: O zaman Almanca konuşurum ortasın*dan*.
'Then I speak German in-between.'
[?cf. germ. *zwischendurch;* stand. turk. *...arada (bir)...*]

In other cases (cf. [19]-[21]; cf. also [8]) of overextended use of the ablative, a tendency to overgeneralise this case seems in evidence which also may well be connected somehow with the distribution of *von* in German.

Conclusions

In conclusion I would like to offer the following comments: firstly, there are good reasons to be suspicious of the value contrastive analysis may have for predicting interference phenomena in the present setting. We have to set out with a descriptive approach. I dare say that the validity of this position is born out by the type of data I have discussed. I see no way in which the specific pattern cropping up could have been predicted in more than very general terms.

Secondly, the syntactical level is not deeply affected by the contact with German. In particular, great designs like the parameter setting theory have no bearing on the issues involved (cf. Pfaff, 1991). Eventually, Turkish as an immigrant language might change more dramatically, i.e., in terms of deep structure, as a result of shifted distributions of variable surface word order. But this is a sociolinguistic subject for an investigation of which the present context of the first language acquisition process is much to narrow a frame-work.

Thirdly, there are two mechanisms through which the influence of German has a more than just superficial impact. First of all, certain types of calques can upset global distributions of parameters like surface word order (e.g., the examples [14]-[16]). We could even speculate that in the long run these characteristics will affect the competence of the speakers of later generations, that is, result in new rules of syntax and word formation (e.g., lack of agreement marking as in [4], or a possible development towards aktionsart marking in Germanic fashion as in [5] and [6]). Moreover, it seems clear that one of the basic features of the process of first language acquisition are certain simplifications of linguistic structure, both of a syntagmatic and paradigmatic nature. The transfer of characteristics of a second language might come in here, as seems clear from the connection of some Turkish structures with the German preposition *von*. The patterns are basically lexically motivated.

Fourthly, there is no reason for assuming that the patterns described are valid for present-day German-Turkish contact, although some of them might be more generally valid than others.

Finally, Child language researchers must acknowledge that bilingual acquisition research cannot be conducted without extensive sociolinguistic research to back it up. In fact, in a case like the contact situation presently discussed sociolinguistics and acquisition research cannot be separated.

References

Backus, A., 1992. *Patterns of language mixing. A study in Turkish-Dutch bilingualism.* Wiesbaden: Harrassowitz.

Boeschoten, H., 1990. *Acquisition of Turkish by Immigrant Children. A multiple case study of Turkish children in the Netherlands aged 4 to 6.* Wiesbaden: Harrassowitz.

Boeschoten, H. & A. Backus, forthcoming. Code-switching and ongoing linguistic change. To appear in: B. Rona (ed.), *Proceedings of the 5th Conference on Turkish Linguistics,* London 1990.

Boeschoten, H. & P. Broeder, (forthcoming). Zum Interferenzbegriff in seiner Anwendung auf die Zweisprachigkeit türkischer Migranten. In: L. Johanson & J. Rehbein (eds), *Das Türkische im Kontakt mit dem Deutschen.*

Bowerman, M., 1982. Starting to talk worse: Clues to language acquisition from Children's Late Speech Errors. In: S. Strauss (ed.), *U-shaped Behavioral Growth,* 101-145. New York: Academic Press.

Johanson, L., 1971. *Aspekt im Türkischen. Vorstudien zu einer Beschreibung des türkeitürkischen Aspektsystems.* Uppsala: Acta Universitatis Upsaliensis, Studia Turcica Upsaliensia 1.

Johanson, L., 1992. Code-copying in immigrant Turkish. In: G.Extra & L.Verhoeven (eds), *Immigrant Languages in Europe: A Sociolinguistic Perspective.* Clevedon: Multilingual Matters (to appear).

Pfaff, C., 1991. Turkish in contact with German: Language maintenance and loss among immigrant children in Berlin (West). *International Journal of the Sociology of Language* 90, 97-129.

Verhoeven, L., 1991. Acquisition of Turkish in a mono- and bilingual setting. In: H. Boeschoten & L. Verhoeven (eds), *Turkish Linguistics Today,* 113-149. Leiden: Brill.

First language influence on second language acquisition:
Turkish and Moroccan adults in the Netherlands

Under the auspices of the European Science Foundation in Strasbourg (France) a longitudinal and cross-linguistic multiple case study on adult second language acquisition was carried out simultaneously in France, Germany, Great Britain, the Netherlands and Sweden (see Perdue, 1984, 1993). Source and target languages (SL and TL respectively) were represented pairwise in the following way:

TL	Swedish		French		Dutch		German		English	
	/ \		/ \		/ \		/ \		/ \	
SL	Finnish	Spanish		Arabic		Turkish		Italian		Punjabi

The chosen source languages belong to the major immigrant languages in the Western European countries under consideration. Four out of the five target languages are Germanic, and three out of the six source languages are non-Indo-European. For each pair of source and target language, four kernel informants were followed from their initial stage of second language acquisition during almost two-and-a-half years, with approximately one month intervals between data collection points (N_{total} = 10 x 4 = 40 informants). Each informant took regularly part in a comparable variety of language activities. Data collection resulted in an extensive computerized data bank which is centrally stored and maintained at the Max Planck Institute for Psycholinguistics in Nijmegen, the Netherlands (cf. Feldweg, 1991).

The project focused on adult language learners, because this is a rather neglected area of research compared to the work on both first and second language acquisition by children. Although there is a growing interest in universal principles of language acquisition, most of the research deals with cross-linguistic evidence on children. Studies on adult language use can offer an essential contribution to our understanding of universal principles of language acquisition. Given the fact that in such a condition language development and cognitive maturation are no longer indissolubly interwoven, we will have a chance to take a closer look at language development per se. On the basis of such studies, developmental characteristics can be taken into account that are independent of a specific target language, source language or age of acquisition. A combination of such independencies would obviously provide the strongest indications of universal principles.

After a brief outline of our informants and data base, the focus of this paper will be on one particular domain of analysis: the acquisition of word formation devices. Data derived from a series of related studies will be used. Both target and source language derived principles of lexical innovation, compounding vs. derivation, and head-final (modifier-head) vs. head-initial (head-modifier) arrangements will be taken into account.

Informants and data base

In the L2 Dutch part of the study, four kernel informants were selected for extensive data analysis: the Turkish informants Mahmut and Ergün, and the Moroccan informants Fatima and Mohamed. For each of these informants a socio-biographical profile will be presented in the following.

Mahmut

Mahmut was born in a small town 150 km from Ankara, Turkey. He attended primary school and then worked as a mechanic. At the age of nineteen he went to the Netherlands to join his wife, who had been living there for about four years. He joined the project nine months after his arrival. Mahmut first lived with his parents-in-law. However, at the beginning of the data collection period he moved to a rented house next door to his parents-in-law. During the first year of his stay in the Netherlands he was unemployed. After a year he found a job in a meat factory on a ten-month contract. This contract has been renewed since. His contacts with native speakers were limited to Dutch colleagues, authorities, hospital staff and doctors (in the third cycle he was in hospital for a week, suffering from a liver problem and he regularly saw his doctor), and people in second-hand car markets (as a former mechanic he was very interested in cars). Mahmut often reflected on his second language proficiency. He was fully aware of his shortcomings in Dutch, but also knew that owing to his family responsibilities (after a stay in the Netherlands of one-and-a-half years his daughter was born) he was unable to attend a target language course.

Ergün

After five years of primary school Ergün started working as a mechanic in Turkey. At the age of seventeen he left Turkey and joined his parents in Tilburg, who had been living in the Netherlands for some years. Soon after his arrival he attended a target language course for two hours a week for a period of five months. His attendance was rather irregular and at the beginning of the data collection period his command of Dutch was judged to be very limited. After five months he found a job as a factory worker on a temporary basis. Afterwards he was alternately employed and unemployed. At the time of the first session in the ESF project, Ergün had been living in the Netherlands for about eleven months. He was still very much a teenager at this stage. His contacts with native speakers resembled Mohamed's, one of the Moroccan learners of Dutch. Being a youngster and living with his family, he enjoyed life very much: visiting friends, going to discotheques, playing football in a mixed Turkish/Dutch team, and meeting Turkish and Dutch friends. After two years, because of many parental rows, he moved to Groningen, a city in the northern part of the Netherlands. He started working there as a car-wrecker at a breaker's yard. Given the fact that there are not many immigrants living in Groningen, Ergün's contacts with native speakers of Dutch increased even more.

Mohamed

Mohamed was born in Casablanca. After primary school he attended secondary school for only two years. Afterwards he was trained to become a mechanic, but this activity did not lead to a diploma. At the age of nineteen he and most of his family left Morocco to join his father, who had been living in the Netherlands for almost fourteen years. Soon after his arrival he found a job as a factory worker, which he remained throughout the data collection period, only temporary interrupted by a short period of unemployment. He joined the ESF project eight months after his arrival. As a youngster, living in a small town near Tilburg with relatively few immigrants he soon had lots of contacts with native target language speakers, from authorities to customers in discotheques and bars. The relation with his parents detoriated over time. He regularly stayed with his uncle for a while. After a year-and-a-half he moved in with his Dutch girlfriend at her parents' place. At the end of the data collection he was living with another Dutch girl. He had not taken part in any language course at all.

Fatima

In Kenitra, a town in Western Morocco, Fatima attended primary school for only two years, after which she received sewing and knitting lessons. For some years she was a successful seamstress. She had a little shop and taught other women. At the age of twenty-four she married a Moroccan who had been living in the Netherlands for twelve years. She joined him in Tilburg. At the time of the first encounter in the ESF project Fatima had been living in the Netherlands for one year and her proficiency in Dutch was almost zero, although she had taken part in a voluntary training course for migrant women for two hours a week, and continued to do so. This was a very basic course and had a primarily social function. She had a part-time job as a cleaning woman in the kitchen of a motel with other Moroccan and Turkish women. Her contacts with native speakers of Dutch were very limited, except for a short period at the end of the first year of her stay in the Netherlands when her husband was abroad. Her son was born when she had been in the Netherlands for two years.

In the final stage of selecting these four kernel informants, our global prognosis on their rate of L2 acquisition was taken into account. Fatima and Mahmut were selected as relatively slow learners, whereas Mohamed and Ergün were selected as relatively fast learners. The rationale behind this decision was to get a data base representing a spectrum of different types of development and a wide range of developmental stages.

For these kernel informants, data collection took place over a period of 27 months. Apart from summer holidays and other disruptions, there were regular intervals of 25-35 days between each moment of data collection, resulting in 27 sessions of one to two hours per informant. These 27 sessions were organized in the form of three successive cycles, each cycle consisting of nine sessions. These nine sessions contained the same set of speech elicitation tasks. By repeating speech elicitation activities in the form of cycles, comparable data over time become available for analysis. Various types of elicitation tasks were used: free conversations, pre-structured play acting, commenting on or retelling video fragments of films (in particular silent movies), and small-scale experiments for eliciting more standardized data related to specific linguistic domains.

The resulting data base was so extensive that the analyses had to be derived from (various) subsets of the data, depending upon the particular topic of analysis. To give an impression of the size of the data base, the estimated number of word tokens over all cycles is given in Table 1 for both the four informants and their native interlocutors.

Table 1. Estimated number of word tokens over all cycles for informants and their native interlocutors.

	Informant	Native interlocutor	Total
Fatima	31 500	44 500	76 000
Mohamed	56 000	48 500	104 500
Ergün	64 000	55 000	119 000
Mahmut	61 000	45 500	106 500
Total	212 500	193 500	406 000

Table 1 shows that the number of word tokens for Fatima is rather low. The number of word tokens in the utterances of the native speakers seems to be rather constant over the informants. The total number of word tokens is fairly high for a data base of spoken language. For instance, the data base used in De Jong (1979) for counting word frequencies in spoken native Dutch only contains 120.000 tokens.

Acquisition of word formation devices: main hypotheses

Language would be a rather uneconomical means of communication if we only could use unrelated word forms for the concepts we want to express. Take the Dutch verb stem 'teken' *(draw)* which refers to an activity. It would be hard for any language learner if reference to this activity in the past, to a male or female agent of this activity, or to the object of this activity had to be expressed by totally unrelated words. In fact, past reference, (fe)male agent reference, and object reference are expressed by different suffixes with wider applicabilities, i.e., 'tekende', 'teken-aar', 'teken-ares', and 'teken-ing' respectively. Moreover, the combinatory possibilities of words provide the language learner with expedient devices to use a restricted set of words efficiently. Consider the following compounds with 'teken': 'teken-boek' *(drawing book)*, 'teken-bord' *(drawing board)*, 'teken-doos' *(drawing case)* and 'tekentafel' *(drawing table)*.

Broadly speaking, we can divide the basic word-stock of the target language under consideration into an extensive set of free morphemes (lexemes) and a restricted set of bound morphemes (affixes). Various processes may be applied by our learners to extend this basic wordstock, e.g.:

1. creation of new word roots;
2. combination of two (or more) already existing lexemes;
3. combination of lexemes and one or more affixes; (derivation);
4. conversion of existing lexemes to other word classes (zero derivation).

We will focus on the processes mentioned under (2) and (3), and in particular on word formation processes for reference to entities. Addition of quantification or temporal information (inflection) will not be considered in the context of this paper.

The composition of lexemes (also called compounding) is generally referred to as a semantically transparent word formation process and derivation as an opaque one. In the case of derivation, the language learner has to combine free morphemes with abstract bound morphemes. The latter ones never occur as independent words, they consist most commonly of unstressed, minimal speech units, and they have rather subtle - and sometimes also ambiguous - meanings (for Dutch, see De Kleijn & Nieuwborg, 1983: 363-375.

With respect to spontaneous adult language acquisition we can therefore formulate the two following hypotheses:

H1: Given the transparency of composition and the opaqueness of derivation, the former devices will precede the latter in language acquisition.

H2: Learners will make a creative and innovative use of a variety of compositional means, also in expressing reference to entities where native speakers of the target language would prefer derivational means.

With respect to composite word formation processes, a distinction must be made between hierarchical and non-hierarchical (or linear) compounds. Hierarchical compounds are based on a right- or left-hand head rule (see Selkirk, 1982: 19-27 or, to put it differently, on head-final vs. head-initial patterns. The basic pattern for combining nouns in Dutch can be described in terms of modifier plus head, but other patterns may occur as well. Rather infrequently, there may be no hierarchical relationship between the lexemes (e.g., 'hotel-restaurant'). Moreover, more than two lexemes can be involved (e.g., 'house door bell'). In addition, another composing device is operative and productive in Dutch by which two nouns are connected by a preposition (often 'van' *(of, from))* and the head precedes the modifying part. This type of word formation device does not occur in Turkish; compounding in Turkish basically consists of modifier-head patterns. Arabic, however, mainly combines nouns in a head-modifier way by connecting head and modifier by prepositions. Derived from these different word order principles, we formulate the following hypothesis:

H3: *Given the opposite preference of word order principles for expressing nominal heads and modifiers in Turkish and Arabic, and given the ambivalent order of these devices in Dutch, Turkish and Moroccan learners of Dutch will show differential source language effects in approaching the target language norm.*

A final hypothesis can be formulated on the use of connective elements in noun-noun compounds. In Dutch these elements consist of binding phonemes like /s/, sjwa or - most commonly - zero. We formulate the following hypothesis:

H4: *Given the dominance of zero-connectors in Dutch noun-noun compounds, learners of Dutch will prefer and overgeneralize this principle.*

For testing these hypotheses, we made use of a core and extended data base in a series of related studies. For each informant, the core data base consisted of two different language activities (free conversation and film retelling) in three different cycles (N_{total} = 4 x 2 x 3 = 24 activities). The computerized storage of the complete data base made it possible to search for additional evidence on specific word formation processes in a systematic way. Scanning of specific semantic domains was done by means of the Oxford Concordance Program.

Noun-noun word formation

In this section data are discussed on word formation devices with nouns derived from our core data base. The analysis focused on developmental and distributional characteristics of noun-noun word formation types which refer to entities; token frequencies were not taken into account. The criterion for marking a combination of nouns in the data base as a composite device was that the composing parts might occur separately as meaningful lexical units. As a consequence, fossilized compounds like 'Christmas' or 'Sunday' were not taken into account.
  In Table 2 we present basic findings in the L2 Dutch data on noun-noun composition types, including N+prep+N constructions and complex head-final constructions (X+N+N). The types are distinguished according to the position of the head noun and the modifying noun.

Table 2. Number of N-N composition types in the learner varieties.

Form	Order	Fatima			Mohamed			Ergün			Mahmut		
		C1	C2	C3	C1	C2	C3	C1	C2	C3	C1	C2	C3
N+N	head-final	11	11	4	2	5	4	20	9	7	25	16	16
X+N+N	head-final	0	0	0	0	0	0	2	3	0	4	4	4
N+N	linear	1	0	0	0	0	0	1	0	0	1	2	1
N+N	head-initial	0	0	2	0	1	0	2	0	1	3	1	1
N+prep+N	head-initial	6	8	2	0	5	1	0	0	0	0	0	0
total		18	19	8	2	11	5	25	12	8	33	23	22

Table 2 shows that N+N compositions, and in particular head-final compositions, predominate in all L2 Dutch learner varieties. Nevertheless, opposite principles in Arabic and Turkish do indeed show up in distinct preferences. Only Ergün and Mahmut, the two Turkish learners, make use of head-final oriented compositions with a complex modifier. Some examples are given in Table 3.

Table 3. Use of head-final compositions (Turkish learners).

	learner variety		target variety	
Ergün				
C1	allemaal-kleine-kinder-feest	all-little-children-party	feest met allemaal kleine kinderen	party with all little children
C2	auto-monteur-werk	car-mechanic-work	werk als automonteur	work as car mechanic
Mahmut				
C3	politie-bureau-directeur	police-office director	chef van het politiebureau	director of the police office
C3	andere-mensen garage	other-people-garage	garage van andere mensen	other people's garage

Fatima and Mohamed use relatively less N+N formation devices; instead, our Moroccan learners have constructions in which the head is on the left side by using N+prep+N. Such head-initial constructions with a preposition are common in spoken Arabic, but they occur only in rare cases in spoken Turkish. In standard Dutch these constructive devices would commonly be expressed by head-final compounds. Compare the occurrences of our Moroccan informants in Table 4.

Table 4. Use of head-final compositions (Moroccan learners).

	learner variety		target variety	
Fatima				
C1	kerk van Marokko	church of Mor.	moskee	mosque
C1	kleren van baby	clothes of baby	babykleren	baby-clothes
C2	auto van *police*	car of *police*	politie-auto	police car
C2	sleutel van fiets	key of bike	fietssleutel	bike-key
C2	winkel van sigaret	shop of sigaret	sigarenwinkel	cigar shop
C3	brief van werk	letter of work	arbeidscontract	labour contr.
C3	kleren van kinder	clothes of childern	kinderkleren	children cl.
Mohamed				
C2	brief van werk	letter of work	arbeidscontract	labour contr.
C2	baas van winkel	boss of shop	winkeleigenaar	shopkeeper
C2	directeur van die ge-vangenis	director of that prison	gevangenis-directeur	director of prison
C2	man van die disco	man of that disco	disc jockey	disc jockey
C2	meneer van die winkel	mister of that shop	winkeleigenaar	shopkeeper
C3	fabriek van boten	factory of ships	scheepswerf	shipyard

The data show clear evidence of a source language effect, an effect which was also found in related studies (e.g., Van Helmond & Van Vugt, 1984; Hughes, 1979). When learners make innovative compounds, and if the target language structure allows the possibility, then they resort to source-language based compounding.

Linear compounds occur only infrequently. Table 5 gives the occurrences that were found in the Dutch data.

Table 5. Use of linear compositions.

	learner variety		target variety	
Ergün				
C1	vader-moeder	father-mother	ouders	parents
Mahmut				
C2	vader-moeder	father-mother	ouders	parents
C2	broer-zus	brother-sister	'Geschwister'	'Geschwister'
C2	oma-opa	grandfather-grandmother	grootouders	grandparents
C3	vader-moeder	father-mother	ouders	parents
Fatima				
C1	vader-moeder	father-mother	ouders	parents

All occurrences derive from the domain of kinship reference. 'Vader-moeder' *(father-mother)* and 'opa-oma' *(grandfather-grandmother)* seem to be used to compensate for lack of cover terms. There is no cover term available in standard Dutch for 'broer-zus' *(brother-sister)*. The kinship compounds again show the innovative use of composition by our learners.

Connective elements in noun-noun compositions

From the learner examples of compositions given in the preceding section it is evident that in head-initial constructions prepositions are used as connective elements. In general, our learners do not seem to have problems in catching the function of a preposition in compositions, especially not if their source language has a similar connective device. On the other hand, binding phonemes between a modifier and its head seem to be absent most of the time. In standard Dutch three binding phonemes, including zero-marking, can be distinguished in head-final N-N compositions. No systematic predictions can be made for the selection of a specific binding phoneme (see Botha, 1969). The relevant data for our learners of Dutch are presented in Table 6.

Table 6. Use of binding phonemes in head-final compositions.

	Ergün			Mahmut			Fatima			Mohamed		
	C1	C2	C3	C1	C2	C3	C1	C2	C3	C1	C2	C3
zero	20	9	7	25	15	16	10	11	4	2	6	4
-e-	-	-	-	-	1	-	1	-	-	-	-	-
-s-	-	-	-	-	-	-	-	-	-	-	-	-

The almost exclusive pattern is based on zero-marking. In most cases this pattern is in accordance with the target language norm. However, overextensions can be observed in Table 7.

Table 7. Overextentions of binding phonemes in head-final compositions.

	learner variety	target variety	
Ergün			
C1	paard-man	'paard-e-man'	rider
C1	stad-plein	stad-s-plein	city square
C2	varken-vlees	varken-s-vlees	pork
Mahmut			
C1	arbeid-bureau	arbeid-s-bureau	labour exchange
C1	paard-auto	'paard-e-auto'	'horse car'
C1	paard-vlees	paard-e-vlees	horse flesh
C1	varken-vlees	varken-s-vlees	pork
C2	arbeid-bureau	arbeid-s-bureau	labour exchange
Fatima			
C1	koe-vlees	'koei-e-vlees'	beef
C1	vark-vlees	varken-s-vlees	pork

These reconstructive compositions in our learner data are additional evidence for the fact that compounds are not acquired as unanalysed lexical units. The only occurrences of sjwa-binding are 'kopp-e-pijn' *(headache)* (Mahmut, cycle 2) and 'schap-e-vlees' *(mutton)* (Fatima, cycle 1). The first utterance is not in accordance with the target language norm ('koppijn'), the second one is a direct imitation of the native interlocutor.

Derivational processes

Derivational means have been investigated in the same dataset as used in the preceding sections (i.e., the core data base consisting of 6 conversations/retellings per informant). However, hardly any trace of productive derivation could be found, despite the variety in types of derivational nouns represented in the data set (see Broeder et al., 1988).

The following sequence, taken from Fatima in cycle 3, clearly shows the opaque character of derivational means. Fatima uses non-agent 'bakkerij' *(bakery)* for agent reference to 'bakker' *(baker):*

FA	die ander vrouw gezien die meisje	that other woman seen that girl
NS	ja	yes
FA	zeg van die bakker/ bakkerij	says of that baker/ bakery
NS	ja	yes
FA	die bakkerij loop achter die meisje	that bakery walk after that girl
NS	ja en dan?	yes and then?
FA	dan die bakkerij pak die meisje	then that bakery take that girl

Occasionally, some suffixes can be found. In most cases it is doubtful whether these devices are used productively. Most suffixes can be considered as unanalysed lexicalizations or formulas, or they are in fact direct imitations of the native interlocutor.

Innovative reference to agents, instruments, and places

The use of productive word formation devices has been investigated more thoroughly in the extended data base. All 27 encounters (nine per cycle) of our four kernel informants were scanned for such systematic word formation patterns. The analysis focused on innovative reference to a selected list of agents, instruments, and places. With respect to agents, the following lexemes were investigated in the extended data base: 'mens' *(person)*, 'man' *(man)*, 'vrouw' *(woman)*, 'jongen' *(boy)*, 'meisje' *(girl)*, 'vriend' *(friend)*, 'vriendin' *(girl friend)*, 'baas' *(boss)*, 'meneer' *(mister)*, 'baby', 'persoon' *(person)*. In Table 8 we present the innovative compositions that were found in referring to these agents.

Table 8. Innovative compositions for reference to agents.

	learner variety		target variety	
Mohamed,,	boer-mensen	farmer-people	boeren	farmers
Mahmut	boerderij-mensen	farm-people	boeren	farmers
,,	verzekeringmensen	insurance-people	verzekeringsagenten	insurance agents
,,	buitenlandmensen	foreign-people	buitenlanders	foreigners
,,	dorpmensen	village-people	dorpelingen	villagers
,,	zwart-mensen	black-people	zwarten	blacks
	wit-mensen	white-people	blanken	whites
Fatima	bakker-man	baker-man	bakker	baker
Fatima +				
MohamedErg	kapitalist-man	capitalist-man	kapitalist	capitalist
ün	repar-man	repair-man	fietsenmaker	bicycle repairman
Fatima	vrucht-vrouw	foetus-wife	vroedvrouw	midwife
,,	vroeg-vrouw	early-wife	vroedvrouw	midwife
Mahmut	koning-vrouw	king-wife	koningin	queen
Mohamed	hoer-meisje	whore-girl	prostituee	prostitute
,,	moslim-meisje	moslim-girl	moslimmeisje	moslim girl
Mahmut	fabriek-vrienden	factory-friends	vrienden op de fabriek	friends at the factory
Mohamed	baas van winkel	boss of shop	winkeleigenaar	shopkeeper
,,	baas van Turks	boss of Turkish	Turkse president	Turkish president
Mahmut	fiets-baas	bicycle boss	fietsenhandelaar	bicycle dealer
,,	politie-baas	police-boss	politiecommissaris	police commissioner
,,	baas Turkije	boss-Turkey	baas in Turkije	boss in Turkey
,,	Turkije-baas	Turkey-boss	baas in Turkije	boss in Turkey
,,	brood-baas	bread-boss	bakker	baker
,,	bus-baas	bus-boss	buschauffeur	bus driver
,,	gemeente-baas	municipal-boss	burgemeester	mayor
,,	vrachtwagen-baas	truck-boss	vrachtwagenchauff.	truck driver
,,	voor-baas	fore-boss	voorman	foreman
,,	kantoor-baas	office-boss	kantoorchef	office manager
,,	kantoor-chef-baas	office-chef-boss	kantoorchef	office manager
Mahmut +	fabriek-baas	factory-boss	fabriekseigenaar	factory owner
Ergün				
Mahmut	bril-meneer	spectacle-mister	brildrager	'spectacle bearer'

Innovative reference to instruments and places did yield far less systematic results. The only exception is the word 'kamer' *(room)*. Parts of a house can be referred to in standard Dutch by using 'kamer' *(room)* as the head preceded by a specification of its function. All four language learners used the following referential means according to standard conventions: 'slaap-kamer' *(sleeping-room),* 'zit-kamer' *(sitting-room).* In addition, the innovations presented in Table 9 could be observed.

Table 9. Innovative compositions for reference to rooms.

	learner variety		target variety	
Mahmut	koe-kamer	cow-room	koeiestal	cow shed
,,	schaap-kamer	sheep-room	schapestal	sheep fold
,,	douche-kamer	douche-room	douche	douche
,,	keuken-kamer	kitchen-room	keuken	kitchen
,,	dak-kamer	roof-room	zolderkamer	loft room
,,	bed-kamer	bed-room	slaapkamer	bedroom
,,	fiets-kamer	bicycle-room	fietsenhok	bicycle shed
,,	opereer-kamer	operation-room	operatiekamer	operating room
Mohamed	salon-kamer	saloon-room	salon	saloon
,,	kamer voor slaap	room for sleep	slaapkamer	bedroom

Especially Mahmut makes again a productive use of 'X + kamer' *(X + room).* It can be concluded that all learners have discovered the creative possibilities of combining lexemes. However, in many cases the use of particular innovative devices was found to be both a lexeme-specific and informant-specific strategy. Similar innovative phenomena were observed by Clark & Hecht (1982) in first language acquisition processes.

Innovative reference to inhabitants

It was expected that from the beginning adult learners of Dutch would frequently need lexical items in the domain of reference to inhabitants. Standard Dutch is based on a rather complex and irregular derivational system for referring to inhabitants. Table 10 illustrates this on the basis of countries and their inhabitants that the Turkish and Moroccan informants frequently referred to during the period of data collection.

Table 10. Reference to countries and their inhabitants in standard Dutch.

Country	English equivalent	Inhabitant male	Inhabitant female	Inhabitants plural
Nederland	The Netherlands	Nederland-er	Nederland-se	Nederland-ers
Holland	The Netherlands	Holland-er	Holland-se	Holland-ers
Duitsland	Germany	Duits-er	Duit-se	Duits-ers
Turkije	Turkey	Turk	Turk-se	Turk-en
Frankrijk	France	Frans-man	Fran-se	Frans-en
Marokko	Morocco	Marokk-aan	Marokkaan-se	Marokk-anen

Detailed descriptions of the standard Dutch system for reference to inhabitants are given by Geerts et al. (1984: 1209-1246) and Donaldson (1981: 248-256). The word forms presented in Table 12 show that both composition and derivation are used to refer to countries and their inhabitants in standard Dutch. In order to find evidence about (non)-standard reference in this particular domain, a systematic computer search in all 27 encounters per informant was carried out. In this way we could trace the ways in which this domain was progressively built up. The following picture emerges for our learners of Dutch.

Again, all informants have a high preference for composition instead of derivation. During all cycles they consistently refer to inhabitants by means of the simple head-final device 'X + mens/mensen/man/vrouw' *(X + person/people/man/woman).* This construction provides our language learners with a regular, transparent and productive device for reference to inhabitants. For three informants, Mahmut, Ergün and Fatima, it remains the most important device for referring to inhabitants during the whole three year period of observation, e.g., 'Marokkaans-mensen' *(Moroccan people),* 'Nederland-vrouw' *(Netherland wife).* Standardlike derivational devices can hardly be observed when our learners refer to inhabitants.

In the early encounters the Turkish informants Mahmut and Ergün occasionally use the lexemes in reverse order, resulting in head-initial devices, e.g., 'mensen-Turkse' *(people Turkish)* pro 'Turk-en' *(Turk-s),* and 'mensen-*Belçika*' *(people Belgian)* pro 'Belg-en' *(Belgian-s).* For Ergün a remarkable use of the word form 'Nederlander' *(Dutchman)* can be found. It is hardly used at all for standardlike reference to an inhabitant of the Netherlands, but mostly expresses a locative referential meaning, i.e., 'in Nederland' *(in the Netherlands).*

Only in a later stage do the informants unravel the linguistic means and referential functions of derivational devices. Mohamed is in many regards the most advanced learner of our four kernel informants. This can also be traced back in the way his lexical field for reference to inhabitants develops. In the early encounters, the same picture emerges for Mohamed as for the other informants: derivational devices are still missing and there is a marked preference for head-final devices. Over time, however, successive standard derivational devices are used for referring to inhabitants. First Mohamed discovers the derivational devices '-en' and '-aan'.

These devices result in the use of the standard word forms 'Marokkaan' *(Moroccan)*, 'Marokkanen' *(Moroccans)* and 'Turken' *(Turks)* instead of 'Marokkaans-mens/man' *(Moroccan person/man)*, 'Marokkaans-mensen' *(Moroccan people)* and 'Turks-mensen' *(Turkish people)* respectively. Next, Mohamed discovers the derivational device '-er', resulting in the use of 'Duitser' *(German)* and 'Hollanders' *(Dutchmen)* instead of 'Duits-mens' *(German person)* and 'Hollands-mensen' *(Dutch people)* respectively. Apart from the successive build-up of derivational devices, head-final compounds can still be found regularly. Finally, the use of standard-like derivations has become the rule and the use of innovative compositions the exception.

Innovative reference to kinship

A promising domain for the study of word formation in learner varieties is kinship reference. Although the devices for kinship reference belong to the most well-defined and extensively studied examples of semantic fields (cf. Barnard & Good, 1984; Lambek, 1986; Allen, 1989), studies dealing with the acquisition of kinship terms are rather scarce. Most acquisition studies have dealt with child language (cf. Carter, 1984; Haviland & Clark, 1974). Child language, however, is a less revealing area for the acquisition of kinship reference. Children will acquire the basic terms for close kins at a relatively early stage. References to relatives outside the nuclear family will only be needed at a later stage, at which time such reference is commonly accomplished in a standardlike fashion. Adult learners, however, will feel the need to refer to both close and distant kins in an early stage of acquisition. The most important conceptual dimensions on which reference to kinship relations can vary cross-linguistically, are the following:

– generation: i.e., kins of the same generation, ancestors, and descendants;
– blood relationship: i.e., consanguineal vs. affinal kins;
– degree: i.e., first, second and third degree kins;
– gender of ego, relative (alter), and connecting relative.

Table 11 contains basic kinship terms in standard Dutch derived from these conceptual distinctions.

Table 11. Basic kinship terms in standard Dutch (1/2/3 = generation).

G	Consanguineal				Affinal	
	Direct		Collateral			
	Male	*Female*	*Male*	*Female*	*Male*	*Female*
+3	over-grootvader	over-grootmoeder				
+2	opa grootvader	oma grootmoeder	oudoom grootoom	oudtante groottante		
+1	papa vader	mama moeder	oom	tante	schoonvader	schoonmoeder
0	broer	zus(ter)	neef	nicht	schoonbroer zwager	schoonzus(ter)
-1	zoon	dochter			schoonzoon	schoon-dochter
-2	kleinzoon	kleindochter	achterneef	achternicht		
-3	achter-kleinzoon	achter-kleindochter				

The standard Dutch system for kinship reference has separate lexemes for six nuclear kinship types: 'vader' *(father)*, 'moeder' *(moeder)*, 'broer' *(broer)*, 'zus(ter)' *(sister)*, 'zoon' *(son)* and 'dochter' *(daughter)*. In addition, there are four more intimate kinship terms: 'papa' *(daddy)*, 'mama' *(mommy)*, 'opa' *(grandpa)* and 'oma' *(grandma)*. Kins outside the nuclear family are referred to by a transparent system of word-formation devices in which specific classes of additional preposed morphemes correspond with specific kinship types:

– direct ancestors are referred to by means of *groot* (+2) and *over-groot* (+3);
– direct descendants are referred to by means of *klein* (-2) and *achter-klein* (-3);
– collateral ancestors are referred to by means of *oud* (+2);
– collateral descendants are referred to by means of *achter* (-2);
– affinal relations are expressed by preposing *schoon* to nuclear basic terms; however, apart from *schoonbroer*, there is also a separate basic lexeme for brother-in-law, i.e., *zwager*.

With respect to some nuclear kinship types, Dutch has coverterms in which the gender distinction is neutralized, i.e., 'ouders' *(parents)* and 'kind' *(child)*. However, Dutch has no such coverterm for reference to siblings. In Broeder & Extra (1991) an extensive analysis is given of kinship reference in the total Dutch data base. All relevant word-tokens were scanned, together with their verbal context and frequency of use. Finally, the referential function was established for each word-token. In this way, the list of word-tokens could be reduced to a list of expressive devices which refer to specific kinship types. Table 12 shows the final result.

Table 12. Survey of standard (SD) vs. non-standard devices (NSD) for kinship types.

	Mahmut		Ergün		Mohamed		Fatima	
	SD	NSD	SD	NSD	SD	NSD	SD	NSD
Direct kins	411	24	335	18	275	3	254	19
Collateral kins	3	43	73	12	57	14	13	20
Affinal kins	63	24	32	6	--	4	19	3
Total	477	91	440	36	332	21	286	42

As can be expected, direct kins are more frequently referred to than collateral or affinal kins. Moreover, however, direct kins are commonly referred to with standard devices, whereas non-standard devices frequently emerge for reference to collateral or affinal devices.

Most non-standard devices are based on the utilization of an initial core word-stock of consanguineal-direct kinship terms. The structure of these devices used for reference to direct, collateral and affinal kins is summarized in Table 13. Both linear and hierarchical constructions are represented. The latter are divided into head-final constructions and head-initial constructions.

Table 13. Linear (Lin), head-initial (HI), and head-final (HF) non-standard devices for kinship reference.

	Mahmut			Ergün			Mohamed			Fatima		
	Lin	HI	HF	Lin	HI	HF	Lin	HI	HF	Lin	HI	HF
Direct kins	23	-	-	15	1	2	3	-	-	-	-	-
Collateral kins	-	-	43	-	-	10	-	13	-	-	14	-
Affinal kins	9	-	20	-	-	5	-	5	-	2	14	2

A mirror-like division emerges between our Turkish and Moroccan learners of Dutch, according to different principles in their respective source languages. Whereas Mahmut and Ergün prefer non-standard head-final constructions, such as 'vader zus' *(father's sister)*, 'vader broer zoon' *(father's brother son)* and 'zuster dochter' *(sister's daughter)*, Mohamed and Fatima prefer head-initial constructions such as 'broer van vader' *(brother of father)*, 'dochter van tante' *(daughter of aunt)*, or 'vrouw mijn oom' *(wife my uncle)*. The expressive devices referring to 'aunt' are summarized in Table 14.

Table 14. Expressive devices for reference to aunt.

Type	Learner variety	F A	M O	M A	E R	English equivalent
Standard deriva-tion	tante	2	8	3	5	aunt
	oom-a	4	0	0	0	uncle-a (fem. suffix)
Head-final	vader zus	0	0	1	0	father sister
	moeder-zus(je)	0	0	1	2	mother sister
	moeder en zus	0	0	0	1	mother and sister
	oom vrouw	0	0	0	1	uncle wife
Head-initial	zus(ter) van (mijn) moeder	2	2	0	0	sister of (my) mother
	zuster van vader of moeder	0	1	0	0	sister of father/mother
	vrouw van mijn oom	0	1	0	0	wife of my uncle

In particular Mahmut consistently produces head-final compositions. He even uses several times a three-step left-branching combination of nouns: 'vader zus dochter' *(father sister daughter* = 'niece'), 'vrouw broer zoon' *(wife brother son* = 'nephew'). Ergün applies on two other occasions the same connective device as in 'moeder en zus' *(mother and sister)* in Table 14. He apparently tries to express the intended relationship by concatenating nouns by the connective 'en' *(and)*.

A very striking innovative use of a derivational device for reference to 'aunt' can be observed for Fatima: i.e., the Arabic feminine gender suffix '-a'. Fatima uses the word 'oma', which literally means 'grandma' in Dutch, but her expressive device actually consists of the bilingual combination 'oom-a', i.e., 'uncle-a' *(aunt)*. It is one of the very few examples in our data base of a direct derivational source language effect: the standard Dutch kinship term 'oom' (male reference) is combined with an Arabic suffix '-a' (female suffix). Such use of 'oom-a' obviously will lead to misunderstandings in native non-native communication, as can be observed in session 5 (cycle 1) where Fatima shows family photos to her native interlocutor:

FA	uh haar zus van mijn moeder	er her sister of my mother
NS	zus van je moeder?	sister of your mother?
FA	ja	yes
NS	met allemaal kindertjes	with all little children
FA	van deze	of these
NS	ja	yes
FA	Amal	Amal <=proper name of aunt>
NS	ja	yes
FA	van haar dochter/uh zoon	of her daughter/ er son
	deze van dochter deze uh	these of daughter these er
NS	ja	yes
FA	mijn neef	my cousin
NS	neef ja	cousin yes
FA	ja oom-*a* kind van oom-*a*	yes uncle-*a* child of uncle-*a*
NS	kind van?	child of?
FA	*mon oncle*	*my uncle*
NS	ja van jouw oom ja + ja	yes of your uncle yes + yes
	leuk oom-*a* als vrouwelijk	funny uncle-*a* as the feminine form
	van oom ja + 't kind van je/	of uncle yes + the child of your/
	+ jouw neef ja jouw neefje	+ your cousin yes your little cousin

One other example of such code-mixing emerges. Fatima once uses the word 'doctor-a' for reference to a female doctor in Dutch (see Broeder, 1991: 179).

Tables 13 and 14 make clear that the primary device for the Turkish learners is head-final composition without any additional connectors. The Moroccan learners rely almost completely on the head-initial order in which they use a preposition as a connecting device. The domain of kinship reference clearly shows how our learners compound new lexical units in a creative and innovative way.

Conclusions

We now return to our main hypotheses on the acquisition of word formation devices specified before. The four hypotheses will be discussed on the basis of the evidence derived from various parts of our core and extended data base.

H1: Given the transparency of composition and the opaqueness of derivation, the former devices will precede the latter in language acquisition.

Derivational means of word formation for both agent and non-agent reference to entities only play a minor role in early learner varieties:
- most suffix types are represented by only one or few different word forms per informant;
- several occurrences are direct imitations of the native interlocutor;

- various suffix types are in fact lexicalisations or formulas.

Not surprisingly, derivational innovations hardly show up at all in our learners data.

H2: Learners will make a creative and innovative use of a variety of compositional means, also in expressing reference to entities where native speakers of the target language would prefer derivational means.

The results clearly show that our adult learners make a creative and innovative use of a variety of compositional means in approaching the target language norm. Noun-noun composition is by far the most productive word formation process. Within this category, head-final combinations dominate over head-initial combinations, whereas linear compounds are rare. Head-final compounds are the most common pattern in the target language under consideration and the dominance of this pattern in early learner varieties is an accurate reflection of this phenomenon. Cross-linguistic evidence of lexical innovation was found in a whole range of word formation devices. In specific semantic domains, in particular kinship reference, differences between the Moroccan and Turkish learners of Dutch are more pronounced.

H3: Given the opposite preference of word order principles for expressing nominal heads and modifiers in Turkish and Arabic, and given the ambivalent order of these devices in Dutch, Turkish and Moroccan learners of Dutch will show differential source language effects in approaching the target language norm.

In the case of our Turkish and Moroccan learners of Dutch a remarkably systematic variation emerges. The order preferences can be traced back to the interplay between the source and target language systems. This effect has also been noted by Broeder (1991: 184) for the other SL-TL pairs in the ESF-project. Learners seem to analyse language input for the typological possibilities of their source language. This conclusion is in favour of the alternation hypothesis proposed by Jansen et al. (1981).

H4: Given the dominance of zero-connectors in Dutch noun-noun compounds, learners of Dutch will prefer and overgeneralize this principle.

The realization of differential binding phonemes in Dutch noun-noun compounds is an additional analytic and synthetic task for second language learners. One solution of this task in early learner varieties is based on zero-marking, whether or not in accordance with the target language norm. Zero-marked and other overextensions of binding principles are additional evidence for the fact that compounds are not acquired as unanalysed wholes.

In sum, composition precedes derivation in adult language acquisition processes.

In expanding their lexicon, adult language learners make a creative and innovative use of a variety of compositional means. In doing so, they rely both on source-language related principles and on target-language related principles. Although there is clear evidence of source-language related influence in building compounds in adult second-language use (see also Van Helmond & Van Vugt, 1984; Hughes, 1979), a similar order of acquisition of compositional before derivational word formation devices, and - to a great extent - a similar innovative use of early compounds have been observed in children learning a first language. Clark (1992) showed on the basis of a variety of child language data that transparent, simple, regular, and productive word formation devices appear early in language acquisition. At the same time, these early devices compensate for opaque, complex, irregular, and unproductive ones. A preference of compositional over derivational word formation devices can also be observed in processes of pidginization and creolization (cf. Mühlhaüsler, 1986; Schumann et al., 1987). These similarities are striking evidence of universal processes of language acquisition that are independent of a specific source language, target language, and age.

References

Allen, N., 1989. The evolution of kinship terminology. *Lingua,* 7, 173-186.

Barnard, A. & A. Good, 1984. *Research practices in the study of kinship.* London: Academic Press.

Botha, R., 1969. Bindfonemen: grammatische, linguïstische en wetenschapsfiloso-fische problemen. *De Nieuwe Taalgids,* 62, 101-114.

Broeder, P., 1991. Talking about people. A multiple case study on adult language acquisition. Amsterdam: Swets & Zeitlinger (= European Studies on Multilingualism 1).

Broeder, P. & G. Extra, 1991. Acquisition of kinship reference. A study on word formation processes of adult language learners. *International Journal of Applied Linguistics,* 1, 209-227.

Broeder, P., G. Extra, R. van Hout, S. Strömqvist & K. Voionmaa, 1988. Processes in the developing lexicon. (=Final Report to the European Science Foundation, III). Strasbourg: ESF.

Carter, A., 1984. The acquisition of social deixis: children's usages of 'kin' terms in Maharashta, India. *Journal of Child Language,* 11, 179-201.

Clark, E., 1992. *The acquisition of lexicon.* Cambridge: Cambridge University Press.

Clark, E. & B. Hecht, 1982. Learning to coin agent and instrument nouns. *Cognition,* 12, 1-24.

Donaldson, B., 1981. *Dutch reference grammar.* The Hague: Nijhoff.

Feldweg, H., 1991. *The European Science Foundation second language data bank.* Nijmegen: Max-Planck-Institut für Psycholinguistik.

Geerts, G., W. Haserijn, J. de Rooij & M. van den Toorn, 1984. *Algemene Neder-*

landse Spraakkunst. Groningen: Wolters-Noordhoff.

Haviland, S. & E. Clark, 1974. 'This man's father is my father's son': a study of the acquisition of English kin terms. *Journal of Child Language, 1,* 23-47.

Helmond, K. van & M. van Vugt, 1984. On the transferability of nominal compounds. *Interlanguage Studies Bulletin, 8,* 5-34.

Hughes, A., 1979. Aspects of a Spanish adult's acquisition of English. *Interlanguage Studies Bulletin, 4,* 49-65.

Jansen, B., J. Lalleman & P. Muysken, 1981. The alternation hypothesis: acquisition of Dutch word order by Turkish and Moroccan foreign workers. *Language Learning, 31,* 315-336.

Jong, E. de, 1979. *Spreektaal. Woordfrequenties in gesproken Nederlands.* Utrecht: Bohn, Scheltema & Holkema.

Kleijn, P. de & E. Nieuwborg, 1983. *Basiswoordenboek Nederlands.* Leuven: Wolters-Noordhoff.

Lambek, J., 1986. A production grammar for English kinship terminology. *Theoretical Linguistics, 13,* 19-36.

Mühlhaüsler, P., 1986. *Pidgin and creole linguistics.* Oxford: Blackwell.

Perdue, C. (ed.), 1984. *Second language acquisition by adult immigrants.* A field manual. Rowley, Mass.: Newbury House.

Perdue, C. (ed.), 1993. *Adult language acquisition: Cross-linguistic perspectives, Volume I Field methods, Volume II The results.* Cambridge: Cambridge University Press.

Schumann, J., M. Sokolik & P. Master, 1987. *The experimental creation of a pidgin language* (UCLA Working Paper).

Selkirk, E., 1982. *The syntax of words,* Cambridge: MIT Press.

Authors and affiliations

Jeroen Aarssen
Tilburg University
Research Group on Language and Minorities
P.O. Box 90153
5000 LE Tilburg
The Netherlands

Abdelâli Bentahila
University of Fes
Dept. of English
p/a Villa 133 Mimosas
Avenue Moulay Kamel
Fes
Morocco

Hendrik Boeschoten
Tilburg University
Research Group on Language and Minorities
P.O. Box 90153
5000 LE Tilburg
The Netherlands

Petra Bos
Tilburg University
Research Group on Language and Minorities
P.O. Box 90153
5000 LE Tilburg
The Netherlands

Peter Broeder
Tilburg University
Research Group on Language and Minorities
P.O. Box 90153
5000 LE Tilburg
The Netherlands

Eirlys Davies
University of Fes
Dept. of English
p/a Villa 133 Mimosas
Avenue Moulay Kamel
Fes
Morocco

Annick De Houwer
University of Antwerpen
p/a Galgestraat 123
B 1785 Merchem
Belgium

Özden Ekmekçi
Çukurova University
Centre for Foreign Languages
Adana
Turkey

Guus Extra
Tilburg University
Research Group on Language and Minorities
P.O. Box 90153
5000 LE Tilburg
The Netherlands

Kenji Hakuta
Stanford University
School of Education
California, P.O. Box 94305
USA

Hanneke van der Heijden
Tilburg University
Research Group on Language and Minorities
P.O. Box 90153
5000 LE Tilburg
The Netherlands

Roeland van Hout
Tilburg University
Research Group on Language and Minorities
P.O. Box 90153
5000 LE Tilburg
The Netherlands

Aldo di Luzio
Universität Konstanz
Fachgruppe Sprachwissenschaft
Postfach 5560
D-7750 Konstanz 1
Germany

Barry McLaughlin
University of California
Dept. of Psychology
399 Kerr Hall
Santa Cruz, CA 95064
USA

Lucinda Pease-Alvarez
University of California
Dept. of Psychology
399 Kerr Hall
Santa Cruz, CA 95064
USA

Carol Pfaff
Freie Universität Berlin
JFK Institut
Lansstrasse 7-9
D-1000 Berlin 22
Germany

Anneli Schaufeli
Nijmegen University
Dept. of Applied Linguistics
P.O. Box 9103
6500 HD Nijmegen
The Netherlands

Åke Viberg
Stockholms Universitet
Centre for Research on Bilingualism
S-106 91 Stockholm
Sweden

Ludo Verhoeven
Tilburg University
Research Group on Language and Minorities
P.O. Box 90153
5000 LE Tilburg
The Netherlands

Kathleen Wodala
Szeged
Barát U. 5/A
6725
Hungary

Authors and affiliations